Teaching and Learning at a Distance
Foundations of Distance Education

GARRETT COMMUNITY
COLLEGE LIBRARY

WITHDRAWN

D0209492

Michael Simonson
Nova Southeastern University

Sharon Smaldino
University of Northern Iowa

Michael Albright
Iowa State University

Susan Zvacek
Old Dominion University

Merrill
an imprint of Prentice Hall
Upper Saddle River, New Jersey   Columbus, Ohio

Library of Congress Cataloging-in-Publication Data

Teaching and learning at a distance : foundations of distance
  education / Michael Simonson . . . [et al.].
     p.   cm.
  Includes bibliographical references and index.
  ISBN 0-13-769258-7
  1. Distance education.   I. Simonson, Michael R.
LC5800.T43   2000
371.3'5—dc21   99-21229
                                                CIP

Editor: Debra A. Stollenwerk
Editorial Assistant: Penny S. Burleson
Production Editor: Mary Harlan
Design Coordinator: Diane C. Lorenzo
Photo Coordinator: Anthony Magnacca
Text Design and Project Coordination: Carlisle Publishers Services
Cover Designer: Tanya Burgess
Cover art: © Stephan Schildbach
Production Manager: Pamela D. Bennett
Illustrations: Carlisle Communications, Ltd.
Director of Marketing: Kevin Flanagan
Marketing Manager: Meghan Shepherd
Marketing Coordinator: Krista Groshong

This book was set in Minion by Carlisle Communications, Ltd. and was printed
and bound by R. R. Donnelley & Sons Company. The cover was printed by Phoenix
Color Corp.

© 2000 by Prentice-Hall, Inc.
Pearson Education
Upper Saddle River, New Jersey 07458

All rights reserved. No part of this book may be reproduced, in any form or by any
means, without permission in writing from the publisher.

Photo Credits: AT&T Photo Center, p. 3; Audio-Technica, p. 89 (*upper left*);
Canon U.S.A., Inc., p. 88 (*middle*); VTEL Corporation, pp. 4, 6, 12, 14-15, 19, 49, 69, 83,
86, 88 (*upper left, upper right, and bottom*), 89 (*upper right and bottom*), 90, 95, 113,
127, 129, 132, 139, 142, 147, 151, 175, 181, 185, 191, 205, 218, 225.

Printed in the United States of America

10 9 8 7 6 5 4 3 2 1

ISBN: 0-13-769258-7

Prentice-Hall International (UK) Limited, *London*
Prentice-Hall of Australia Pty. Limited, *Sydney*
Prentice-Hall of Canada, Inc., *Toronto*
Prentice-Hall Hispanoamericana, S. A., *Mexico*
Prentice-Hall of India Private Limited, *New Delhi*
Prentice-Hall of Japan, Inc., *Tokyo*
Prentice-Hall (Singapore) Pte. Ltd., *Singapore*
Editora Prentice-Hall do Brasil, Ltda., *Rio de Janeiro*

preface

Everett Rogers, in his landmark book *Diffusion of Innovations,* defined an innovation as "an idea, practice, or object that is perceived as new by an individual. . . ." Certainly, distance education is new to most of us. This text attempts to link what teachers and trainers know and understand about the learning and teaching process to what is new—the idea of learners in different locations and times. The authors of *Teaching and Learning at a Distance* feel that once educators become familiar with the innovation called distance education, they will find out how important and how much fun it really is.

Teaching and Learning at a Distance is written for use in an introductory distance education course for preservice or in-service teachers, and for those in training programs who wish to teach at a distance or manage distance education systems. It provides readers with the basic information they need in order to be a knowledgeable distance educator.

The teacher or trainer who uses this book will be able to distinguish between appropriate uses of distance education and those uses best met by other techniques. In this text we take the following philosophical position:

◆ Students prefer not to learn at a distance. Certainly, there are times when the convenience of distance education outweighs other considerations, but if given a legitimate choice, sitting in a classroom, laboratory, or conference room with other learners and the instructor is preferable to almost everyone.

◆ It is well documented that students do not learn any better at a distance, nor do they learn any less. Considerations other than distance have greater impact on learning. Many feel that as technologies mature and develop, the concept of distance will become relatively unimportant.

◆ Distance education is a dramatic idea. It may change, even restructure, education, but only if it is possible to make the experience of the distance learner as complete, satisfying, and acceptable as that of the local learner. If distance education is to be a successful and mainstream approach, then distance education systems should be based on the belief that the more equivalent the learning experience of the distant student is to that of the local student, the more equivalent will be the outcomes of the learning experience.

◆ The field should not promote distance education as the next great technological solution to education's problems, or make grand claims about the impact of telecommunications. Rather, those in the field should strive to use technology and technological approaches to make the experiences of distant and local learners positive and equivalent.

Organization of the Text

Teaching and Learning at a Distance has two categories of chapters—foundation chapters and application chapters. Chapters 1 through 4 are designed to provide a conceptual, theoretical, and research-based foundation for the rest of the text. Chapters 5 through 12 are designed to provide educators with practical skills and information that they need in order to function immediately in a distance learning environment.

Chapter 1 discusses the status of distance education for the educator who may not be familiar with this idea. Chapter 1 also explains what distance education is and what impact it has on education. The chapter concludes with a vision for schools and learning that is possible because of distance education.

Chapter 2 reviews definitions of distance education that have been, and still are being, used. Since distance education is a field with a long history, that background is discussed. Beginning with correspondence study, the chapter reviews the field up to the current period. Finally, theories related to the practice of distance education are presented, including a proposed American theory of distance education—equivalency theory.

Chapter 3 reviews the extensive research on distance education, including specific areas of the practice of the field as well as more general and comprehensive summaries of what the research says. *Teaching and Learning at a Distance* is a research-based textbook. The positions taken by the authors are based on a thorough study of the empirical information about distance. This research-based approach is found in all chapters, but is emphasized in Chapter 3.

Chapter 4 presents comprehensive information about the technologies used in distance education systems. Technology is broadly defined, and this chapter includes discussions, explanations, and many visuals to provide the reader with a working knowledge of how information is communicated and how distance education systems operate.

Chapter 5, the first of the application chapters, deals with copyright. Distance educators transmit information, much of which may be copyrighted. Chapter 5 discussed the rules, regulations, and procedures that the distance educator needs to understand.

Chapter 6 presents the basic intellectual technique of the technology-using educator—instructional design. Instructional design is the systematic process followed by educators using technology. This chapter presents the procedures to be followed when courses or components of courses are designed for distance delivery.

Chapters 7 and 8 explain the unique responsibilities of the learner and instructor involved in distance education. The authors of *Teaching and Learning at a Distance* feel that learning and teaching at a distance are more similar to than different from traditional education. However, there are some special responsibilities and expectations of those involved in distance education. These two chapters discuss learning and teaching at a distance.

Chapter 9 may be the most important chapter of the book. Handouts, study guides, and visuals are important tools and techniques of the effective educator, generally, and distance educator, specifically. The interactive study guide with its word pictures, visual analogies, and visualization is a significant tool used in distance education systems of all kinds.

Chapter 10 provides an in-depth coverage of the Internet and the World Wide Web as delivery mechanisms. The Internet and Web are explained, discussed, and evaluated. Finally, procedures for designing Inter/Web-based courseware are discussed.

The final two chapters discuss two very important and closely related topics: (1) assessment of learning and learners and (2) evaluation of teaching and systems. Assessment and evaluation are closely related, but their importance is special to the distance educator. These chapters discuss procedures for assessment and evaluation and give specific examples of procedures to follow.

Features

Each chapter has goals and objectives to provide an organization plan for the student. Chapters usually have from three to seven subsections that structure the information of the chapter for each study. Visuals are used liberally when appropriate in an attempt to *show* the reader in addition to *telling*. Each chapter has self-test questions and answers that review key ideas. Most self-test questions are divided into two sections. The first part of the question is a fact, idea, or concept that is important. The second part of each question requires an analysis that may not have a specific answer, and that is best answered by participating in a group discussion with classmates or with the instructor. Finally, each chapter has a comprehensive list of references and additional readings. In some instances, nonprint resources, especially World Wide Web locations, are provided.

Additional Resources

Three categories of additional resources are available to support the user of *Teaching and Learning at a Distance:*

1. A series of 11 videos
2. A collection of interactive study guides
3. A series of PowerPoint presentations

Videos.   The following 11 videos are available for use during class and outside of class. They were developed to support courses such as this one.

Introductory Video Title: *A Room With a View*
Description: Distance education offers significant new opportunities to learners of all
    ages. With construction of the Iowa Communications Network, linking more
    than 100 educational sites, Iowa has demonstrated its commitment to a high-
    quality, innovative educational system. This video discusses the opportunities
    offered by this new technology and presents vignettes from actual distance
    education classrooms. *15 min.*

Foundations and Applications of Distance Education

Foundations

Definitions and Background	The historical development of distance education and the definition of distance education. *12 min.*
Research and Theory	The implications of research for distance education practice. *13 min.*
Technologies and Terminology	An explanation of telecommunications technologies. *14 min.*
The Classroom	The hardware of a typical two-way interactive distance education classroom. *14 min.*
Distance Education Costs	The costs involved in constructing a distance education system, including distance education classrooms. *12 min.*

Applications

The Teacher	The skills needed for successful distance teaching. *18 min.*
The Student	The skills needed for successful distance education. *7 min.*
The Curriculum	How distance education can support and enrich the curriculum. *11 min.*
ICN	The purpose, structure, and capabilities of Iowa's 3,000-mile fiber optic network. *12 min.*
Three Statewide Approaches	How distance education is practiced in three states—Kentucky, Mississippi, and Iowa. *18 min.*

These videos are available from the Association for Educational Communications and Technology, 1025 Vermont Avenue, NW, Suite 820. Washington, DC 20005 (202-347-7839).

Interactive Study Guides and PowerPoint Presentations.   These materials are designed to be used together during classroom presentations. The titles include

1. Copyright
2. Definitions, Theories, and Research
3. Distance Education and the WWW
4. Distance Education Systems
5. Handouts and Study Guides
6. Instructional Design
7. Interaction
8. Internet and the WWW
9. Teaching Techniques

The masters for the interactive study guides are in the *Instructor's Manual,* which is available to adopters from your Merrill/Prentice Hall representative or directly from the publisher.

ACKNOWLEDGMENTS

While this text has four authors, a number of others participated in the development of many of the ideas presented. In particular, Dan Hanson, Nancy Maushak, Charles Schlosser, and Mary Anderson of the Technology Research and Evaluation Group at Iowa State University contributed a great deal to the development of *Teaching and Learning at a Distance*. We would also like to thank the reviewers for their comments and suggestions: Franklin R. Koontz, The University of Toledo; S. Kim MacGregor, Louisiana State University; Mike Moore, Virginia Tech; Farhad Saba, San Diego State University; Janice R. Sandiford, Florida International University; and Caryl Sheffield, California University of Pennsylvania.

Distance education is a new concept to many. It is possible that distance education as an idea may provide educators in rural, isolated, or economically disadvantaged areas the opportunity to overcome the problems inherent in their situations. *Teaching and Learning at a Distance* is offered to give teachers and trainers the background and skills needed to function effectively and critically in the educational environment of the 21st century. Remember,

Make no little plans; they have no magic to stir the blood.

Michael Simonson
Sharon Smaldino
Michael Albright
Susan Zvacek

Discover the Companion Website Accompanying This Book

www.prenhall.com/simonson

The Prentice Hall Companion Website: A Virtual Learning Environment

Technology is a constantly growing and changing aspect of our field that is creating a need for content and resources. To address this emerging need, Prentice Hall has developed an online learning environment for students and professors alike—Companion Websites—to support our textbooks.

In creating a Companion Website, our goal is to build on and enhance what the textbook already offers. For this reason, the content for each user-friendly website is organized by topic and provides the professor and student with a variety of meaningful resources. Common features of a Companion Website include:

For the Professor

Every Companion Website integrates **Syllabus Manager™,** an online syllabus creation and management utility.

▶ **Syllabus Manager™** provides you, the instructor, with an easy, step-by-step process to create and revise syllabi, with direct links into Companion Website and other online content without having to learn HTML.

▶ Students may log on to your syllabus during any study session. All they need to know is the web address for the Companion Website and the password you've assigned to your syllabus.

▶ After you have created a syllabus using **Syllabus Manager™,** students may enter the syllabus for their course section from any point in the Companion Website.

▶ Class dates are highlighted in white and assignment due dates appear in blue. Clicking on a date, the student is shown the list of activities for the assignment. The activities for each assignment are linked directly to actual content, saving time for students.

▶ Adding assignments consists of clicking on the desired due date, then filling in the details of the assignment—name of the assignment, instructions, and whether or not it is a one-time or repeating assignment.

▶ In addition, links to other activities can be created easily. If the activity is online, a URL can be entered in the space provided, and it will be linked automatically in the final syllabus.

▶ Your completed syllabus is hosted on our servers, allowing convenient updates from any computer on the Internet. Changes you make to your syllabus are immediately available to your students at their next log-on.

For the Student

▶ **Topic Overviews**—outline key concepts in topic areas

▶ **Electronic Blue Book**—send homework or essays directly to your instructor's e-mail with this paperless form

▶ **Message Board**—serves as a virtual bulletin board to post—or respond to—questions or comments to/from a national audience

▶ **Web Destinations**—links to www sites that relate to each topic area

▶ **Professional Organizations**—links to organizations that relate to topic areas

▶ **Additional Resources**—access to topic-specific content that enhances material found in the text

To take advantage of these and other resources, please visit the *Teaching and Learning at a Distance* Companion Website at **www.prenhall.com/Simonson.**

contents

PART II ◆ APPLICATIONS   93

PART I

FOUNDATIONS

chapter 1

Foundations of Distance Education

CHAPTER GOAL

The purpose of this chapter is to discuss the importance of distance education and the impact that distance education has on the improvement of education.

CHAPTER OBJECTIVES

After reading and reviewing this chapter, you should be able to

1. Explain the reason why students demand to learn at a distance even though they prefer to learn in the classroom with the teacher and their classmates.
2. Define *distance education*.
3. Explain Coldeway's quadrants.
4. Discuss Richard Clark's "mere vehicles" quote as it relates to distance education.
5. Explain how Jim Finn might compare stirrups with distance education.
6. Give examples of how distance education is being used in several locations of the world and in the United States.
7. Explain a vision for education and schooling in the future.

◆ CHEMISTRY AT A DISTANCE? A TRUE STORY

Chemistry is a hands-on, laboratory-based course that many consider to be one of the most rigorous in the average high school curriculum. Many students dread taking chemistry, and in many small communities there is only one chemistry teacher in the school.

Recently, four high school chemistry teachers decided that they could improve their basic chemistry course if they collaborated and team-taught. The only problem was that their schools were about 60 miles from each other.

This did not stop them, however, because their schools were connected with a fiber-optic network that permitted full-motion video signals to be sent between the four schools. The network also carried a high-speed Internet connection that allowed easy access to the World Wide Web.

Not only did the four teachers want to collaborate, but more importantly they wanted their students to collaborate. To accomplish this they decided on some basic objectives and then planned the curriculum.

The teachers decided that they would teach concepts cooperatively, act as laboratory supervisors for each other's students, and serve as partners with student collaborators. They also decided upon another important goal: to have their students cooperate across schools. Finally, they decided that the chemistry projects should be authentic and deal with local, real-world issues.

Increasingly, courses like chemistry are being taught to distant and local learners simultaneously.

Next, the four teachers met to plan their curriculum. They identified eight modules that could be shared among the four schools. These modules were taught by one or two of the four chemistry teachers, and required collaboration by the students from the four schools. The modules included live television instruction presented by one of the teachers, collaborative work by students who communicated with each other by television and the Internet, and class assignments that dealt with various aspects of the same chemistry concept, such as the local ecology. Students investigated their portion of the problem and then shared results with their distant classmates. Each module ended with a live, interactive discussion, presentation, and sharing of information over the fiber-optics television network.

For all practical purposes, the students in the four schools became one large class, with subgroups of students who worked with classmates from their own school and also with distant friends. The teachers served as presenters some of the time, but most often as tutors who worked with subgroups of students. The Internet and e-mail were used to keep everyone communicating outside of class, and even outside of school.

By any measure the course was a huge success. Students learned chemistry; test scores showed that. They also discovered how to collaborate as real scientists with colleagues at distant locations, and they discovered the power of distance education to open up their school to resources available elsewhere.

Telecommunications technology made this possible. Their chemistry classroom became a "room with a view," connected to other chemistry classrooms and to the resources of the world available through the Internet. The course became more like real chemistry—chemistry practiced to solve actual problems outside the school involving experts from a number of areas brought together because of their expertise, without regard for geography or time.

Distance education is one of the most dramatic of the recent technology-based innovations influencing education. The scenario above is just one of thousands of examples of how distance education is changing learning and teaching.

◆ DISTANCE EDUCATION TODAY AND TOMORROW

In the last few years, distance education has become a major topic in education. In 1998, there were over 50 conferences dealing with some aspect of distance education, and almost every professional organization's publications and conferences have shown a huge increase in the number of distance education-related articles and papers.

Many educators are making grand claims about how distance education is likely to change education and training. Certainly, the concept of distance education is exciting, and recent hardware and software innovations are making telecommunications distance education systems more available, easier to use, and less costly. Distance education has begun to enter the mainstream.

However, distance educators are being confronted by two conflicting pressures. First, *students say they do not really want to learn at a distance*. When asked, they say

Compressed videos systems that use regular telephone lines make it possible to originate or receive distance education courses from virtually anywhere.

they prefer meeting with the learning group and the instructor in the classroom, the lecture hall, the seminar room, or the laboratory. Students report that they value the presence of a learning group, and that the informal interactions that occur before and after, and sometimes during, a formal class are valuable components of the total learning experience. Second, and conversely, there is evidence that *students are increasingly demanding to be allowed to learn at a distance.* They want to be able to supplement, and even replace, conventional learning experiences with distance education experiences. Learners say this is because there are many other considerations besides personal preferences that motivate them, especially about where and when they learn.

These opposing preferences pose a dilemma for the educational community. Should resources be dedicated to improving the traditional educational infrastructure of buildings, classrooms, laboratories, and offices, and should students be transported to these facilities? Or should money be used to develop modern and sophisticated telecommunications systems? The trend seems to be toward telecommunications.

Because of advances in technology, effective educational experiences can be provided for learners, no matter where they are located. In other words, technologies are now available to develop cost-effective distance learning systems.

The practice of distance education has dramatically changed in the last decade. Traditional approaches to distance education based on the delivery of print and broadcast media technologies are no longer as relevant to the field as it is practiced in the United States as they once were. As a matter of fact, a redefinition of distance education has occurred. Distance education is now often defined as

> institution-based, formal education where the learning group is separated geographically, and where interactive telecommunications systems are used to connect learners, resources, and instructors.

◆ WHAT IS DISTANCE EDUCATION?

It is the nature of questions that they are easier to ask than to answer. This is true of the question "What is distance education?" for at least several reasons. First, *distance* has multiple meanings. Distance can mean geographical distance, time distance, and possibly even intellectual distance.

Second, the term *distance education* has been applied to a tremendous variety of programs serving numerous audiences via a wide variety of media. Some use print, some use telecommunications, and many use both. Finally, rapid changes in technology challenge the traditional ways in which distance education is defined.

Dan Coldeway, of Canada's Athabasca University, provided a framework useful in helping to define four ways in which education can be practiced. This framework, which considers the two variables of time and place, gives insight into different approaches to the practice of education and distance education. Combinations of time and place result in four approaches to education. The four are same-time, same-place education (ST-SP), different-time, same-place education (DT-SP), same-time, different-place education (ST-DP), and different-time, different-place education (DT-DP).

Traditional education takes place at the same time in the same place. This is typically the regular self-contained classroom that most often is teacher-centered. Different-time, same-place education means that individual learning occurs in a learning center, or that multiple sections of the same classes are offered so students can attend the class in the same place at a time they chose. This is education that is available at different times to students but in the same place, such as the media center or computer laboratory.

The last two categories focus on education occurring in different places. Instruction can take place in different places at the same time when telecommunications systems are used. Often, television is used to connect the local classroom with the teacher and students to learners at a distance. Satellite, compressed video, and fiber-optics systems are increasingly used for same-time, different-place education. This approach is also called *synchronous* distance learning.

Students can also learn at different times and in different places. Dan Coldeway has said that the purest form of distance education occurs at different times and in different places. In other words, learners choose when and where to learn and when and where to access instructional materials. Recently, World Wide Web courses have been offered to learners anywhere they have access and whenever they choose. This approach is called *asynchronous* distance learning.

◆ MEDIA IN EDUCATION—EARLIER DEBATES

The discussion about distance education is somewhat reminiscent of a recent debate in the educational technology field that began when Richard Clark, a researcher and theorist, published a classic article containing his now famous "mere vehicles" analogy. Clark summarized over six decades of educational media research. It was obvious to him that many researchers were reporting about flawed studies involving media. Clark believed that many educators did not understand the last 60 years of research about media and learning.

It was even more alarming that many practitioners were making unrealistic claims about the impact of technology on learning. According to Clark, there was a large segment of the educational community who felt that mediated instruction was inherently better than teaching when media were not used.

In 1983, Clark wrote in volume 53 of the *Review of Educational Research* that

the best current evidence is that media are *mere vehicles* that deliver instruction but do not influence student achievement any more than the truck that delivers our groceries causes changes in nutrition . . . only the content of the vehicle can influence achievement. (p. 445)

Clark's article went on to convincingly claim that instructional media were excellent for storing educational messages and for delivering them almost anywhere. However, media were not responsible for a learning effect. Learning was not enhanced because instruction was media-based. Rather, the content of the instruction, the method used to promote learning, and the involvement of the learner in the instructional experience were what, in part, influenced learning.

While many did not, and still do not, agree with Clark, his article caused a reassessment of how educators looked at the impact of media. Clark continued to implore the education community to "give up your enthusiasm for media effects on learning," which was the theme of a more recent publication on this topic (Clark, 1994). "Give up your enthusiasm" has become the new rallying cry for those who do not believe there is a media effect.

Certainly, some distance educators claim that distance education is the best way to learn because it allows students to acquire knowledge when it is most relevant to them. However, most who have studied distance learning make few claims about the approach being better. Rather, they say it is a viable and important approach to learning and teaching that should be one option of many available.

A second analogy by another great technology pioneer also has relevance to distance education. In the 1960s, Jim Finn from the University of Southern California talked about the stirrup as a technological innovation that changed society. He often told a story that went like this:

The Anglo-Saxons, a dominating enemy of Charles Martel's Franks, had the stirrup but did not truly understand its implications for warfare. The stirrup made possible the emergence of a warrior called the knight who understood that the stirrup enabled the rider not only to keep his seat, but also to deliver a blow with a lance having the combined weight of the rider and charging horse. This simple concept permitted the Franks to conquer the Anglo-Saxons and change the face of western civilization. Martel had a vision to seize the idea and to use it. He did not invent the stirrup, but knew how to use it purposefully. (Finn, 1964, p. 24)

Finn (1964) summarized the implications of this story as follows:

The acceptance or rejection of an invention, or the extent to which its implications are realized if it is accepted, depends quite as much upon the condition of society, and upon the imagination of its leadership, as upon the nature of the technological item itself. . . . The Anglo-Saxons used the stirrup, but did not comprehend it; and for this they paid a fearful price. . . . It was the Franks alone—presumably led by Charles Martel's genius—who fully grasped the possibilities inherent in the stirrup and created in terms of it a new type of warfare supported by a novel structure of a society which we call feudalism. . . . For a thousand years feudal institutions bore the marks of their birth from the new military technologies of the eighth century. (p. 24)

What Clark strongly proposed with his "mere vehicles" and "give up your enthusiasm" arguments was that media and technology did not directly affect learning. He forcefully argued that educators should not claim that technology-based learning, such as modern distance education systems, had any inherent advantage (or disadvantage for that matter) over other methods of learning. Like Finn, Clark proposed that technologies may provide ways of accomplishing tasks that are new and not readily obvious.

Finn advocated that practitioners should attempt to identify unique approaches for change by using new technologies in new ways. Finn's story explained that the stirrup not only made getting on and off a horse easier, but also made possible a new, previously unheard-of consequence, the emergence of the knight, and it was the knight who caused significant and long-lasting changes in society. Perhaps the correct application of distance education will significantly change and restructure learning and teaching on par with the societal change called feudalism needed to support the knight.

The implication of the arguments of these two educators is that when new technologies emerge, they often allow users to be more efficient. However, it is not technologies themselves that cause changes; rather changes occur because of new ways of doing things that are enabled by technologies. The stirrup made riding horses easier and more efficient, but it was the knight who changed medieval society.

◆ STATUS OF DISTANCE EDUCATION

Worldwide Examples

Distance education has a major and varied impact worldwide. While politics and economics influence how distance education is employed, there is a strong demand in the world for distance education opportunities. The three examples that follow illustrate some of the factors that influence distance education and show the demand for distance learning opportunities.

1. In Sub-Saharan Africa, political instability and economic depression have caused a decline in educational standards in some countries. As the population increased in these countries, there was a tremendous classroom shortage, and both the number of qualified teachers and the availability of instructional materials became inadequate.

Distance education is seen as having the potential to contribute to national reconstruction by providing economically feasible educational opportunities to many people. Collaboration with a variety of international distance education organizations has provided expertise and support for the practice of distance education. As a result, distance education at a basic level, as it is practiced in many regions of Africa, has expanded quite sharply. However, while growth in distance education in Sub-Saharan African countries is evident, it does not yet have a wide impact. Lack of funding prevents distance education institutions from reaching many potential students.

2. China developed a national higher distance education program in the late 70s and early 80s in response to a growth in population and a high cost per capita for the craft-like approach to regular higher education in the country. Because China could not afford to meet the higher education needs of the expanding population, a national radio and TV university system was developed. By 1985, China had over 30,000 TV classes throughout the country and employed almost 25,000 academics. One in five students studying in higher education was enrolled in a radio and TV university. This national system incorporated a centralized approach to course development, delivery, and examinations. However, despite an increase in offerings, there has been a significant decrease in student numbers. Recently, only 1 in every 13 students in higher education was enrolled in a radio and TV university.

Socioeconomic factors have caused changes in the mass market for higher education in China. The centralized approach to course development and delivery no longer meets the diverse needs of learners and does not adapt itself quickly to the new conditions. In response, China's radio and TV universities have changed from a central system of course development and delivery to a regionally responsive system that provides a wide variety of both diploma and non-diploma courses (Ding, 1994, 1995).

3. Distance education has had a long history in European countries. The continuation of this tradition is evident in the vast array of programs offered by European Union countries. Enrollment in these programs recently was almost 2¾ million. In some countries open distance teaching universities offer the majority of the country's distance education programming. Spain's Universidad Nacional de

Educacion a Distancia is Europe's largest distance teaching university, with a current enrollment of about 130,000 students. In other countries, traditional universities deliver the majority of the courses. France, for example, has no national distance teaching university, but offers higher distance education through 22 offices within traditional universities. Recently, 34,000 students were enrolled in these programs. In some cases governments provide substantial distance education training opportunities that do not lead to a university degree. France is a leader in this area, providing over 350,000 students a year with opportunities at a range of levels: elementary school, high school, technical and professional qualifications, teacher training, and university-level and postgraduate courses. In addition, 250,000 students are served by proprietary distance training providers in France (Keegan, 1994).

Distance instruction in the European Union uses a wide variety of media to deliver courses. These range from traditional correspondence delivery, to computer conferencing, to two-way audio and video virtual classrooms (Holmberg, 1995; Keegan, 1995). Using these technologies, the established distance education and training organizations of Europe will continue to play a significant role in education in and beyond the European Union.

United States

In the United States, the emergence of new technologies has brought on increased interest in distance education and learning.

> Electronic mail, electronic bulletin boards, facsimiles, and interactive computer networks now augment or replace mail carriers in delivering curricular materials, textbooks, and examinations to distance learners. New transmission media capable of providing two-way, full-motion, real-time (live) interaction between the student and teacher replace non-interactive, one-way systems. (Tompkins, 1993, pp. 265–266)

At the university level it is reported that distance education enrollments are in the high six figures nationally. This includes enrollment in courses offered by traditional universities and those offered by distance learning universities. The United States military is heavily involved in distance education technology because distance education is viewed as a cost-efficient way to deliver technical training to a large number of soldiers. The development of new weapons systems and other technologies increases the demand for this type of training. The Army's Interactive Teletraining Network, the Navy's Video Teletraining Network, and the Air Force's Teleteach Expanded Delivery System all provide distance training opportunities for personnel across the United States and around the world.

A focus on education in the primary and secondary schools separates American distance education from traditional European distance education. This emphasis on kindergarten through Grade 12 (K–12) students is demonstrated in the federally funded Star Schools projects. The U.S. Department of Education began the Star

American distance education often focuses on students in primary and secondary schools.

Schools program "to encourage improved instruction in mathematics, science, foreign languages, literacy skills, and vocational education for underserved populations through the use of telecommunications networks" (Simonson, 1995, pp. 3–4). While these projects are not limited to K–12 programming, their primary emphasis is on K–12 students and teachers. A variety of network technologies including satellite, cable, fiber optics, microcomputer-based laboratories, multimedia, and electronic networking technologies have been used to deliver instructional programming to over 6,000 schools nationwide through the Star Schools project (U.S. Department of Education, 1995).

Typically the Star Schools project has funded programs that provide satellite delivery of instruction to a large number of students in many states. One of the largest is the Connections 2000 Star Schools Project of Los Angeles County Office of Education, which is a consortium of education and public television agencies in over 10 states. The consortium provides math, science, social science, language arts, and technology programming to over 1,300 school sites and 125,000 students in Grades 4 through 7. In addition, the project provides professional development opportunities for over 4,000 teachers. The Star Schools project funds a number of similar satellite-based projects.

The Star Schools project has sponsored three special statewide projects that fund the development of statewide infrastructures, allowing for synchronous interaction between students and instructors. The most comprehensive is in the state of Iowa. Currently, Iowa's 3,000-mile statewide fiber-optic network connects more than 500 educational sites, with over 350 more sites to be added in the next few years. Hundreds of thousands of hours of K–12 programming are provided each year, in addition to teacher professional development and higher education course opportunities. Kentucky and Mississippi have joined Iowa in the development of statewide systems that promote personalized interactive instruction and learning.

As the examples described above show, distance education has a major impact worldwide. In addition to economics and politics, the growth and impact of distance education is directly linked to the availability of new technologies. "As technology links distant sites in an electronic web of information and new communication channels, people around the globe are pulled together" (Thach & Murphy, 1994). This type of communication has contributed to globalization. Globalization implies that people are connected more or less contemporaneously with distant events. The new computer-mediated communications and telecommunications technologies contribute to globalization. Distance educators will be challenged both by globalization and by the emerging technologies. How they take advantage of these opportunities will give new meaning to the practice of distance education.

◆ CHARACTERISTICS OF DISTANCE EDUCATION— A VISION

Recently, a number of advances have been made in the study of learning and teaching that are providing educators with strategies for improving the educational experience. Often, these advances are considered to be in opposition to the common practices of distance education because of the misconception that teachers lecture to distant learners. This is changing dramatically however, as distance education systems attempt to provide a learning site that is a *room with a view.*

This emerging approach that relies strongly on distance education suggests a scenario detailing the school and classroom of the future similar to the following scenario, which implies that classrooms of the future will be technology-rich and will continue to have teachers who are responsible for the learning events that occur.

In every community and neighborhood there are schools surrounded by playgrounds and sports fields with trees and grass. The schools themselves look modern but very familiar. The schools are open 24 hours per day, everyday, all year. Each is a part of a locally controlled and supported district that is one of several hundred that make up a technology-rich statewide educational system. Classrooms are considered rooms with a view. Every learner and teacher possesses a high-powered multimedia computer that is connected to a worldwide network containing virtually unlimited educational resources. The network connects the learner to multisensory multimedia resources that are accessible from school, home, and business. Education is learner- and learning-centered and technology-supported. Schools are small,

Training of staff located at remote sites is facilitated and made cost-effective by using teleconferencing systems.

with about 600 to 800 students, and classes never exceed 25. In the evenings the classrooms are converted to learning laboratories that are used by the entire community. Each classroom has full-motion video links to state and national networks that permit true interactive learning. Students have desktop video access through their computers, also. The educational philosophy of this school is to promote authentic, student-centered learning activities that are cognitively situated whenever possible in real-world events. The school and its classrooms are a community resource.

This scenario could be considered a dream rather than a vision. However, it is based on the following widely available and general accepted techniques and technologies.

First, instruction is learner-centered. The networked computer permits the learner to access events of instruction that can be tailored to meet individual needs. Second, multimedia instruction is routine via technology, especially networked computer and video systems. Interactive instruction is possible because the technologies used permit the learner to contact databases, information sources, instructional experts, and other students in real-time and interactive ways. For example, individual students can use their computers to contact other students or individuals who have information they need. Also, the entire class can participate in interactive video sessions with teachers from remote sites or with groups of students from other schools. Instruction is

Students can interact with students from other schools.

Distance education is used on the plant floor, anytime outside expertise is needed.

authentic because it is not teacher-centered; rather it is content- and learner-centered. The teacher orchestrates the individual learning activities of students who collaborate with classmates, with distant learners, with the teacher, and with multimedia technology available locally or from the World Wide Web. Finally, the learning environment of the future encourages collaboration without the limitations inherent in the self-contained classroom.

Much of this is possible because of the concept of distance education, which is the bringing of learners and the content of instruction together no matter where each is located. Interactive, real-time, on-demand, learner-centered, authentic, and learner-constructed events will characterize the educational environment of the future. Ultimately the concept of distance will disappear as insignificant and the idea of interaction will replace it.

◆ SUMMARY

Separation of the student and the teacher is a fundamental characteristic of distance education. Increasingly, educators are using technology to increase the access of the distant learner to the local classroom, to improve access of all learners to resources, and to make the experience of the remote student comparable to the experience of the local learner.

Distance education is a dramatic idea. It may change, even restructure, education, but only if it is possible to make the experience of the distant learner as complete, satisfying, and acceptable as the experience of the local learner. If distance education is to be a successful and mainstream approach, then it is imperative that distance education systems be designed to permit equivalent learning experiences for distant and local students.

Distance education using telecommunications technologies is an exciting emerging field. However, practitioners should not promote distance education as the next great technological solution to education's problems, nor make grand claims about the impact of telecommunications systems. Rather, students of the area should strive to understand technology and technological approaches that make the experiences of distant and local learners positive and equivalent, at least until someone's genius identifies an approach to learning using telecommunications systems to change education, just as Charles Martel's use of the stirrup changed society.

Self-Test Questions

1. What are Coldeway's quadrants, and which quadrant did Coldeway consider the purest form of distance education? What are the pros and cons of dividing educational events into one of Coldeway's four categories?
2. What is the fundamental characteristic of distance education? Discuss what this means. What are the various kinds of distance?
3. True/False. Learners prefer not to learn at a distance. Explain your answer.

4. Richard Clark says media are "mere vehicles that deliver instruction but do not influence student achievement." Discuss Clark's analogy and decide if it is accurate. Are media vehicles? What does the word *mere* imply?
5. What do stirrups and distance education have in common? Discuss the concept of innovations and how they are used or not used. Has the computer changed teaching and learning?
6. Write a vision for a school 10 years from today.

Answers to Self-Test Questions

1. Coldeway's quadrants for education are ST-SP (same time, same place), ST-DP (same time, different place), DT-SP (different time, same place), and DT-DP (different time, different place). Coldeway considered DT-DP as the purest form of distance education. In many new applications of distance education in the United States, telecommunications technologies are being used for ST-DP teaching and learning.
2. Separation (of the learner and the teacher) is the fundamental characteristic of distance education.
3. True. However, learners often demand to be allowed to learn at a distance because of other constraints such as availability, time, or cost.
4. Clark made this claim in 1983 when he published a review of a number of decades of media research. Clark's position has been attacked by others.
5. Stirrups, according to Finn, were an invention that permitted a person to ride a horse easier. However, Charles Martel took this simple idea and created something new and unique—the knight, who used the stirrup in a way that no one had ever thought of before. Distance education permits learners to take classes and courses at a distance, but it may prove to significantly change education, even if right now no one is quite sure how.
6. A vision should be a dream for how education will look and what it will do. The vision should create a mental image in the reader's mind.

References

Clark, R. (1983). Reconsidering research on learning from media. *Review of Educational Research, 53*(4), 445–459.

Clark, R. (1994). Media will never influence learning. *Educational Technology Research and Development, 42*(2), 21–29.

Ding, X. (1994). China's higher distance education—Its four systems and their structural characteristics at three levels. *Distance Education, 15*(2), 327–346.

Ding, X. (1995). From Fordism to new-Fordism: Industrialisation theory and distance education—a Chinese perspective. *Distance Education, 16*(2), 217–240.

Finn, J. (1964). The Franks had the right idea. *NEA Journal, 53*(4), 24–27.

Holmberg, B. (1995). The evolution of the character and practice of distance education. *Open Learning, 10*(2), 47–53.

Keegan, D. (1994). *Distance training in the European Union* (ZIFF Papiere). Hagen, Germany: Institute for Research into Distance Education, Fern Universitat. (ERIC Documentation Reproduction Service No. ED 381 684)

Keegan, D. (1995). *Distance education technology for the new millennium: Compressed video teaching.* (ERIC Document Reproduction Service No. ED 389 931)

Simonson, M. (1995). Overview of the Teacher Education Alliance, Iowa Distance Education Alliance research plan. In C. Sorensen, C. Schlosser, M. Anderson, & M. Simonson (Eds.), *Encyclopedia of distance education research in Iowa* (pp. 3–6). Ames, Iowa: Teacher Education Alliance.

Thach, L., & Murphy, L. (1994). Collaboration in distance education: From local to international perspectives. *The American Journal of Distance Education, 8*(3), 5–21.

Tompkins, L. S. (1993). A new light on distance learning—fiber optics. *Journal of Educational Technology Systems, 21*(3), 265–275.

U.S. Department of Education. (1995). *The Star Schools program.* (Available from Star Schools, U.S. Department of Education, 555 New Jersey Avenue NW, Washington, DC 20208-5644)

Additional Readings

Hanna, D. (1995). *Mainstreaming distance education.* Conference of the National Association of State University and Land Grant Colleges, Madison, WI.

Jurasek, K. (1993). *Distance education via compressed video.* Unpublished master's thesis, Iowa State University, Ames.

Kozma, R. (1994). Will media influence learning: Reframing the debate. *Educational Technology Research and Development Journal, 42*(2), 7–19.

Schlosser, C., & Anderson, M. (1994). *Distance education: Review of the literature.* Washington, DC: Association for Educational Communications and Technology.

Simonson, M. (1996). *Reinventing distance education.* Paper presented at the Annual Convention of the U.S. Distance Learning Association. Washington, DC.

Simonson, M., & Schlosser, C. (1995). More than fiber: Distance education in Iowa. *Tech Trends, 40*(3), 13–15.

Willis, B. (1994). *Distance education: Strategies and tools.* Englewood Cliffs, NJ: Educational Technology Publications.

chapter 2

Definitions, History, and Theories of Distance Education

CHAPTER GOAL

The purpose of this chapter is to review the definitions, history, and theories of distance education.

CHAPTER OBJECTIVES

After reading and reviewing this chapter, you should be able to

1. Discuss the reason for different definitions of distance education.
2. Describe the various definitions of distance education that have been offered.
3. List and explain the five main elements of the various definitions of distance education given by Keegan.
4. Give the emerging definition of distance education that is appropriate for the United States.
5. Outline the general history of distance education, explaining how it began with correspondence study and evolved into the use of electronic communications media.
6. Discuss the emergence of distance teaching universities.
7. Explain the various theoretical approaches to distance education, including theories of independence, industrialization, and interaction and communication.
8. Synthesize the various theories of distance education.
9. Describe the emerging theory of distance education that relates to equivalence of learning experiences.
10. Explain Fordism, neo-Fordism, and post-Fordism.

◆ DEFINING DISTANCE EDUCATION

Distance education was defined in Chapter 1 as

> institution-based, formal education where the learning group is separated geographically, and where interactive telecommunications systems are used to connect learners, resources, and instructors.

This definition is not the only one and certainly is not the first offered for distance education. As a matter of fact, distance education has been defined from a number of perspectives over the years. For example, Rudolf Manfred Delling said,

> Distance education is a planned and systematic activity which comprises the choice, didactic preparation and presentation of teaching materials as well as the supervision and support of student learning and which is achieved by bridging the physical distance between student and teacher by means of at least one appropriate technical medium.

For Hilary Perraton (1988), distance education is an educational process in which a significant proportion of the teaching is conducted by someone removed in space and/or time from the learner.

The U.S. Department of Education's Office of Educational Research and Improvement defines distance education as "the application of telecommunications and electronic devices which enable students and learners to receive instruction that originates from some distant location." Typically, the learner may interact with the instructor or program directly, and may meet with the instructor on a periodic basis.

Grenville Rumble (1989) offered the following four-part definition of distance education:

◆ In any distance education process there must be: a teacher; one or more students; a course or curriculum that the teacher is capable of teaching and the student is trying to learn; and a contract, implicit or explicit, between the student and the teacher or the institution employing the teacher, which acknowledges their respective teaching-learning roles.

◆ Distance education is a method of education in which the learner is physically separate from the teacher. It may be used on its own, or in conjunction with other forms of education, including face-to-face.

◆ In distance education learners are physically separated from the institution that sponsors the instruction.

◆ The teaching/learning contract requires that the student be taught, assessed, given guidance and, where appropriate, prepared for examinations that may or may not be conducted by the institution. This must be accomplished by two-way communication. Learning may be undertaken either individually or in groups; in either case it is accomplished in the physical absence of the teacher.

For Desmond Keegan (1986), the following four definitions were central to an attempt to identify the elements of a single, unifying definition of distance education:

- The French government, as part of a law passed in 1971, defined distance education as education which either does not imply the physical presence of the teacher appointed to dispense it in the place where it is received or in which the teacher is present only on occasion or for selected tasks.
- According to Börje Holmberg, distance education covers the various forms of study at all levels which are not under the continuous, immediate supervision of tutors present with their students in lecture rooms or on the same premises but which, nevertheless, benefit from the planning, guidance and teaching of a supporting organization.
- Otto Peters emphasized the role of technology, saying that distance teaching/education (Fernunterricht) is a method of imparting knowledge, skills and attitudes which is rationalized by the application of division of labor and organizational principles as well as by the extensive use of technical media, especially for the purpose of reproducing high quality teaching material which makes it possible to instruct great numbers of students at the same time wherever they live. It is an industrialized form of teaching and learning.
- For Michael Moore, the related concept of "distance teaching" was defined as the family of instructional methods in which the teaching behaviors are executed apart from the learning behaviors, including those that in a contiguous situation would be performed in the learner's presence, so that communication between the teacher and the learner must be facilitated by print, electronic, mechanical or other devices.

Keegan identified five main elements of these definitions, using them to compose a comprehensive definition of distance education:

- The quasi-permanent separation of teacher and learner throughout the length of the learning process (this distinguishes it from conventional face-to-face education).
- The influence of an educational organization both in the planning and preparation of learning materials and in the provision of student support services (this distinguishes it from private study and teach-yourself programs).
- The use of technical media—print, audio, video or computer—to unite teacher and learner and carry the content of the course.
- The provision of two-way communication so that the student may benefit from or even initiate dialogue (this distinguishes it from other uses of technology in education).
- The quasi-permanent absence of the learning group throughout the length of the learning process so that people are usually taught as individuals and not in groups, with the possibility of occasional meetings for both didactic and socialization purposes.

Garrison and Shale (1987) argued that, in light of advances in distance education delivery technologies, Keegan's definition was too narrow and did not correspond to the existing reality as well as to future possibilities. While declining to offer a definition of distance education, Garrison and Shale offered the following three criteria they regarded as essential for characterizing the distance education process:

- Distance education implies that the majority of educational communication between (among) teacher and student(s) occurs noncontiguously.
- Distance education must involve two-way communication between (among) teacher and student(s) for the purpose of facilitating and supporting the educational process.
- Distance education uses technology to mediate the necessary two-way communication.

Keegan's definition and the definitions preceding it define the traditional view of distance education. Rapid changes in society and technology are challenging these traditional definitions.

Emerging Definitions

The contemporary period is often characterized as one of unpredictable change. Globalization, brought on by supersonic air travel, satellite television, computer communications, and societal changes, has inspired new ways of looking at distance education. Edwards (1995) uses the term *open learning* to describe a new way of looking at education in a quickly changing and diverse world. He indicates that distance education and open learning are two distinct approaches to education. While he does not define the two, he states that distance education provides distance learning opportunities using mass-produced courseware to a mass market. In contrast, open learning places greater emphasis on the current specific needs and/or markets available by recognizing local requirements and differences instead of delivering an established curriculum. Open learning shifts from mass production and mass consumption to a focus on local and individual needs and requirements. Edwards states that this can occur outside of the traditional organization of education. This is a major difference between his description of open learning and the previous definitions of distance education.

◆ A BRIEF HISTORY OF DISTANCE EDUCATION

Distance education seems a new idea to most educators of today. However, the concepts that form the basis of distance education are more than a century old. Certainly, there has been a growth and change in distance education recently, but it is the long traditions of the field that continue to give it direction for the future. This section offers a brief history of distance education, from correspondence study, to electronic communications, to distance teaching universities.

Correspondence Study

The roots of distance education are at least 160 years old. An advertisement in a Swedish newspaper in 1833 touted the opportunity to study "Composition through the medium of the Post." In 1840, England's newly established penny post allowed Isaac Pitman to offer shorthand instruction via correspondence. Three years later, instruction was formalized with the founding of the Phonographic Correspondence Society, precursor of Sir Isaac Pitman's Correspondence Colleges.

Distance education, in the form of correspondence study, was established in Germany by Charles Toussaint and Gustav Langenscheidt, who taught language in Berlin. Correspondence study crossed the Atlantic in 1873 when Anna Eliot Ticknor founded a Boston-based society to encourage study at home. The Society to Encourage Studies at Home attracted more than 10,000 students in 24 years. Students of the classical curriculum (mostly women) corresponded monthly with teachers, who offered guided readings and frequent tests.

From 1883 to 1891, academic degrees were authorized by the state of New York through the Chautauqua College of Liberal Arts to students who completed the required summer institutes and correspondence courses. William Rainey Harper, the Yale professor who headed the program, was effusive in his support of correspondence study, and confident in the future viability of the new educational form:

> The student who has prepared a certain number of lessons in the correspondence school knows more of the subject treated in those lessons, and knows it better, than the student who has covered the same ground in the classroom.
>
> The day is coming when the work done by correspondence will be greater in amount than that done in the classrooms of our academies and colleges; when the students who shall recite by correspondence will far outnumber those who make oral recitations.

In 1891, Thomas J. Foster, editor of the *Mining Herald,* a daily newspaper in eastern Pennsylvania, began offering a correspondence course in mining and the prevention of mine accidents. His business developed into the International Correspondence Schools, a commercial school whose enrollment exploded in the first two decades of the 20th century, from 225,000 in 1900 to more than 2 million in 1920.

In 1886, H. S. Hermod, of Sweden, began teaching English by correspondence. In 1898 he founded Hermod's, which would become one of the world's largest and most influential distance teaching organizations.

Correspondence study continued to develop in Britain with the founding of a number of correspondence institutions, such as Skerry's College in Edinburgh in 1878 and University Correspondence College in London in 1887. At the same time, the university extension movement in the United States and England promoted the correspondence method. Among the pioneers in the field were Illinois Wesleyan in 1877 and the University Extension Department of the University of Chicago in 1892.

Illinois Wesleyan offered bachelor's, master's, and doctoral degrees as part of a program modeled on the Oxford, Cambridge, and London model. Between 1881 and 1890, 750 students were enrolled; and in 1900, nearly 500 students were seeking degrees. However, concerns about the quality of the program prompted a recommendation that it be terminated by 1906.

Correspondence study was integral to the University of Chicago. The school, founded in 1890, created a university extension as one of its five divisions, the first such division in an American university. The extension division was divided into five departments: lecture study, class study, correspondence teaching, library, and training.

The correspondence study department of the University of Chicago was successful, at least in terms of numbers. Each year, 125 instructors taught 3,000 students enrolled in 350 courses. Nevertheless, enthusiasm within the university for the program waned, partly for financial reasons.

At the University of Wisconsin, the development of the "short course" and farmers' institutes in 1885 formed the foundation for university extension. Six years later, the university announced a program of correspondence study led by the eminent historian, Frederick Jackson Turner. However, as at the University of Chicago, faculty interest waned. Further, public response was minimal, and the correspondence study program was discontinued in 1899. Correspondence study would have to wait another seven years to be reborn under a new, stronger, correspondence study department within the school's university extension division.

Distance education began to enrich the secondary school curriculum in the 1920s. Students in Benton Harbor, Michigan, were offered vocational courses in 1923, and six years later, the University of Nebraska began experimenting with correspondence courses in high schools.

In France, the Ministry of Education set up a government correspondence college in response to the impending Second World War. Although the Centre National d'Enseignement par Correspondences was established for the education of children, it has since become a huge distance teaching organization for adult education.

The original target groups of distance education efforts were adults with occupational, social, and family commitments. This remains the primary target group today. Distance education provided the opportunity to widen intellectual horizons, as well as the chance to improve and update professional knowledge. Further, it stressed individuality of learning and flexibility in both the time and place of study.

Two philosophies of distance education became identifiable. The full liberalism of programs offered by Hermod's, in Sweden, emphasized the free pacing of progress through the program by the student. Other programs, such as those offered by the University of Chicago, offered a more rigid schedule of weekly lessons.

Electronic Communications

In Europe, there was a steady expansion of distance education, without radical changes in structure, but with gradually more sophisticated methods and media employed. Audio recordings were used in instruction for the blind and in language teaching for all students. Laboratory kits were used in such subjects as electronics and radio engineering. Virtually all large-scale distance teaching organizations were private correspondence schools.

In the United States, advances in electronic communications technology helped determine the dominant medium of distance education. In the 1920s, at least 176 radio stations were constructed at educational institutions, although most were gone by the end of the decade. The surviving stations were mostly at land grant colleges.

In the early 1930s, experimental television teaching programs were produced at the University of Iowa, Purdue University, and Kansas State College. However, it was not until the 1950s that college credit courses were offered via broadcast television: Western

Reserve University was the first to offer a continuous series of such courses, beginning in 1951. Sunrise Semester was a well-known televised series of college courses offered by New York University on CBS from 1957 to 1982.

Satellite technology, developed in the 1960s and made cost-effective in the 1980s, enabled the rapid spread of instructional television. Federally funded experiments in the United States and Canada, such as the Appalachian Education Satellite Project (1974–1975), demonstrated the feasibility of satellite-delivered instruction. However, these early experiments were loudly criticized for being poorly planned. More recent attempts at satellite-delivered distance education have been more successful. The first state educational satellite system, Learn/Alaska, was created in 1980. It offered six hours of instructional television daily to 100 villages, some of them accessible only by air. The privately operated TI-IN Network, of San Antonio, Texas, has delivered a wide variety of courses via satellite to high schools across the United States since 1985.

In the late 1980s and early 1990s the development of fiber-optic communication systems allowed for the expansion of live, two-way, high-quality audio and video systems in education. While the initial cost of fiber-optic systems may be high, the long-term savings and benefits of the technology outweigh the initial costs. Many now consider fiber-optic delivery systems as the least expensive option for the high-quality, two-way audio and video required for live two-way interactive distance education. The state of Iowa has the largest statewide fiber-optic system. Currently the Iowa Communications Network (ICN) provides full-motion, two-way interactive video, data (Internet), and voice services to over 600 Iowa classrooms. In the near future, all school districts, area education agencies, and public libraries in Iowa will have classrooms connected to the fiber optics of the ICN. The ICN also serves as the backbone for computer telecommunications, and asynchronous, Internet-based programs are being offered to distant learners. Over 100,000 hours of formal educational opportunities were offered during the first 18 months of the network's service. Recently, 100,000 hours were being offered every month.

Distance education opportunities are quickly growing through the use of computer-mediated communications. Tens of thousands of networks are connected to the Internet, with millions of people using the Internet worldwide (Ackermann, 1995). Both credit and noncredit courses have been offered over computer networks since the mid-1980s. In most cases, a teacher organizes the course materials, readings, and assignments. The students read the material, complete assignments, and participate in on-line discussions with other classmates. The advent of computer conferencing capabilities has had an impact on the traditional approach to the design of distance education instruction. Computer conferencing increases the potential for interaction and collaborative work among the students. This type of collaboration among students was difficult with previous forms of distance education.

In addition, computer networks are a convenient way to distribute course materials to students around the world. Many faculty members now use the convenient user interface of the World Wide Web to make course materials available to their students. The British Open University, Fern Universität of Germany, and the University of Twente in the Netherlands are some of the leading providers of on-line courses in Europe. In the United States, the American Open University, Nova Southeastern University, and the University of Phoenix have been traditional leaders in providing distance education. They, along with many other universities, are now offering hundreds of courses on-line.

Distance Teaching Universities

The 1962 decision that the University of South Africa would become a distance teaching university brought about a fundamental change in the way distance education was practiced in much of the world. Another landmark was the founding, in 1971, of the Open University of the United Kingdom, a degree-giving distance teaching university offering full degree programs, sophisticated courses, and the innovative use of media (Holmberg, 1986). The Open University brought heightened prestige to distance education, and spurred the establishment of similar institutions in industrial nations such as West Germany, Japan, and Canada, as well as in such lesser developed nations as Sri Lanka and Pakistan.

While the distance teaching universities shared numerous similarities, they were not identical in their mission or practice. Two of the largest and most influential, the Open University of the United Kingdom and the German Fern Universität, differ widely. The British school favors employed, part-time students of above normal study age, and allows them to enroll without formal entrance qualifications. By 1984, some 69,000 of its students had completed work for the bachelor of arts degree.

The German Fern Universität, founded in 1975, offers a more rigorous program than its British counterpart. Despite strict, formal entrance requirements, it had 28,000 students in 1985. However, the dropout rate is very high, and in its first decade, only 500 students completed the full curricula for a university degree.

Holmberg (1986) offers numerous political, economic, and educational reasons for the founding of distance teaching universities, including

◆ The need felt in many countries to increase the offerings of university education generally
◆ A realization that adults with jobs, family responsibilities, and social commitments form a large group of prospective part-time university students
◆ A wish to serve both individuals and society by offering study opportunities to adults, among them disadvantaged groups
◆ The need found in many professions for further training at an advanced level
◆ A wish to support educational innovation
◆ A belief in the feasibility of an economical use of educational resources by mediated teaching

◆ THEORY AND DISTANCE EDUCATION

Most students, and many teachers, cringe at the thought of a discussion of theory. This need not be the case. This section is designed not to intimidate or to bore, but to inform. Theory is important to the study of distance education because it has a direct impact on the practice of the field.

Traditionally, theories of distance education have come from sources external to America. Recently, the field in the United States has matured to the point where indigenous definitions and theories have begun to emerge.

The Need for Theory

Although forms of distance education have been in existence since the 1840s and attempts at theoretical explanations of distance education had been undertaken by leading scholars in the field, the need for a theory base of distance education was still largely unfulfilled in the 1970s. Holmberg (1986) stated that further theoretical considerations will contribute results that will give distance educators a firmly based theory, a touchstone against which decisions can be made with confidence. In 1988, Holmberg continued to recognize the need for theoretical considerations:

> One consequence of such understanding and explanation will be that hypotheses can be developed and submitted to falsification attempts. This will lead to insights telling us what in distance education is to be expected under what conditions and circumstances, thus paving the way for corroborated practical methodological application. (p. 3)

Moore (1994) was concerned that the progress of distance education would be hindered by the lack of attention to what he called the "macro factors." He indicated that in this area of education there was a need to describe and define the field, to discriminate between the various components of the field, and to identify the critical elements of the various forms of learning and teaching.

Keegan (1988) implied the continued need for a theory of distance education when he lamented the lack of it:

> Lack of accepted theory has weakened distance education: there has been a lack of identity, a sense of belonging to the periphery and the lack of a touchstone against which decisions on methods, on media, on financing, on student support, when they have to be made, can be made with confidence. (p. 63)

More recently, Keegan stated his ideas about what the theory should encompass: According to Keegan, a firmly based theory of distance education will be one which can provide the touchstone against which decisions—political, financial, educational, social—when they have to be taken, can be taken with confidence. This would replace the ad hoc response to a set of conditions that arises in some "crisis" situation of problem-solving, which normally characterizes this field of education.

In a general sense, theory is taken to mean a set of hypotheses logically related to one another in explaining and predicting occurrences. Holmberg (1985) stated that

> the aim of the theoretician is to find explanatory theories; that is to say, the theories which describe certain structural properties of the world, and which permit us to deduce, with the help of initial conditions, the effects to be explained. . . . Theoretical, to bring explanation, on the other hand practical, to provide for application or technology. (p. 5)

Keegan added (1995):

> A theory is something that eventually can be reduced to a phrase, a sentence or a paragraph and which, while subsuming all the practical research, gives the foundation on which the structures of need, purpose and administration can be erected. (p. 20)

In 1995 Holmberg gave a more specific definition of the concept of theory. He stated that a theory means

> a systematic ordering of ideas about the phenomenon of our field of inquiry and an overarching logical structure of reasoned suppositions which can generate intersubjectively testable hypotheses. (p. 4)

Holmberg suggested that distance education has been characterized by a trial and error approach with little consideration being given to a theoretical basis for decision making. He suggested that the theoretical underpinnings of distance education are fragile. Most efforts in this field have been practical or mechanical and have concentrated on the logistics of the enterprise.

To some, distance education represents a deviation from conventional education. Holmberg claimed it was a distinct form of education. Keegan (1986) concluded that distance education is a distinct field of education, parallel to and a complement of conventional education. Shale (1988) countered that all of what constitutes the process of education when teacher and student are able to meet face-to-face also constitutes the process of education when the teacher and student are physically separated.

Cropley and Kahl (1983) compared and contrasted distance education and face-to-face education in terms of psychological dimensions and claimed neither set of principles emerged in a pure form. Peters (1988) strongly stated:

> Anyone professionally involved in education is compelled to presume the existence of two forms of instruction which are strictly separable: traditional face-to-face teaching based on interpersonal communication and industrialized teaching, which is based on objectivized, rationalized technologically-produced interaction. (p. 20)

In his landmark work, *The Foundations of Distance Education,* Keegan (1986) classified theories of distance education into three groups:

- Theories of independence and autonomy
- Theories of industrialization of teaching
- Theories of interaction and communication

A fourth category seeks an explanation of distance education in a synthesis of existing theories of communication and diffusion, as well as philosophies of education.

Theory of Independent Study—Charles Wedemeyer

For Wedemeyer, the essence of distance education was the independence of the student. This was reflected in his preference for the term *independent study* for distance education at the college or university level. Wedemeyer was critical of contemporary patterns of higher education. He believed that outdated concepts of learning and teaching were being employed, and that they failed to utilize modern technologies in ways that could alter the institution.

Wedemeyer set forth a system with 10 characteristics emphasizing learner independence and adoption of technology as a way to implement that independence. According to Wedemeyer, the system should

◆ Be capable of operation any place where there are students—or even only one student—whether or not there are teachers at the same place at the same time
◆ Place greater responsibility for learning on the student
◆ Free faculty members from custodial-type duties so that more time can be given to truly educational tasks
◆ Offer students and adults wider choices (more opportunities) in courses, formats, and methodologies
◆ Use, as appropriate, all the teaching media and methods that have been proved effective
◆ Mix media and methods so that each subject or unit within a subject is taught in the best way known
◆ Cause the redesign and development of courses to fit into an "articulated media program"
◆ Preserve and enhance opportunities for adaptation to individual differences
◆ Evaluate student achievement simply, not by raising barriers concerned with the place, rate, method, or sequence of student study
◆ Permit students to start, stop, and learn at their own pace

Wedemeyer proposed the separation of teaching from learning as a way of breaking education's "space-time barriers." He suggested six characteristics of independent study systems:

◆ The student and teacher are separated.
◆ The normal processes of teaching and learning are carried out in writing or through some other medium.
◆ Teaching is individualized.
◆ Learning takes place through the student's activity.
◆ Learning is made convenient for the student in his or her own environment.
◆ The learner takes responsibility for the pace of his or her own progress, with freedom to start and stop at any time.

Wedemeyer noted four elements of every teaching-learning situation: a teacher, a learner or learners, a communications system or mode, and something to be taught or learned. He proposed a reorganization of these elements that would accommodate physical space and allow greater learner freedom. Key to the success of distance education, Wedemeyer believed, was the development of the relationship between student and teacher.

Theory of Independent Study—Michael Moore

Formulated in the early 1970s, Moore's theory of distance education, which he calls "independent study," is a classification method for distance education programs. Shaped in part by Moore's adult education and university extension experience, it examines two variables in educational programs: the amount of learner autonomy and the distance between teacher and learner.

For Moore, distance is composed of two elements, each of which can be measured. First is the provision for two-way communication (dialog). Some systems or programs offer greater amounts of two-way communication than others. Second is the extent to which a program is responsive to the needs of the individual learner (structure). Some programs are very structured, while others are very responsive to the needs and goals of the individual student.

In the second part of his theory, Moore addresses learner autonomy. He notes that in traditional school settings learners are very dependent on teachers for guidance, and that in most programs, conventional and distance, the teacher is active, while the student is passive.

In distance education, there is a gap between teacher and student, so the student must accept a high degree of responsibility for the conduct of the learning program. The autonomous learner needs little help from the teacher, who may be more of a respondent than a director. Some adult learners, however, require help in formulating their learning objectives and in identifying sources of information and in measuring objectives.

Moore classifies distance education programs as "autonomous" (learner-determined) or "nonautonomous" (teacher-determined), and gauges the degree of autonomy accorded the learner by answers to the following three questions:

◆ Is the selection of learning objectives in the program the responsibility of the learner or of the teacher (autonomy in setting of objectives)?
◆ Is the selection and use of resource persons, of bodies and other media, the decision of the teacher or the learner (autonomy in methods of study)?
◆ Are the decisions about the method of evaluation and criteria to be used made by the learner or the teacher (autonomy in evaluation)?

Theory of Industrialization of Teaching—Otto Peters

In a major treatise on education, Otto Peters of Germany developed a view of distance education as an industrialized form of teaching and learning. He examined a research base that included an extensive analysis of the distance teaching organizations of the 1960s. This led him to propose that distance education could be analyzed by comparing it with the industrial production of goods. He stated that from many points of view conventional, oral, group-based education was a preindustrial form of education. His statement implied that distance teaching could not have existed before the industrial era. Using economic and industrial theory, Peters proposed the following new categories (terminology) for the analysis of distance education.

◆ **Rationalization.** The use of methodical measures to reduce the required amount of input of power, time, and money. In distance education, ways of thinking, attitudes, and procedures can be found which only established themselves in the wake of an increased rationalization in the industrialization of production processes.
◆ **Division of labor.** The division of a task into simpler components or subtasks. In distance education, the tasks of conveying information, counseling, assessment, and recording performance are performed by separate individuals. To Peters, the division of labor is the main prerequisite for the advantages of distance education to become effective.

◆ **Mechanization.** The use of machines in a work process. Distance education, Peters noted, would be impossible without machines. Duplicating machines and transport systems are prerequisites, and later forms of distance teaching have the additional facilities of modern means of communication and electronic data processing installations.

◆ **Assembly line.** Commonly, a method of work in which workers remain stationary, while objects they are working on move past them. In traditional distance education programs, materials for both teacher and student are not the product of an individual. Rather, instructional materials are designed, printed, stored, distributed, and graded by specialists.

◆ **Mass production.** The production of goods in large quantities. Peters noted that because demand outstrips supply at colleges and universities, there has been a trend toward large-scale operations not entirely consistent with traditional forms of academic teaching. Mass production of distance education courses, however, can enhance quality. Peters believed that the large number of courses produced forced distance teaching organizations to analyze the requirements of potential distance learners far more carefully than in conventional teaching and to improve the quality of the courses.

◆ **Preparatory work.** Determining how workers, machines, and materials can usefully relate to each other during each phase of the production process. Peters believed that the success of distance education depended decisively on a preparatory phase. The preparatory phase concerns the development of the distance study course involving experts in the various specialist fields with qualifications often higher than those of other teachers involved in distance study.

◆ **Planning.** The system of decisions which determines an operation prior to it being carried out. Peters noted that planning was important in the development phase of distance education, as the contents of correspondence units, from the first to the last, must be determined in detail, adjusted in relation to each other, and represented in a predetermined number of correspondence units. The importance of planning is even greater when residential study is a component of a distance education program.

◆ **Organization.** Creating general or permanent arrangements for purpose-oriented activity. Peters noted the relationship between rational organization and effectiveness of the teaching method. Organization makes it possible for students to receive exactly predetermined documents at appointed times, for an appropriate university teacher to be immediately available for each assignment sent in, and for consultations to take place at fixed locations at fixed times. Organization, Peters pointed out, was optimized in large distance education programs.

◆ **Scientific control methods.** The methods by which work processes are analyzed systematically, particularly by time studies, and in accordance with the results obtained from measurements and empirical data. The work processes are tested and controlled in their elementary details in a planned way, in order to increase productivity, all the time making the best possible use of working time and the staff available. In distance education, some institutions hire experts to apply techniques of scientific analysis to the evaluation of courses.

- **Formalization.** The predetermination of the phases of the manufacturing process. In distance education, all the points in the cycle, from student, to distance teaching establishment, to the academics allocated, must be determined exactly.
- **Standardization.** The limitations of manufacture to a restricted number of types of one product, in order to make these more suitable for their purpose, cheaper to produce, and easier to replace. In distance education, not only is the format of correspondence units standardized, so are the stationery for written communication between student and lecturer, the organizational support, and also the academic content.
- **Change of function.** The change of the role or job of the worker in the production process. In distance education, change of function is evident in the role of the lecturer. The original role of provider of knowledge in the form of the lecturer is split into that of study unit author and that of marker; the role of counselor is allocated to a particular person or position. Frequently, the original role of lecturer is reduced to that of a consultant whose involvement in distance teaching manifests itself in periodically recurrent contributions.
- **Objectification.** The loss, in the production process, of the subjective element which used to determine work to a considerable degree. In distance education, most teaching functions are objectified as they are determined by the distance study course as well as technical means. Only in written communication with the distance learner or possibly in a consultation or the brief additional face-to-face events on campus has the teacher some individual scope left for subjectively determined variants in teaching method.
- **Concentration and centralization.** Because of the large amounts of capital required for mass production and the division of labor, there has been a trend to large industrial concerns with a concentration of capital, a centralized administration, and a market that is monopolized. Peters noted the trend toward distance education institutions serving very large numbers of students. The Open University of the United Kingdom, for instance, recently had more than 70,000 students. It is more economical to establish a small number of such institutions serving a national population, rather than a larger number of institutions serving regional populations.

Peters concluded that for distance teaching to become effective, the principle of the division of labor is a constituent element of distance teaching. The teaching process in his theory of industrialization is gradually restructured through increasing mechanization and automation. He stated that

- The development of distance study courses is just as important as the preparatory work taking place prior to the production process.
- The effectiveness of the teaching process is particularly dependent on planning and organization.
- Courses must be formalized and expectations from students standardized.
- The teaching process is largely objectified.
- The function of academics teaching at a distance has changed considerably vis-à-vis university teachers in conventional teaching.
- Distance study can only be economical with a concentration of the available resources and a centralized administration.

According to Peters, within the complex overall distance teaching activity one area has been exposed to investigation that had been regularly omitted from traditional analysis. New concepts were used to describe new facts that merit attention. He did not deny there were disadvantages to a theory of the industrialization of teaching; but in any exploration of teaching, the industrial structures characteristic of distance teaching need to be taken into account in decision making.

Theory of Interaction and Communication— Börje Holmberg

Holmberg's theory of distance education, what he calls guided didactic conversation, falls into the general category of communication theory. Holmberg noted that his theory had explanatory value in relating teaching effectiveness to the impact of feelings of belonging and cooperation as well as to the actual exchange of questions, answers, and arguments in mediated communication.

Holmberg offers seven background assumptions for his theory:

♦ The core of teaching is interaction between the teaching and learning parties; it is assumed that simulated interaction through subject matter presentation in preproduced courses can take over part of the interaction by causing students to consider different views, approaches, and solutions and generally interact with a course.

♦ Emotional involvement in the study and feelings of personal relation between the teaching and learning parties are likely to contribute to learning pleasure.

♦ Learning pleasure supports student motivation.

♦ Participation in decision making concerning the study is favorable to student motivation.

♦ Strong student motivation facilitates learning.

♦ A friendly, personal tone and easy access to the subject matter contribute to learning pleasure, support student motivation, and thus facilitate learning from the presentations of preproduced courses, i.e., from teaching in the form of one-way traffic simulating interaction, as well as from didactic communication in the form of two-way traffic between the teaching and learning parties.

♦ The effectiveness of teaching is demonstrated by students' learning of what has been taught.

These assumptions, Holmberg believes, are the basis of the essential teaching principles of distance education. From these assumptions he formed his theory:

> Distance teaching will support student motivation, promote learning pleasure and make the study relevant to the individual learner and his/her needs, creating feelings of rapport between the learner and the distance-education institution (its tutors, counselors, etc.), facilitating access to course content, engaging the learner in activities, discussions and decisions and generally catering for helpful real and simulated communication to and from the learner.

Holmberg himself notes that this is admittedly a leaky theory. However, he adds, it is not devoid of explanatory power: it does, in fact, indicate essential characteristics of effective distance education.

In 1995 Holmberg significantly broadened his theory of distance education. His new comprehensive theory of distance education is divided into eight parts. This expanded theory encompasses the theory just stated above, and stated that

◆ Distance education serves individual learners who cannot or do not want to make use of face-to-face teaching. These learners are very heterogeneous.

Distance education means learners no longer have to be bound by decisions made by others about place of study, division of the year into study terms and vacations, timetables, and entry requirements.

Distance education thus promotes students' freedom of choice and independence.

◆ Society benefits from distance education, on the one hand, from the liberal study opportunities it affords individual learners, and, on the other hand, from the professional/occupational training it provides.

Distance education is an instrument for recurrent and lifelong learning and for free access to learning opportunities and equity.

◆ All learning concerned with the acquisition of cognitive knowledge and cognitive skills as well as affective learning and some psychomotor learning is effectively provided for by distance education. Distance education may inspire metacognitive approaches.

◆ Distance education is based on deep learning as an individual activity. Learning is guided and supported by noncontiguous means. Teaching and learning rely on mediated communication, usually based on preproduced courses.

◆ Distance education is open to behaviorist, cognitive, constructivist, and other modes of learning. It has an element of industrialization with division of labor, use of mechanical devices, electronic data processing, and mass communication, usually based on preproduced courses.

◆ Personal relations, study pleasure, and empathy between students and those supporting them (tutors, counselors, etc.) are central to learning in distance education. Feelings of empathy and belonging promote students' motivation to learn and influence the learning favorably. Such feelings are conveyed by students being engaged in decision making; by lucid, problem-oriented conversation-like presentations of learning matter that may be anchored in existing knowledge; by friendly, noncontiguous interaction between students and tutors, counselors, and others supporting them; and by liberal organizational-administrative structures and processes.

◆ While it is an effective mode of training, distance education runs the risk of leading to mere fact learning and reproduction of accepted "truths." However, it can be organized and carried out in such a way that students are encouraged to search, criticize, and identify positions of their own. It thus serves conceptual learning, problem learning, and genuinely academic ends.

◆ In sum, the above represents, on the one hand, a description of distance education and, on the other hand, a theory from which hypotheses are generated and which has explanatory power in that it identifies a general approach favorable to learning and to the teaching efforts conducive to learning.

A Synthesis of Existing Theories—Hilary Perraton

Perraton's theory of distance education is composed of elements from existing theories of communication and diffusion, as well as philosophies of education. It is expressed in the form of 14 statements, or hypotheses. The first five of these statements concern the way distance teaching can be used to maximize education:

◆ You can use any medium to teach anything.
◆ Distance teaching can break the integuments of fixed staffing ratios which limited the expansion of education when teacher and student had to be in the same place at the same time.
◆ There are circumstances under which distance teaching can be cheaper than orthodox education, whether measured in terms of audience reached or of learning.
◆ The economies achievable by distance education are functions of the level of education, size of audience, choice of media, and sophistication of production.
◆ Distance teaching can reach audiences who would not be reached by ordinary means.

The following four statements address the need to increase dialog:

◆ It is possible to organize distance teaching in such a way that there is dialog.
◆ Where a tutor meets distance students face-to-face, the tutor's role is changed from that of a communicator of information to that of a facilitator of learning.
◆ Group discussion is an effective method of learning when distance teaching is used to bring relevant information to the group.
◆ In most communities there are resources that can be used to support distance learning to its educational and economic advantage.

The final five statements deal with method:

◆ A multimedia program is likely to be more effective than one that relies on a single medium.
◆ A systems approach is helpful in planning distance education.
◆ Feedback is a necessary part of a distance learning system.
◆ To be effective, distance teaching materials should ensure that students undertake frequent and regular activities over and above reading, watching, or listening.
◆ In choosing between media, the key decision on which the rest depend concerns the use of face-to-face learning.

Equivalency Theory—An Emerging American Theory of Distance Education

The impact of new technologies on distance education is far-ranging. Desmond Keegan (1995) suggests that electronically linking instructor and students at various locations creates a virtual classroom. Keegan goes on to state that

> The theoretical analyses of virtual education, however, have not yet been addressed by the literature: Is it a subset of distance education or to be regarded as a separate field of educational endeavor? What are its didactic

structures? What is the relationship of its cost effectiveness and of its educational effectiveness to distance education and to conventional education? (p. 21)

It is in this environment of virtual education that the equivalency theory of distance education has emerged. Simonson theorizes that for distance education to be successful in the United States

Its appropriate application should be based on the belief that the more equivalent the learning experiences of distant students are to that of local students, the more equivalent will be the outcomes of the learning experience.

This theory is based on the emerging definition of distance education as formal, institutionally based education that takes place using two-way interactive telecommunication systems. Simonson (1996) in elaborating on this theory states

It should not be necessary for any group of learners to compensate for different, possibly lesser, instructional experiences. Thus, those developing distance educational systems should strive to make equivalent the learning experiences of all students no matter how they are linked to the resources or instruction they require.

One key to this theoretical approach is the concept of equivalency. Local and distant learners have fundamentally different environments in which they learn. It is the responsibility of the distance educator to design learning events that provide experiences with equal value for learners. Just as a triangle and a square may have the same area and be considered equivalent even though they are quite different geometrical shapes, the experiences of the local learner and the distant learner should have equivalent value even though these experiences might be quite different.

Another key to this approach is the concept of the learning experience. A learning experience is anything that promotes learning, including what is observed, felt, heard, or done. It is likely that different students in various locations, learning at different times, may require a different mix of learning experiences. Some will need a greater amount of observing, and others a larger dosage of doing. The goal of instructional planning is to make the sum of experiences for each learner equivalent. Instructional design procedures should attempt to anticipate and provide the collection of experiences that will be most suitable for each student or group of students.

This approach is supported by Shale (1988), who argued that distance education is not a distinct field of education. He states that the process of education when students and teacher are face-to-face is the same as when students and teachers are at a distance.

A Theoretical Framework for Distance Education— Desmond Keegan

Keegan (1986) suggested that the theoretician had to answer three questions before developing a theory of distance education:

◆ *Is distance education an educational activity?* Keegan's answer was that, while distance education institutions possess some of the characteristics of businesses, rather than of traditional schools, their educational activities are dominant. Distance education is a more industrialized form of education. The theoretical bases for distance education, Keegan pointed out, were within general education theory.

◆ *Is distance education a form of conventional education?* Keegan believed that, because distance education was not based on interpersonal communication and is characterized by a privatization of institutionalized learning (as is conventional education), it is a distinct form of education. Therefore, while the theoretical basis for distance education could be found within general education theory, it could not be found within the theoretical structures of oral, group-based education.

However, Keegan considered virtual systems based on teaching face-to-face at a distance a new cognate field of study to distance education. He believes that a theoretical analysis of virtual education still needs to be addressed.

◆ *Is distance education possible, or is it a contradiction in terms?* Keegan points out that if education requires intersubjectivity—a shared experience in which teacher and learner are united by a common zeal—then distance education is a contradiction in terms. Distance *instruction* is possible, but distance *education* is not.

Again, the advent of virtual systems used in distance education challenges the traditional answer to this question.

Central to Keegan's concept of distance education is the separation of the teaching acts in time and place from the learning acts. Successful distance education, he believes, requires the reintegration of the two acts:

> The intersubjectivity of teacher and learner, in which learning from teaching occurs, has to be artificially recreated. Over space and time, a distance system seeks to reconstruct the moment in which the teaching-learning interaction occurs. The linking of learning materials to learning is central to this process.

Reintegration of the act of teaching at a distance is attempted in two ways. First, learning materials, both print and nonprint, are designed to achieve as many of the characteristics of interpersonal communication as possible. Second, when courses are presented, reintegration of the teaching act is attempted by a variety of techniques, including communication by correspondence, telephone tutorial, on-line computer communication, comments on assignments by tutors or computers, and teleconferences.

The process of reintegrating the act of teaching in distance education, Keegan suggests, results in at least five changes to the normal structure of oral, group-based education:

◆ The industrialization of teaching
◆ The privatization of institutional learning
◆ Change of administrative structure
◆ Different plant and buildings
◆ Change of costing structures

Keegan offers three hypotheses drawn from his theoretical framework:

◆ Distance students have a tendency to drop out of those institutions in which structures for the reintegration of the teaching acts are not satisfactorily achieved.
◆ Distance students have difficulty in achieving quality of learning in those institutions in which structures for the reintegration of the teaching acts are not satisfactorily achieved.
◆ The status of learning at a distance may be questioned in those institutions in which the reintegration of the teaching acts is not satisfactorily achieved.

◆ FORDISM, NEO-FORDISM, POST-FORDISM: A THEORETICAL DEBATE

Recently, Peters's view of distance education has received renewed attention. His theory of industrialized education is a point of departure, and is extended and revised based on contemporary industrial transformation in a debate on the future of distance education. *Fordism* and *post-Fordism* are the terms borrowed from industrial sociology to classify the opposing views of the debate. This debate deals with changes in the practice of distance education and represents wider debates about the nature of change in the contemporary period (Edwards, 1995). While not all would agree that the Fordist framework applies to distance education (Rumble, 1995a, 1995b, 1995c), it has become the mainstream theory of distance education in international literature and provides a useful analogy in debating the practice of distance education.

The term *Fordism* is derived from Henry Ford's approach to the mass production for mass consumption of automobiles early in the 20th century. *Fordism, neo-Fordism,* and *post-Fordism* are terms that represent three ways to conceptualize the production of distance education. Each of these ideal-type models suggests very different social, political, and educational outcomes. Badham and Mathews (1989) provide a clear model for understanding the three categories of distance education production.

They proposed that a firm's production process and its production strategy can be defined in terms of these three variables—product variety, process innovation, and labor responsibility—and they suggested that a production paradigm represents an exemplary model of efficient production which guides organizational strategy.

In looking at the three variables—product variety, process innovation, and labor responsibility—Fordism would be described as having low product innovation, low process variability, and low labor responsibility. Neo-Fordism would have high product innovation and high process variability, but would maintain the low labor responsibility of the Fordism definition. High product innovation, high process variability, and high labor responsibility would typify the post-Fordism model. Campion (1995) illustrated how these three different production processes relate to distance education:

The Fordist strategy for distance education suggested a fully centralized, single-mode, national distance education provider, gaining greater economies of scale by offering courses to a mass market, thereby justifying a greater investment in more expensive course materials. Rationalization of this kind allows for increased administrative control and a more extreme division of labor as the production process is fragmented in an increasing number of component tasks.

The neo-Fordist strategy extends the Fordist system by allowing much higher levels of flexibility and diversity, and by combining low volumes with high levels of product and process innovation. However, neo-Fordist production retains a highly centralized Fordist approach to labor organization and control. A neo-Fordist expression of distance education might well be represented by a centrally controlled, perhaps multinational, yet locally administered model of distance education. By also using self-instructional course materials for teaching on-campus students, it has the potential to massively reduce costs across the whole student population. However, and most important, a neo-Fordist manifestation of distance education bears a strong relationship to that of the Fordist route inasmuch as it has an overall despoiling effect on academic staff.

The post-Fordist strategy is characterized by high levels of all three variables: product innovation, process variability, and labor responsibility. It is opposed to neo-Fordism and to Fordism, dispensing with a division of labor and rigid managerial control and deliberately fostering a skilled and responsible workforce. A post-Fordist model of distance education would be decentralized and retain integration between the study modes. Academic staff would, however, retain autonomous control of their administered courses, and in so doing, would be able rapidly to adjust course curriculum and delivery to the changing needs of students.

In general, Fordist distance education involves mass production for mass consumption. There is centralized control, a division of work tasks associated with distance education, and the creation of management for the division of the work tasks. Courses are developed by a small core of skilled workers and delivered centrally with a de-skilling effect on the teacher. In a neo-Fordist system course development, delivery, and administration are mixed between a centralized office and regional or local offices. This allows for more flexibility in course development and delivery. In the neo-Fordist model the teacher is still given little responsibility beyond delivering the developed materials. The post-Fordist approach to distance education would focus on the consumer rather than the product. Administration would be decentralized, democratic, and participatory, and the division of labor would be informal and flexible. Teachers would have a high responsibility to develop curriculum and respond to the learning needs of their students.

Much of education as it developed over the past century fits the Fordist paradigm. Renner (1995) states that education became a formalized system of production which could be monitored, maintained, and controlled in the same way as the factory. The practice of distance education has also been greatly influenced by the Fordist paradigm. It has been argued that Fordism is still the dominant international paradigm in distance education.

Distance education has been influenced by the Fordist paradigm because it is the model that has been most successful in business throughout this century. Evans (1995) states that distance education can be seen as both a product and a process of modernity. Its administrative systems, distribution networks, and print production processes are characteristic of modern societies with developed mass production, consumption, and management. The Fordist approach to distance education provides cost-efficiencies and quality production of materials unachievable outside of the Fordist model. In addition, global competition in distance education will favor the marketing power of large educational providers. The Fordist approach to the practice of distance education provides obvious advantages.

However, major concerns about the continuation of the Fordist paradigm in distance education have been expressed. These concerns revolve around the following themes:

1. Mass markets for delivered instruction have changed, reducing the demand for centrally produced instruction for mass delivery.
2. The Fordism model is unable to adapt to the needs of a fast-changing society.
3. The focus on instructional production and the systematic use of preprogrammed curricula are incompatible with higher levels of educational quality.

With heightened competition, diversification of demand, and rapid developments in communication and information technology, the Fordist rationale, which presumes a uniform mass market to support mass production, is inappropriate. As a result, the cost-effectiveness and cost-efficiency of centrally developed and delivered instruction has declined. Ding (1995) in reporting on China's distance education system indicates that the market for many of the traditional disciplines is close to saturation while there are many demands for specific disciplines and specialties. However, Ding states that there is a relatively small demand in each specialty, such as English for foreign trade, tourist economics, manufacture of household appliances, and so on. In addition, different regions of the country report differing needs. Renner concludes that open education markets are becoming more fragmented, competitive, and specialized. A search for more efficient and flexible forms of organizational structure is an inescapable outcome.

The Fordist structure is not well suited to easily adapt to the changing needs in society. If we combine an increasingly differentiated consumer market with the power and speed of contemporary interactive computer communications technologies and add to this a more highly educated workforce, then the bureaucratic practices of the past would seem far from sustainable. This new environment requires a flexible structure in which ideas are readily tried and shared. In China, Ding found that the Fordist structure could not adapt itself to the new conditions of the market immediately and quickly. He stated that the Fordist structure could not adapt curricula to the regional needs of the country or alter the structure and content of the course to the needs of the students. The answer according to Renner is to place an emphasis on labor flexibility that would allow individual academics to produce and deliver quality curriculum more readily customized to student needs. It is felt that post-Fordist systems of distance education would be able to rapidly respond to the needs of society.

Renner's statement that the systematic use of preprogrammed curricula is incompatible with higher levels of educational quality suggests a controversy that goes beyond the debate on Fordism. Preprogrammed curricula used in the Fordist approach to distance education are products of instructional design based on behaviorism.

Post-Fordism is directly linked to constructivism. Renner states that the relationship between constructivism and post-Fordism is intimate. The constructivist believes that the individual gives meaning to the world through experience. Ideally, it is a process of personal and cooperative experimentation, questioning, and problem solving through which meaning can be constructed. This approach to learning is viewed as incompatible with mass production of instructional curricula developed with instructional design methods based in behaviorism that assume a more passive approach to learning. For constructivist learning to occur, teaching must remain flexible and sensitive to learner needs, from intellectual, cognitive, and psychological perspectives. Centrally devised educational courseware that dictates teaching sequences to students and de-skilled tutor-grade staff discourage the customization and construction of knowledge.

For the advocates of post-Fordism, neo-Fordism is no more acceptable than Fordism. While there is higher product innovation and process variability, labor responsibility is still low. It is this view of the role of labor that divides the new-Fordist approach from the post-Fordist approach. The neo-Fordism division of labor leaves the teacher and the academic staff divorced from research, curriculum development, and scholarly inquiry. They simply deliver the curriculum prepared for them. Proponents of the post-Fordist paradigm have two disagreements with this approach. First, this approach again assumes a behavioral-based instructional design method for curricula development. The preceding paragraph outlined the post-Fordist's concerns about this method. Second, post-Fordists would see this approach as being exploitative of the worker. High product innovation and high process variability put additional demands on the worker without additional compensation. The neo-Fordism and post-Fordism approaches to distance education are fundamentally different.

The debate about Fordism is intricate, heated, and tied in with differing political, economic, aesthetic, ethical, and educational perspectives. The issues raised in this debate are important because policymakers introduce regulations, generate institutional structures, and effectively organize workplace practices on the basis of such paradigms. How students learn, and frequently what they learn, is a product of these decisions. As the role of distance education is defined in a changing society, these issues need to be given careful consideration.

There is little involvement in the Fordism/post-Fordism debate by American distance educators. In the United States local control, small classes, rapport between teachers and students, and highly personalized instruction are hailed as important characteristics of its highly respected educational system (Simonson, 1995). This approach to education is diametrically opposed to the mass production, centralized control advocated by a Fordist approach to distance education. While Thach and Murphy (1994) suggest that there is a need for national coordination of higher distance education and that local and state control of education inhibit opportunities for collaboration at a distance among institutions, the United States' traditional approach to education is prevalent. This focus on student needs, personalized instruction, and interaction is evident in the following statement by Michael Moore (1994):

> In a typical United States course that uses teleconferencing technologies to link, let us say, six sites, the curriculum problem is how to integrate the local interests and needs, as well as the local knowledge that lies at each site, into the content to be taught.

◆ SUMMARY

In the rapidly changing and diverse environment in which distance education is practiced, many questions remain unanswered. In this environment it is difficult to arrive at one definition or agree on a theory of how to practice and do research in the field of distance education. New technologies, globalization, and new ideas about student learning challenge the traditional approaches to the practice of distance education. This theme of change is evident in the discussions of distance education and its definition, history, status, and theory.

Numerous definitions of distance education have been proposed. Most include the separation of teacher and learner, the influence of an educational organization, the use of media to unite teacher and learner, the opportunity for two-way communication, and the practice of individualized instruction. The traditional definitions describe distance education as taking place at a different time and in a different place, while recent definitions, enabled by new interactive technologies, stress education that takes place at the same time but in a different place. The role of educational organizations in the distance education process has also been challenged. For example, open learning is a form of distance education which occurs without the influence of an educational organization. These issues will continue to be debated as distance educators seek definitions that fit a changing world.

Investigating the relatively brief history of distance education reveals both a diversity and an ongoing change in its practice. Historically, diverse practices of distance education have been developed according to the resources and philosophies of the organizations providing instruction. The history also shows that key changes in distance education have been promoted by advances in technology. These changes have been most evident in the rapid development of electronic communications in recent decades. How the future of distance education will be shaped by the integration of its history and these new technologies is yet to be seen.

Changes in society, politics, economics, and technology are impacting the status of distance education around the world. In some cases, distance education is seen as an answer to inadequate educational opportunities caused by political and/or economic instability. In other situations, established distance education providers are being required by a changing society to convert from mass instruction to a more decentralized approach to meet the diverse needs of their students. In many countries, the need for continuing education or training and access to degree programs is accelerated by the demands of a changing society. Students in rural or isolated parts of the world look to distance education for opportunities to "keep up" with the outside world. Again, technology advances are a major influence for change in distance education worldwide. The globalization of the world enabled by these new technologies will challenge distance educators to rethink the practice of distance education to take advantage of these new opportunities.

The changing and diverse environment in which distance education is practiced has inhibited the development of a single theory upon which to base practice and research. A variety of theories have been proposed to describe traditional distance education. They include theories that emphasize independence and autonomy of the learner, industrialization of teaching, and interaction and communication. These traditional theories emphasize that distance education is a fundamentally different form of education. Recent emerging theories, based on the capabilities of new interactive audio and video systems, state that distance education is not a distinct field of education. Both utilization of existing educational theory and the creation of like experiences for both the distant and local learner are emphasized. Traditional distance education theorists will need to address the changes to distance education facilitated by new technologies. Advocates of the new theories will need to consider their impact on the traditional strengths of distance education. Specifically, the focus of the new theories on face-to-face instruction eliminates the advantage of time-independent learning that traditional theories of distance education value. The debate on these theoretical issues will only increase in the face of continued change.

One indication of the impact of change in distance education theory is the Fordist/post-Fordist/neo-Fordist debate. Fordist distance education is administered centrally and involves mass production of curricula for mass consumption. Rapid changes in society have resulted in diverse market needs. The Fordist paradigm is unable to respond quickly to these needs. The post-Fordist paradigm implements a decentralized, democratic administration that focuses on the consumer. In this paradigm, teachers have a high responsibility to respond to individual needs of students. Central to the debate between Fordists and post-Fordists are changing views about how learning occurs. The Fordist approach is based in behaviorism learning theory in which knowledge is delivered to the learner. The constructivist approach to learning in which individuals give meaning to the world through experience underlies the post-Fordist position. The debate on these differences will continue as distance education adapts to meet the needs of a changing society.

An environment in which technology, society, economics, politics, and theories of learning are all in transition suggests that definitions, theories, and the practice of distance education will continue to be contested. This theme of change will both challenge and motivate distance educators and researchers as they strive to understand and develop effective ways to meet the needs of learners around the world.

Self-Test Questions

1. Why are there different definitions of distance education? Discuss and develop the definition that you feel is most appropriate.
2. List Desmond Keegan's five main elements of the various definitions of distance education. Write a paragraph explaining which of the elements is most critical and which is least critical.
3. True/False. Many believe that in the near future the concept of distance will become relatively unimportant. What do you think this means?
4. True/False. Correspondence study is a relatively recent form of distance education that developed during World War II. Is correspondence study still important today?

5. Give at least two reasons for the founding of special distance teaching universities. Why is there no national distance learning university in the United States?

6. True/False. Distance education has a long history in European countries. Why is distance learning considered more commonplace in Europe than in the United States?

7. True/False. Keegan believes that the lack of an accepted theory of distance education has weakened the field. Discuss the importance of theory and how theory helps the practitioner of distance education.

8. List at least two of Wedemeyer's six characteristics of independent study systems. Why would Wedemeyer's perspective be important to American educators?

9. Explain the concept of the assembly line as it relates to the industrialization of teaching. Will industrialized education ever be important in American education? Explain.

10. Give Simonson's emerging theory of distance education. List learning experiences that are different for local and distant learners.

Answers to Self-Test Questions

1. Distance education has evolved as technological media have been developed. Newer technologies make possible different ways to allow students to learn at a distance, and this promotes the development of new definitions of distance education. The practice of a profession determines the definition of the profession.

2. Keegan identified five main elements of these definitions, using them to compose a comprehensive definition of distance education:
   • The quasi-permanent separation of teacher and learner throughout the length of the learning process (this distinguishes it from conventional face-to-face education).
   • The influence of an educational organization both in the planning and preparation of learning materials and in the provision of student support services (this distinguishes it from private study and teach-yourself programs).
   • The use of technical media—print, audio, video, or computer—to unite teacher and learner and carry the content of the course.
   • The provision of two-way communication so that the student may benefit from or even initiate dialogue (this distinguishes it from other uses of technology in education).
   • The quasi-permanent absence of the learning group throughout the length of the learning process so that people are usually taught as individuals and not in groups, with the possibility of occasional meetings for both didactic and socialization purposes.

3. True.

4. False.

5. Holmberg (1986) cites numerous reasons for the founding of distance teaching universities, including

- The need felt in many countries to increase the offerings of university education generally
- A realization that adults with jobs, family responsibilities, and social commitments form a large group of prospective part-time university students
- A wish to serve both individuals and society by offering study opportunities to adults, among them disadvantaged groups
- The need found in many professions for further training at an advanced level
- A wish to support educational innovation
- A belief in the feasibility of an economical use of educational resources by mediated teaching

6. True.
7. True.
8. Wedemeyer proposed the separation of teaching from learning as a way of breaking education's "space-time barriers." He suggested six characteristics of independent study systems:
   - The student and teacher are separated.
   - The normal processes of teaching and learning are carried out in writing or through some other medium.
   - Teaching is individualized.
   - Learning takes place through the student's activity.
   - Learning is made convenient for the student in his or her own environment.
   - The learner takes responsibility for the pace of his or her own progress, with freedom to start and stop at any time.
9. Commonly, the assembly line is a method of work in which workers remain stationary, while objects they are working on move past them. In traditional distance education programs, materials for both teacher and student are not the product of an individual. Rather, instructional materials are designed, printed, stored, distributed, and graded by specialists.
10. For distance education to be successful,

   Its appropriate application should be based on the belief that the more similar the learning experience of the distant student is to that of the local student, the more similar will be the outcomes of the learning experience.

References

Ackermann, E. (1995). *Learning to use the Internet.* Wilsonville, OR: Franklin, Beedle and Associates Inc.

Badham, R., & Mathews, J. (1989). The new production systems debate. *Labour and Industry, 2*(2), 194–246.

Campion, M. (1995). The supposed demise of bureaucracy: Implications for distance education and open learning—More on the post-Fordism debate. *Distance Education, 16*(2), 192–216.

Cropley, A. J., & Kahl, T. N. (1983). Distance education and distance learning: Some psychological considerations. *Distance Education, 4*(1), 27–39.

Ding, X. (1994). China's higher distance education—Its four systems and their structural characteristics at three levels. *Distance Education, 15*(2), 327–346.

Ding, X. (1995). From Fordism to new-Fordism: Industrialisation theory and distance education—a Chinese perspective. *Distance Education, 16*(2), 217–240.

Delling, Rudolf M. (1987). Towards a theory of distance education. *ICDE Bulletin, 13*, 21-25.

Edwards, R. (1995). Different discourses, discourses of difference: Globalisation, distance education, and open learning. *Distance Education, 16*(2), 241–255.

Evans, T. (1995). Globalisation, post-Fordism and open and distance education. *Distance Education, 16*(2), 256–269.

Garrison, D. R., & Shale, D. (1987). Mapping the boundaries of distance education: Problems in defining the field. *The American Journal of Distance Education, 1*(1), 7–13.

Holmberg, B. (1985). *The feasibility of a theory of teaching for distance education and a proposed theory* (ZIFF Papiere 60). Hagen (West Germany): Fern Universität, Zentrales Institute fur Fernstudienforschung Arbeitsbereich. (ERIC Document Reproduction Service No. ED 290 013)

Holmberg, B. (1986). *Growth and structure of distance education.* London: Croom Helm.

Keegan, D. (1986). *The foundations of distance education.* London: Croom Helm.

Keegan, D. (1988). Theories of distance education: Introduction. In D. Sewart, D. Keegan, & B. Holmberg (Eds.), *Distance education: International perspectives* (pp. 63–67). New York: Routledge.

Keegan, D. (1995). *Distance education technology for the new millennium: Compressed video teaching.* (ERIC Document Reproduction Service No. ED 389 931)

Moore, M. (1994). Autonomy and interdependence. *The American Journal of Distance Education, 8*(2), 1–5.

Perraton, H. (1988). A theory for distance education. In D. Sewart, D. Keegan, & B. Holmberg (Eds.), *Distance education: International perspectives* (pp. 34–45). New York: Routledge.

Peters, O. (1988). Distance teaching and industrial production: A comparative interpretation in outline. In D. Sewart, D. Keegan, & B. Holmberg (Eds.), *Distance education: International perspectives* (pp. 95–113). New York: Routledge.

Renner, W. (1995). Post-Fordist visions and technological solutions: Education technology and the labour process. *Distance Education, 16*(2), 285–301.

Rumble, G. (1995a). Labour market theories and distance education I: Industrialisation and distance education. *Open Learning, 10*(1), 10–21.

Rumble, G. (1995b). Labour market theories and distance education II: How Fordist is distance education? *Open Learning, 10*(2), 12–28.

Rumble G. (1995c). Labour market theories and distance education III: Post-Fordism the way forward? *Open Learning, 10*(3), 47–52.

Shale, D. (1988). Toward a reconceptualization of distance education. *The American Journal of Distance Education, 2*(3), 25–35.

Simonson, M. (1995). Overview of the Teacher Education Alliance, Iowa Distance Education Alliance research plan. In C. Sorensen, C. Schlosser, M. Anderson, &

M. Simonson (Eds.), *Encyclopedia of distance education research in Iowa* (pp. 3–6). Ames, IA: Teacher Education Alliance.

Simonson, M. (1996). *Distance education: Does anyone really want to learn at a distance?* Manuscript submitted for publication.

Thach, L., & Murphy, L. (1994). Collaboration in distance education: From local to international perspectives. *The American Journal of Distance Education, 8*(3), 5–21.

Additional Readings

Albright, M. (1988). *A conceptual framework for the design and the delivery of a university-level credit course by communications satellite.* Unpublished doctoral dissertation, Iowa State University, Ames.

Barry, M., & Runyan, G. B. (1995). A review of distance-learning studies in the U.S. military. *The American Journal of Distance Education, 9*(3), 37–47.

Bruder, I. (1989). Distance learning: What's holding back this boundless delivery system? *Electronic Learning, 8*(6), 30–35.

Buckland, M., & Dye, C. M. (1991). *The development of electronic distance education delivery systems in the United States. Recurring and emerging themes in history and philosophy of education.* (ERIC Document Reproduction Service No. 345 713)

Holmberg, B. (1989). *Theory and practice of distance education.* London: Routledge.

Holmberg, B. (1995). *The sphere of distance-education theory revisited.* (ERIC Document Reproduction Service No. ED 386 578)

Johnson, J. K. (1988). *Attitudes of high school students in small rural schools toward interactive satellite instruction.* Unpublished master's thesis, Iowa State University, Ames.

Keegan, D. (1988). On defining distance education. In D. Sewart, D. Keegan, & B. Holmberg (Eds.), *Distance education: International perspectives* (pp. 6–33). New York: Routledge.

Lintz, M., & Tognotti, S. (1996). Distance education on the WWW[World Wide Web]. Available: http://tecfa.unige.ch/edu-ws94/contrib/peraya.fm.html.

Magnus, J. (1996). Distance education in Sub-Saharan Africa: The next five years. *Innovations in Education and Training International, 33*(1), 50–56.

Riel, M., & Harasim, L. (1994). Research perspectives on network learning. *Machine-Mediated Learning, 4* (2–3), 91–113.

Rose, S. N. (1991). Collegiate-based noncredit courses. In B. B. Watkins & S. J. Wright (Eds.), The foundations of American distance education (pp. 67–92). Dubuque, IA: Kendall/Hunt.

Rumble, G. (1989). On defining distance education. *The American Journal of Distance Education, 3*(2), 8–21.

Simonson, M. (1995). Distance education revisited: An introduction to the issue. *Tech Trends, 40*(30), 2.

Simonson, M. (1995). Does anyone really want to learn at a distance? *Tech Trends, 40*(3), 2.

Simonson, M., & Schlosser, C. (1995). More than fiber: Distance education in Iowa. *Tech Trends, 40*(3), 13–15.

Sorensen, C., Maushak, N., & Lozada, M. (1996). *Iowa Distance Education Alliance preliminary evaluation report.* Ames: Iowa State University, Research Institute for Studies in Education.

Tompkins, L. S. (1993). A new light on distance learning—Fiber optics. *Journal of Educational Technology Systems, 21*(3), 265–275.

U.S. Department of Education (1995). *The Star Schools program.* (Available from Star Schools, U.S. Department of Education, 555 New Jersey Avenue NW, Washington, DC 20208-5644)

Watkins, B. L. (1991). A quite radical idea: The invention and elaboration of collegiate correspondence study. In B. L. Watkins & S. J. Wright (Eds.), *The Foundations of American Distance Education* (pp. 1–35). Dubuque, IA: Kendall/Hunt.

Young, J. R. (1995). Classes on the Web. *Chronicle of Higher Education,* November 3, 1995, pp. A27, A32–A33.

chapter 3

Research and Distance Education

CHAPTER GOAL

The purpose of this chapter is to summarize the research on distance education.

CHAPTER OBJECTIVES

After reading and reviewing this chapter, you should be able to

1. Explain research dealing with learning outcomes in distance education environments.
2. Explain research on learner perceptions concerning distance education.
3. Explain research on learner attributes and other variables in distance education situations.
4. Describe research related to interaction in distance education.
5. Summarize research on distance education.

◆ THE FOCUS OF DISTANCE EDUCATION RESEARCH

Emerging technologies have forced a redefinition of distance education. At the same time, the distance education research agenda has also evolved. The focus has shifted to a more learner-centered approach. Researchers are not merely looking at achievement but are examining learner attributes and perceptions as well as interaction patterns and how these contribute to the overall learning environment. While there is continued interest in the technology, the focus is not on which medium is best, but on what attributes of the medium can contribute to a positive, equivalent learning experience. This chapter will provide a review of distance education research literature.

In his 1987 article, "The Development of Distance Education Research," Börje Holmberg, a leading distance education theorist and researcher, suggested that the structure of distance education research include

- ◆ Philosophy and theory of distance education
- ◆ Distance students and their milieu, conditions, and study motivations
- ◆ Subject matter presentation
- ◆ Communication and interaction between students and their supporting organization (tutors, counselors, administrators, other students)
- ◆ Administration and organization
- ◆ Economics
- ◆ Systems (comparative distance education, typologies, evaluation, etc.)
- ◆ History of distance education

Leading researchers attending the Third Distance Education Research Symposium-Conference organized discussions around four areas: course design, instruction, policy and administration, and learners and learning. In the area of course design, the need for evaluation of learner affective reactions, learning, transfer of knowledge to other settings, and impact on the organization was stressed. Research to support the intuitive sense that interaction is important and necessary is needed under research on instruction.

◆ LEARNING OUTCOMES

It is likely that when different media treatments of the same informational content to the same students yield similar learning results, the cause of the results can be found in a method which the two treatments share in common . . . *give up your enthusiasm* [italics added] for the belief that media attributes cause learning. (Clark, 1994, p. 28)

Hundreds of media comparison studies indicate, unequivocally, that there is no inherent significant difference in the achievement effectiveness of media (Clark, 1983). These results support Clark's position summarized in the above quote. The specific medium does not matter. That being the case, the focus of future research should be on instruction itself since it is the truly critical factor in determining student achievement (Whittington, 1987).

Unfortunately, much of the research in distance education is still of the media comparison type. This is to be expected given the rapid development of distance education technology, especially in the area of two-way interactive television systems. With each technological advance, the temptation is to conduct media comparison research on the off chance that the new technology might truly bring about higher student achievement.

A typical study reported by Cheng, Lehman, and Armstrong (1991) compared performance of graduate-level students enrolled in traditional and computer conferencing classrooms. The on-campus class had 25 graduate students, and the off-campus group included 28 in-service teachers. The groups differed significantly only on age, with the average age of the off-campus students being older. A pretest/posttest format was used measuring attitude and knowledge. Results indicated no significant difference in overall course performance or in attitudes.

Bruning, Landis, Hoffman, and Grosskopf (1993) compared learning outcomes of an interactive telecourse in introductory high school Japanese with those of a traditional class. The telecourse originated in Nebraska and was transmitted to 170 schools (911 students) the first year, 255 schools (1,157 students) the second year, and 259 schools (1,330) students the third year. The achievement test had two parts and measured listening and writing.

An evaluation of the first year showed that the achievement of students in the telecourse schools was significantly higher than that of students in the comparison schools for both listening and writing. The results for the second year were similar. It was observed that the older students in the distant class were highly motivated and this had a significant impact on their achievement, much more than the fact that they learned at a distance.

Additional data were collected in the third year to investigate possible effects of motivation (measured by self-efficacy rating) and differences in student characteristics of self-reported grades in school and prior language learning experience. The mean achievement test scores for the telecourse students continued to be significantly higher than those of students in the comparison schools even when the variables of self-efficacy, self-reported ability, and prior language experience were controlled. This indicates that the achievement differences between the telecourse students and the comparison group were not related to motivational, self-reported ability, or prior experience factors.

A study by Martin and Rainey (1993) compared the effectiveness of interactive satellite delivery with that of traditional instruction. There was no important difference between the two groups on the pretest. However, the average posttest score for the experimental group, the students who participated in the course by satellite, was significantly higher than that of the control group.

Bramble and Martin (1995) investigated the effectiveness of teletraining in the military. Participants were 275 individuals enrolled in five different teletraining project courses. Standard multiple-proficiency, criterion-based tests were used where available, and achievement tests were developed for the other courses. In all but one course, both pretests and posttests were administered.

Students were allowed a second chance at taking the proficiency tests, and when these retakes were taken into account, all students reached acceptable performance levels. No comparison data were available from schools offering these courses in traditional settings, but knowledgeable training personnel indicated that this performance is as high as or higher than one would normally expect. In all courses where precourse and postcourse performances were measured, the gain was statistically significant.

Students in all five courses were asked if they felt the teletraining was as effective as live instruction. In all but one of the courses, 75% or more responded in the affirmative. The course that had only a 54% affirmative rate was the first course offered, and adjustments may have been made prior to delivery of the other courses. This pattern was repeated when students were asked if they felt that the instructor was in the same room. For the first class only 78% responded yes, while for subsequent classes 84% or more responded in the affirmative.

While comparative research studies on achievement tend to show no significant difference between different delivery systems and between distance education and traditional education, several recent studies indicate a significant higher achievement level for those learning at a distance. Because the accepted position is that the delivery system affects no inherent difference on achievement (Clark, 1994), future research needs to examine what factors do indeed contribute to this difference in achievement. In general, it is safe to conclude that distant and local learners will achieve at the same level, and that distance education is an effective method for delivering instruction that works. In other words, distance is not a predictor of learning.

◆ LEARNER PERCEPTIONS

Ross, Morrison, Smith, and Cleveland (1991) evaluated two programs for tutoring at-risk elementary school children at a distance: one used a local electronic bulletin board system and the other used Applelink, a national network system featuring both electronic mail and teleconferencing. For both studies, both tutor and tutee attitudes were assessed.

In the first program, student reactions ranged from mixed to negative. More than half of the students did not understand corrections made by their tutors, received little help with their writing skills, did not have enough time with their tutors, found the assignments difficult, and said they did not learn much from their tutors. On the positive side, slightly more than half the students felt they had enough on-line time to complete messages.

Most tutors felt they possessed the computer skills and content knowledge to do the work. They also felt they related well to their tutees and had the materials necessary. A need for more intensive training was expressed, and a majority (67%) said they would have liked more personal contact with their students.

More positive results were found in the second study. Tutees felt they had a positive relationship with their tutors and preferred talking to their tutors instead of their friends. They regretted the limited amount of time for on-line communication.

The tutors, similar to those in the first study, felt they possessed the necessary skills. They cited communication problems as a negative aspect. Many (60%) expressed indecision on whether they had found the experience enjoyable or not.

Distant learner satisfaction is an important dimension in understanding the success of interactive telecourses. Biner, Dean, and Mellinger (1994) conducted two studies to identify the major dimensions of learner satisfaction. In the first study, the telecourse evaluation questionnaire (TEQ), developed by Biner, was administered to 201 students enrolled in live, interactive televised courses at the beginning of the last class meeting. Using factor analysis, the researchers identified seven factors, including satisfaction with

◆ Instructor/instruction
◆ Technology
◆ Course management
◆ At-site personnel
◆ Promptness of material delivery
◆ Support services
◆ Out-of-class communication with the instructor

WITHDRAWN

The second study, conducted the following year, confirmed the results of the preliminary study. The researchers concluded by emphasizing the importance of assessment of learner satisfaction to the overall success of a distance education program.

Jegede and Kirkwood (1994) investigated the anxiety level of distance education students and the factors contributing to anxiety. Two instruments, an anxiety checklist and an opinionnaire on factors that affect learning at a distance, were administered at the beginning of the semester and at the end of the semester. Complete results were obtained from 222 distance education students enrolled at the University of Southern Queensland.

Analysis of data from the anxiety checklist indicated that participants had a high anxiety level and were generally more anxious about their studies at the end of the semester than at the beginning. Results showed a statistically significant difference between the presemester means and the postsemester means.

A factor analysis of the opinionnaire identified seven factors affecting learning at a distance: content, environment, finances, readiness, time, employment, and family support. A comparison of presemester and postsemester opinions showed five factors were significantly different at the end of the class than at the beginning. Students' concerns related to content, finance, and readiness were higher at the beginning of the class than at the end, while concerns related to time and employment increased toward the end of the class (Jegede & Kirkwood, 1994).

The results of this study indicated that anxiety felt by distance education learners played a higher role in attrition than previously considered. The researchers suggested future research on the role of anxiety probably comparing on-campus with off-campus students, along with the introduction of other variables like achievement outcomes and a longer period of study.

As part of a larger study, Sorensen (1995) identified the most important predictors of student satisfaction. Surveys were returned by 210 community college students enrolled in two-way interactive televised courses. In general, the students were satisfied with their distance learning experience.

Fast (1995) investigated multisite instruction of students enrolled in foreign language courses delivered by fiber optics that allowed interactive instruction. Nineteen students participated in the study, 11 at the origination site and 8 at the remote site.

Postinstruction questionnaires administered to all students provided data on three variables: student motivation, perceived learning, and involvement.

Remote students had a significantly more favorable attitude toward interactive TV than the origination-site students. Responses to open-ended questions requesting the likes and dislikes of interactive TV classes help clarify this difference.

Students at both locations cited two reasons for liking the multisite instruction: human interest and facilitation of learning. Students at the remote site felt the delivery system provided opportunities for learning that would not be available otherwise.

The two groups differed strongly on their list of dislikes. A high number (over 40%) of the dislikes identified by the origination-site students were organizational issues. Of special concern was the loss of class time because of the need to transport students to the technology classroom. This was not an issue for the remote site students.

The majority of criticisms (60%) from the remote site students focused on problems with interaction. They disliked the lack of opportunity to interact one-on-one with the instructor. Discussions were difficult because everyone talked at once, and posing questions necessitated interrupting class. Origination-site students also identified the loss of interaction with the instructor as a problem. These results suggested that remote-site students tended to experience difficulty in being accepted as part of the discourse, while origination-site students found it more difficult to share their teacher with the remote-site group. Analysis of questions related to perceived learning showed no important differences between remote site students and on-site students.

A similar situation was found when data about perceptions of interaction were analyzed. While there were no important differences between sites, there was a major difference between learning group levels. Higher level students at the remote site indicated that having the teacher at a distance hindered learning.

Research related to learners' perceptions has focused on identifying factors related to satisfaction, attitudes, and perceived learning and interaction. Factors affecting satisfaction are often considered to be organizational and involve the environment, management, and support services. In other words, there are identifiable factors that relate to distant learners' perceptions about the effectiveness of their instructional experiences, and these factors are similar to those of local, traditional learners.

◆ LEARNER ATTRIBUTES

Coggins (1988), in a study of students associated with the University of Wisconsin System External Degree Program, examined the relationship between personal variables (learning style and demographic data) and program completion rate. She found that completers and noncompleters did not differ significantly on variables related to gender, occupation, marital status, presence or absence of children, distance from campus, or age of entry into the baccalaureate program. However, there was a significant difference between the two groups for a number of other variables. Completers had entered the program with higher levels of education, and they had greater expectations of earning higher grades as well as greater expectations of earning a degree. The two groups of students differed in their preference for course content. Noncompleters tended to be more concrete learners, preferring a content that allowed them to work with things instead of people. Completers preferred a content that involved interviewing and counseling of people.

The relationship between gender and success in distance education courses was the subject of a study by Ross and Powell (1990). Data from Athabasca University, in Alberta, Canada, indicated that a greater percentage of women passed distance education courses. Further, this higher completion trend was visible irrespective of the student's general study area, the specific course selection, the course level, the mode of course delivery, the student's program status, or the number of courses the student had previously taken.

An exploratory analysis assessing demographic, motivational, support, and learning style variables indicated some possible reasons for the gender differences in academic achievement. These include differences in marital status, employment, and use of institutional support between the two groups. An important difference was noted in the motivational variable. Women felt gaining a university credential was critical and the impact of failing was serious.

Dille and Mezack (1991) studied locus of control and learning style as predictors of risk among college distance education students. One hundred fifty-one students enrolled in telecourses completed the study's assessment instruments, which included demographic information, the internal-external locus of control scale (IELC), and the learning style inventory (LSI).

The locus of control measure was a significant predictor of two variables: success, defined as receiving a grade of C or above, and actual letter grade. Students with a more internal locus of control were more likely to be successful and to obtain a higher grade. Students with an external locus of control were less likely to persevere when faced with the perceived tougher challenge of a telecourse.

An analysis of the data from the learning style inventory indicated that students who were more successful had a lower LSI average score measuring concrete experience. On the abstract conceptualization/concrete experience scale where a lower score indicated a more concrete learner, successful students had a significantly higher score than nonsuccessful students. These findings support the idea that the less concrete one's learning style, the better suited one is to learn in the telecourse format. While examining the abstract/concrete scale was helpful in predicting success in a distance learning environment, individual learning style was not found to be a significant predictor of success.

Based on Dille and Mezack's (1991) study, the profile of a high-risk telecourse student would be

- 25 years or older
- Divorced
- Less than 30 college credit hours completed
- GPA less than 3.0–2.9
- Higher than average locus of control score, indicating an internal locus of control
- Lower than average AC-CE score, indicating an abstract learner

Laube (1992) examined the relationship between academic and social integration variables and the persistence of students in a secondary distance education program.

Students were divided into two groups based on persistence. Completer/persisters were those who completed or still persisted in course work one year after enrollment, whereas dropout/nonstarters had dropped out during the same time.

Out of 351 surveys mailed, 181 surveys were returned, 124 in the completer/persister group and 57 in the dropout/nonstarter group. Interestingly, in the nonreturned surveys there were 44 completer/persisters and 126 dropout/nonstarters.

Two variables showed important differences between the groups. Completer/persisters were more likely than dropout/nonstarters (1) to have higher educational goals and (2) to study more than 10 hours a week.

Three variables related to social integration were studied: self-initiated contact with the school, student attitudes toward their tutors, and student attitudes toward missing peer socialization. The two groups differed significantly only in their attitudes toward their tutors, with completer/persisters indicating a more positive attitude. Both groups indicated a positive attitude toward their tutors, but a large percentage of dropout/nonstarters selected undecided as a response, which contributed to the significant results obtained.

Stone (1992) examined the relationship of contact with a tutor and locus of control to course completion rates for students enrolled in print-based, distance training courses. One group received weekly phone calls from the training staff, whereas the second group received only minimal feedback. Results did not show any important difference between the two groups in course completion rates. However, Stone did find that students with relatively external loci of control completed their coursework at significantly faster rates when exposed to regular telephone cues from their tutors.

How study practices and attitudes of students in a distance learning program relate to academic success was examined by Bernt and Bugbee (1993). This study examined approximately 300 students. The most important result reported was that students who were considered high passers were likely to have advanced degrees.

Two types of study strategies with distance education students were also examined. The researchers concluded that those who passed differed significantly from failers in their test strategies, concentration, and time management skills, but were not significantly different in active processing of information, diligence, and positive attitude.

The researchers also found that students with varying education levels differed in their study strategies, notably time management, concentration, and testing strategies. This, they concluded, suggested that distance learning students who have not completed college are "at risk" primarily because they lack metacognitive or executive skills for approaching coursework and taking examinations. Distance education instructors need to be aware that, similar to traditional education students, learners are different and some need more direction and structure than others.

Garland (1993) used ethnographic procedures to identify barriers to persistence in distance education. Building on the framework of Rubenson (1986), Garland classified barriers into four categories: situational, institutional, dispositional, and epistemological. Face-to-face interviews were conducted with 47 students enrolled in primarily print-based introductory academic courses. Participants in the study included 17 students who did not complete the final exam and 30 persisting students, students who took the final exam regardless of outcome.

Barriers to persistence in all four categories were encountered by both withdrawal students and persisting students. Situational barriers included poor learning environment and lack of time. Students indicated that a lack of support from both family and peers contributed to poor learning environments. They also identified resource availability and a quiet place to study as important. Students felt the course took more time than anticipated, especially as many were juggling the demands of work, home, and school.

Cost, institutional procedures, and course scheduling/pacing were reported as institutional barriers. In this study, students said that tuition was not a problem but add-on costs of texts and labs were seen as barriers to persistence. Students who felt the university did not try to meet their needs identified both institutional procedures and course scheduling/pacing as problems. Limited office hours made reaching staff for assistance difficult.

The largest number of barriers to persistence related to the psychological and sociological nature of the student. These barriers included: (1) uncertainty of an educational or professional goal, (2) stress of multiple roles (school, work, home), (3) time management problems, (4) problems associated with learning style differences, and (5) adult pride indicated by overachievement and/or fear of failure.

The study pointed to the individualness of learning, whether at a distance or in a traditional setting. Regardless of the setting, the focus needs to be on creating optimal learning conditions for each individual.

Pugliese (1994) investigated psychological variables as predictors of persistence in telecourses. Variables studied included loneliness, communication apprehension, communication competence, and locus of control. Of those urban commuter students enrolled in telecourses, 306 (a 39% response rate) responded to Pugliese's telephone survey.

The study's results were interesting. In a traditional classroom it would be expected that the students possessing greater social interaction skills would be more likely to persist and complete the course. Results appeared to indicate that telecourses were the social equalizer. Telecourses apparently minimize the impact of social skills.

Fjortoft (1995) similarly investigated predictors of persistence in distance learning programs. Fjortoft developed a model, based on the literature of adult education, that related adult learners to persistence. The variables studied included age, gender, grade point average at the time of college graduation, satisfaction with the college experience, intrinsic job satisfaction, ease of learning on one's own, intrinsic benefits of degree completion, and extrinsic benefits of degree completion. Persistence was defined by active enrollment status.

The 395 students surveyed included those actively enrolled in a distance learning program in pharmacy and those who had been admitted but had withdrawn before completion. The response rate was 50%, with a sample size of 198.

Three variables were significant in predicting persistence in distance learning programs. Results indicated a positive relationship between perceived intrinsic benefits and continued enrollment, whereas a negative relationship between both age and ease of learning on their own and persistence was indicated. An internal desire for more satisfaction and challenge in one's career more than desires for enhanced salary and career mobility motivated adults to continue their education. The respondents ranged in age from the upper 20s to just over 60. Results indicated it was more difficult for the older students to persist in the distance learning program than it was for younger students.

Fjortoft concluded that only individuals who recognized that they possessed the skills necessary to learn on their own elected to enter a distance learning program. Alternatively, adults might not be able to realistically assess their individual learning styles.

Biner, Bink, Huffman, and Dean (1995) investigated the role of personality characteristics in predicting achievement in televised courses. The Sixteen Personality Factor Questionnaire was administered to both traditional-course and televised-course students to determine how the two groups differed and also to identify personality factors predictive of success in televised courses.

The personality profiles of the two groups differed. Telecourse students tended to be more intelligent, emotionally stable, trusting, compulsive, passive, and conforming than traditional students.

Results indicated that several personality characteristics correlated significantly with course achievement. The group-oriented/self-sufficient student was more likely to have high performance, indicating successful telecourse students tended to be self-sufficient. A negative relationship was found between the introvert/extrovert dimension and course performance. This indicated that the more introverted a student was, the better the student performed in a distance education setting.

Higher levels of expedience were associated with higher grades in the telecourse group. This was in contrast to higher levels of conscientiousness associated with higher grades in the traditional course group. Telecourse students tended to be older and were juggling responsibilities of job and home.

A review of the above studies indicates that several learner characteristics have some effect on the success of the learner in a distance education environment. While studies on the effects of gender indicated mixed results, students who were younger and had a higher level of education were more likely to complete a distance education course.

Motivation is important. Intrinsically motivated learners and those with high expectations for grades and completion of a degree tended to have higher success rates. A positive attitude toward the instructor would also be a factor contributing to the success of distant learners.

Dille and Mezack (1991) and Stone (1992) both found locus of control to be a significant factor. More abstract learners with internal locus of control and skills in learning alone tended to be more successful. Providing students possessing external locus of control with regular contact with the instructor increased their chances of success.

Individual learning style was not a significant predictor of success. Distance education systems proved to be adept in providing for the learning needs of students with a variety of learning styles. Once again, the distant learner and the local learner are not generally different from each other.

◆ INTERACTION

Beare (1989) compared the effectiveness of six instructional formats that allowed differing levels of interaction: (1) lecture, (2) lecture with videotape backup, (3) telelecture, (4) audio-assisted independent study, (5) video-assisted independent study, and (6) video on campus. Study participants consisted of 175 nontraditional teacher education students.

Not surprisingly, given the history of media comparison research, individual instructional formats had little effect on student achievement. The amount of interaction also appeared to have had no impact on student achievement.

Course evaluations yielded some interesting results, however. Analysis showed that distant learners found the course just as stimulating, were equally interested in the subject matter, and judged the instructor equally as skilled as did those receiving face-to-face instruction. The on-site students in the telecourse strongly disliked the medium. It was reported that one night, when the electronic equipment failed temporarily, the class spontaneously cheered.

Bauer and Rezabek (1992) compared verbal interaction under three conditions: (1) two-way audio and video, (2) two-way audio, and (3) traditional instruction. The study include 172 students pursuing teacher certification randomly assigned to one of the three treatment groups.

There was no significant difference in total number of interactions between the audio/video group and the audio group. There was, however, a statistically significant difference between the audio/video group and the traditional group as well as between the audio group and the traditional group. Results seem to indicate that merely the addition of video in the distance education format does not increase interaction. This could be a result of the conditioned passive response of individuals to viewing television. Simply measuring interaction may not be the answer in discovering variables contributing to increased interaction.

Souder (1993) investigated interaction and achievement of students in traditional delivery courses compared with students in a distance delivery course. Three groups of students in the same course participated in the study. One group was in a traditional classroom; the second group was on-site with the instructor while the class was broadcast to the third group at a distance. The instructor, the course content, and the course evaluation requirements were the same for each group.

There was no significant difference between the two traditional delivered courses for evaluation questionnaire items addressing face-to-face interaction. However, the responses of the distance group were significantly different from both the on-site group and the traditional group. The students at a distance defended their distance learning experiences. They did not agree that face-to-face instruction with a live instructor was vital, nor did they believe that real-time interactions with other students were vital. The students in traditional settings disagreed and did not feel that a distance class would be of the same quality as the more traditional approach to instruction.

The results seemed to indicate that students at a distance tended to bond more with their fellow classmates and the instructor. They appeared supportive of each other and, in general, felt they performed better than the other two groups. In fact, the overall achievement of the distance group was significantly higher than that of the on-site group.

Souder (1993) concluded:

the distance learners in this study were observed to gain much more than a traditional education from their experiences. They gained a broadened network of valuable colleagues, skills in working with others and collaborating across distances, and many social skills beyond those offered by traditional settings. (p. 50)

Using semistructured personal interviews, May (1993) investigated the contribution of interaction to women's learning experiences in women's studies courses delivered using distance education. Nine women of varied backgrounds and experiences were interviewed. Course delivery was mostly one-way technology, and content focused on the dissemination of knowledge. There was very little interaction.

Students did not appear to miss the interaction or to recognize its potential benefits. The general feeling was that increasing student interaction required arranging face-to-face meetings. Making time for these meetings was not desirable. Distant learners questioned the value and desirability of increased collaboration.

The women in this study did not believe that isolation among distance learners necessitated a negative learning experience. The researcher concluded that increased learner interaction was not an inherently or self-evidently positive educational goal or strategy.

Fulford and Zhang (1993) examined the relationship of perceived interaction and satisfaction in an in-service training course delivered by the Hawaiian Interactive Television System (HITS). One hundred twenty-three students completed surveys at the beginning, midpoint, and end of a 10-week course. Participants responded to questions about three variables: personal interaction, overall interaction, and satisfaction with the value and quality of instruction.

Level of personal interaction was considered only a moderate predictor of satisfaction. Perceived level of overall interaction was almost three times more important. Learner satisfaction was considered to be attributed more to perceived overall interactivity than to individual participation. Probably instructors using interactive television should focus more on building group interaction rather than individual participation.

This study also examined the variable of time. Learners' perceptions of interaction and satisfaction decreased over the length of the course; however, overall interaction was a more stable predictor of satisfaction as learners became more experienced with the technology.

In a follow-up study, Zhang and Fulford (1994) investigated the variable of time. Participants were 260 students enrolled in a course delivered by HITS. While this study also looked at perceived interaction and satisfaction, variables were expanded to include attitude toward interaction and actual interaction time determined by analyzing videotapes of each session.

The correlation between perceived interaction and actual interaction time was nonsignificant. Reserving a considerable portion of TV time for interaction, a common strategy among TV instructors, did not seem to be quite as important as some suggest. This seems to support the work of May (1993) that indicated that more interaction was not necessarily better.

While the correlation between actual interaction time and attitude was clear, the relationship between perceived interaction and attitude was near perfect. Similar relationships were found when correlating actual interaction and perceived interaction with satisfaction. Increasing interaction time merely for more time's sake is not necessary.

Communication and teaching patterns that contributed to student participation were examined in a study by Schoenfelder (1995). Schoenfelder studied 44 students and 11 teachers participating in interactive television courses. A questionnaire was used to measure teachers' and students' perceptions of ways to increase interaction and involvement.

Both teachers and students thought that an enthusiastic teacher with a sense of humor was an important factor in enhancing involvement. They also felt that addressing students by name and providing timely feedback were factors that made a positive contribution to interaction. Specific teaching habits were found to help increase student involvement. These included varying the learning activities and using a variety of visual materials.

Using observations, interviews, and videotapes, Baker (1995) examined the interactive television teaching behaviors of five faculty members teaching courses using distance education technology. Seven broad categories of teaching behaviors were identified:

◆ Nonverbal "immediacy" behaviors
◆ Verbal "immediacy" behaviors
◆ Behaviors that personalize the class
◆ Technology management strategies
◆ Methods for acquiring student feedback
◆ Methods used to manage student participation
◆ Active learning strategies

Nonverbal behaviors that conveyed a feeling of approachability and warmth increased involvement of students at the remote site. Specific behaviors included making eye contact with the camera, using gestures, and using camera angles and shots that allowed students to see facial expressions. Verbal "immediacy" behaviors that were found to contribute to student involvement included the use of humor, frequent positive encouragement, and the frequent sharing of personal examples. Teachers used a variety of methods for acquiring student feedback that improved student involvement. Most of the teachers relied, at least partially, on the nonverbal cues of the students at the origination site. Some used a variety of questioning techniques, while others used more formal, written formative evaluations.

Research regarding interaction and distance education technologies indicates that different technologies allow differing degrees of interaction. However, similar to comparison studies examining achievement, research comparing differing amounts of interaction showed that interaction had little effect on achievement (Beare, 1989; Souder, 1993). Those students who had little or no interaction as part of a course did not seem to miss it (May, 1993).

◆ DISTANCE EDUCATION TECHNOLOGY

Numerous studies have described or examined the efficacy of individual forms of distance education, whereas others have examined aspects or components of those forms. Garrison (1990) used a description of audio teleconferencing to argue for an appropriate concentration on the role of the teacher and the importance of two-way communication in the education process. Along the way, he argued for the appropriate, conservative use of interactive communication technologies.

The core of Garrison's argument was that

education, whether it be at a distance or not, is dependent upon two-way communication. There is an increasing realization in the educational community that simply accessing information is not sufficient. In an educational experience information must be shared, critically analyzed, and applied in order to become knowledge. (p. 13)

A goal of some distance education programs is to make education more student-centered through the prepackaging of instructional materials that students may use when convenient. However, Garrison argued that this approach ignores the essential nature of an educational learning experience. Garrison reported that this simply risked making learning more private and therefore less likely to transform the views and perspectives of the learner in a positive developmental manner.

Garrison argued that the quality and the integrity of the educational process are dependent upon sustained, two-way communication. Such communication, between student and teacher, and between student and student, is the prime benefit of teleconferencing. When this technology is applied to distance education, the result is that distance education is no longer necessarily an independent and isolated form of learning but, instead, begins to approach the interactive ideal of an educational experience.

Garrison supports audio teleconferencing, which he regards as a distinct generation of distance education capable of providing unique and varied teaching and learning possibilities. Independent and isolated study is no longer the hallmark of distance education.

Egan, Welch, Page, and Sebastian (1992) examined graduate students' perceptions of three instructional delivery systems: (1) conventional delivery, (2) closed-circuit microwave system (EDNET), and (3) videotape recordings (Professor Plus). Near the conclusion of the course, 514 students evaluated the delivery systems using the Media Evaluation Survey. This instrument allows individuals the opportunity to evaluate instructional media on 10 elements:

1) amount of material covered, 2) level of difficulty, 3) degree to which the course content was well organized, 4) clarity of the content, 5) degree to which the various programs and instructional activities were relevant to the course objectives, 6) excellence or lack of excellence of the presenter's delivery, 7) extent to which text and weekly assignments were integrated with each week's class, 8) value of slides, films, and other visual materials, 9) value of text screens to support the presenter's delivery, and 10) degree to which the course held the student's interest. (p. 50)

Results showed 6 of the 10 variables to be different for distant learners. The conventional delivery group gave higher ratings to organization, clarity, relevance, integration, value of visuals, and value of text screens. A comparison of conventional delivery to Professor Plus yielded similar results, with significant differences shown on the two additional variables of adequacy of presenter's delivery and student interest, which were rated higher by the conventional delivery group.

A comparison of the two television delivery systems, EDNET and Professor Plus, showed a significant difference for distant learners for only one variable. The average of the EDNET group's ratings on the value of visuals variable was higher than the mean of the Professor Plus group's ratings.

An analysis of the educational attributes of two forms of communication technology was reported by Tuckey (1993). The electronic white board, a form of synchronous audioconferencing, and asynchronous computer conferencing were reviewed. It was not the intent of the analysis to identify one form of communication as better than the other.

Face-to-face interaction was available in the uses of the electronic white board reviewed. Students met in small groups with the aural presence of the instructor. This element provides opportunities for social interaction, for mutual support, and for collaborative learning, and provides more possibilities for group work than does audioconferencing.

Computer conferencing permitted only text-based communication. Several negative aspects, including limits in display capabilities, contributed to difficulties in collaboration. Group work is also difficult due to the asynchronous nature of this technology.

Tuckey concluded that each form of communication has its advantages. There is a need to review the attributes of the technology used for distance education. Visual channels may be more important in subject areas such as mathematics and the sciences, whereas (computer conferencing) may be more suitable in areas requiring extensive discourse.

Ahern and Repman (1994) examined two different delivery technologies and their relationship to interaction. They found that interaction was sometimes inhibited in distance education systems. The attributes of specific delivery technologies may contribute to both the quantity and the quality of teacher-student and student-student interactions.

In the first study, the researchers analyzed videotapes of a class delivered using two-way audio/two-way video technology. Levels of teacher-student interaction were identified. Teachers talked 62% of the time, with students talking 38% of the time. The percent of questions asked was divided almost equally between students and teachers.

In the second study, Ahern and Repman (1994) evaluated computer-mediated communication systems and the impact on interaction. Two versions of software were developed for this study. The first used a graphic-based discussion map; the second was a more traditional text version. Students in the graphic interface produced significantly more messages than students using the textual interface. The students using the graphic version spent approximately 25% more time per visit.

As with any medium used for instruction, it is important to examine attributes and their contribution to the learning outcome. The studies above suggest that different distance education technologies meet different needs. Two-way communication is an essential component of the learning environment. Collaboration with other students and with the instructor is more possible and easier today than previously due to advancements in technology. Continued research needs to examine the setting and context as well as the media attributes to determine variables contributing to learner outcomes.

◆ SUMMARY

While it is always perilous to summarize research in a few sentences, it is also the obligation of those who have studied the literature extensively to provide others with their best estimates of what has been reported.

The distance education literature has several characteristics that make summarization difficult. The largely anecdotal nature of distance education literature, reporting results of a specific project, makes it difficult to generalize. Widely criticized comparison studies continue to be popular. Comparing the achievements of distance learners with those of traditional learners or between distance learners using different technologies continues to show "no significant difference." Subjects tend to be highly motivated, with adult learners providing little help in generalizing to other populations.

In spite of these limitations, it is possible to draw the following tentative conclusions from the research literature. Although these summary statements should be interpreted skeptically, they are supported by the literature.

◆ Distance education is just as effective as traditional education in regard to learner outcomes.
◆ Distance education learners generally have a more favorable attitude toward distance education than do traditional learners, and distance learners feel they learn as well as if they were in a regular classroom.
◆ Successful distance education learners tend traditionally to be abstract learners who are intrinsically motivated and possess internal locus of control.
◆ While interaction seems intuitively important to the learning experience, interaction should not be added without real purpose.
◆ Focusing on building collaboration and group interaction may be more important than focusing on individual participation.
◆ Each form of distance education technology has it own advantages and disadvantages in contributing to the overall quality of the learning experience.

The research clearly shows that distance education is an effective method for teaching and learning. Future research needs to focus on different populations, particularly K–12 students; psychological and social attributes of the learner; the impact of distance education on the organization; and the contributions of different media attributes to learning outcomes.

Self-Test Questions

1. True/False. Many distance education researchers are now concentrating on learner-centered approaches in distance education environments. What are educators saying about the need for learner-centered approaches in regular education?
2. List at least three of Holmberg's categories for how research on distance education should be structured. Discuss whether the research presented in this chapter relates to Holmberg's categories.

3. Why did Richard Clark say "give up your enthusiasm for the belief that media attributes cause learning"? Discuss your opinions about this statement.
4. True/False. Generally speaking, distant learners do not achieve as well as do local, traditional learners. What predicts a distant learner's achievement?
5. True/False. Generally, distant learners feel they learn as much as local, traditional learners. Why might this finding be suspect?
6. Give at least three conclusions from the research literature about distance education. Why do these conclusions have impact on the practice of distance education?
7. List areas where additional distance education research is needed. Why?

Answers to Self-Test Questions

1. True.
2. Börje Holmberg, a leading distance education theorist and researcher, suggested that the structure of distance education research include
   - Philosophy and theory of distance education
   - Distance students and their milieu, conditions, and study motivations
   - Subject matter presentation
   - Communication and interaction between students and their supporting organization (tutors, counselors, administrators, other students)
   - Administration and organization
   - Economics
   - Systems (comparative distance education, typologies, evaluation, etc.)
   - History of distance education
3. Clark was attempting to advocate that there is no inherent significant difference in the educational effectiveness of various media. It is not the medium that influences learner outcomes. Rather, it is the instructional message or the learning event that has a direct impact on outcomes.
4. False. Generally, local and distant learners tend to learn at about the same level.
5. True.
6. While these summary statements should be interpreted skeptically, they are supported by the literature.
   - Distance education is just as effective as traditional education in regard to learner outcomes.
   - Distance education learners generally have a more favorable attitude toward distance education than do traditional learners, and distance learners feel they learn as well as if they were in a regular classroom.
   - Successful distance education learners tend to be abstract learners who are intrinsically motivated and possess internal locus of control.
   - While interaction seems intuitively important to the learning experience, interaction should not be added without real purpose.
   - Focusing on building collaboration and group interaction may be more important than focusing on individual participation.

- Each form of distance education technology has it own advantages and disadvantages in contributing to the overall quality of the learning experience.
7. Future research needs to focus on different populations, particularly K–12 students; psychological and social attributes of the learner; the impact of distance education on the organization; and the contributions of different media attributes to learning outcomes.

References

Ahern, T. C., & Repman, J. (1994). The effects of technology on online education. *Journal of Research on Computing in Education, 26* (4), 537–546.

Baker, M. H. (1995). Distance teaching with interactive television: Strategies that promote interaction with remote-site students. In C. Sorensen, C. Schlosser, M. Anderson, & M. Simonson (Eds.), *Encyclopedia of Distance Education Research in Iowa* (pp. 107–115). Ames, IA: Teacher Education Alliance.

Bauer, J. W., & Rezabek, L. L. (1992). *The effects of two-way visual contact on student verbal interactions during teleconferenced instruction.* (ERIC Document Reproduction Service No. ED 347 972)

Beare, P. L. (1989). The comparative effectiveness of videotape, audiotape, and telelecture in delivering continuing teacher education. *The American Journal of Distance Education, 3*(2), 57–66.

Bernt, F. L., & Bugbee, A. C. (1993). Study practices and attitudes related to academic success in a distance learning programme. *Distance Education, 14*(1), 97–112.

Biner, P. M., Bink, M. L., Huffman, M. L., & Dean, R. S. (1995). Personality characteristics differentiating and predicting the achievement of televised-course students and traditional-course students. *The American Journal of Distance Education, 9*(2), 46–60.

Biner, P. M., Dean, R. S., & Mellinger, A. E. (1994). Factors underlying distance learner satisfaction with televised college-level courses. *The American Journal of Distance Education, 8*(1), 60–71.

Bramble, W. J., & Martin, B. L. (1995). The Florida teletraining project: Military training via two-way compressed video. *The American Journal of Distance Education, 9*(1), 6–26.

Bruning, R., Landis, M., Hoffman, E., & Grosskopf, K. (1993). Perspectives on an interactive satellite-based Japanese language course. *The American Journal of Distance Education, 7*(3), 22–38.

Cheng, H. C., Lehman, J., & Armstrong, P. (1991). Comparison of performance and attitude in traditional and computer conferencing classes. *The American Journal of Distance Education, 5*(3), 51–64.

Clark, R. E. (1983). Reconsidering research on learning from media. *Review of Educational Research, 53*(4), 445–459.

Clark, R. E. (1994). Media will never influence learning. *Educational Technology Research and Development, 42*(2), 21–29.

Coggins, C. C. (1988). Preferred learning styles and their impact on completion of external degree programs. *The American Journal of Distance Education, 2*(1), 25–37.

Dille, B., & Mezack, M. (1991). Identifying predictors of high risk among community college telecourse students. *The American Journal of Distance Education, 5*(1), 24–35.

Egan, M. W., Welch, M., Page, B., & Sebastian, J. (1992). Learners' perceptions of instructional delivery systems: Conventional and television. *The American Journal of Distance Education, 6*(2), 47–55.

Fast, M. (1995, April). *Interaction in technology: Mediated, multisite, foreign language instruction.* Paper presented at the Annual Meeting of the American Educational Research Association, San Francisco, CA.

Fjortoft, N. F. (1995). *Predicting persistence in distance learning programs.* (ERIC Document Reproduction Service No. ED 387 620)

Fulford, C. P., & Zhang, S. (1993). Perceptions of interaction: The critical predictor in distance education. *The American Journal of Distance Education, 7*(3), 8–21.

Garland, M. R. (1993). Student perceptions of the situational, institutional, dispositional, and epistemological barriers to persistence. *Distance Education, 14*(2), 181–198.

Garrison, D. R. (1990). An analysis and evaluation of audio teleconferencing to facilitate education at a distance. *The American Journal of Distance Education, 4*(3), 13–24.

Holmberg, B. (1987). The development of distance education research. *The American Journal of Distance Education, 1*(3), 16–23.

Jegede, O. J., & Kirkwood, J. (1994). Students' anxiety in learning through distance education. *The American Journal of Distance Education, 15*(2), 279–290.

Laube, M. R. (1992). Academic and social integration variables and secondary student persistence in distance education. *Research in Distance Education, 4*(1), 2–5.

Martin, E. E., & Rainey, L. (1993). Student achievement and attitude in a satellite-delivered high school science course. *The American Journal of Distance Education, 7*(1), 54–61.

May, S. (1993). Collaborative learning: More is not necessarily better. *The American Journal of Distance Education, 7*(3), 39–50.

Pugliese, R. R. (1994). Telecourse persistence and psychological variables. *The American Journal of Distance Education, 8*(3), 22–39.

Ross, L. R., & Powell, R. (1990). Relationships between gender and success in distance education courses: A preliminary investigation. *Research in Distance Education, 2*(2), 10–11.

Ross, S. M., Morrison, G. R., Smith, L. J., & Cleveland, E. (1991). *An evaluation of alternative distance tutoring models for at-risk elementary school children.* (ERIC Document Reproduction Service No. ED 335 009)

Rubenson, K. (1986). Distance education for adults: Old and new barriers for participation. In G. van Enckevorrt, K. Harry, P. Morin, and H. G. Schutze (Eds.), *Distance higher education and the adult learner: Innovations in distance education* (Vol. 1), pp. 39–55. Heelern, the Netherlands: Dutch Open University.

Schoenfelder, K. R. (1995). Student involvement in the distance education classroom: Teacher and student perceptions of effective instructional methods. In C. Sorensen, C. Schlosser, M. Anderson, & M. Simonson (Eds.), *Encyclopedia of distance education research in Iowa* (pp. 79–85). Ames, IA: Teacher Education Alliance.

Sorensen, C. K. (1995). Attitudes of community college students toward interactive television instruction. In C. Sorensen, C. Schlosser, M. Anderson, & M. Simonson (Eds.), *Encyclopedia of distance education research in Iowa* (pp. 131–148). Ames, IA: Teacher Education Alliance.

Souder, W. E. (1993). The effectiveness of traditional vs. satellite delivery in three management of technology master's degree programs. *The American Journal of Distance Education, 7*(1), 37–53.

Stone, T. E. (1992). A new look at the role of locus of control in completion rates in distance education. *Research in Distance Education, 4*(2), 6–9.

Tuckey, C. J. (1993). Computer conferencing and the electronic white board in the United Kingdom: A comparative analysis. *The American Journal of Distance Education, 7*(2), 58–72.

Whittington, N. (1987). Is instructional television educationally effective? A research review. *The American Journal of Distance Education, 1*(1), 47–57.

Zhang, S., & Fulford, C. P. (1994). Are interaction time and psychological interactivity the same thing in the distance learning television classroom? *Educational Technology, 34*(6), 58–64.

Additional Reading

Moore, M. G. (1995). The 1995 distance education research symposium: A research agenda. *The American Journal of Distance Education, 9*(2), 1–6.

chapter 4

Distance Education Technologies

CHAPTER GOAL

The purpose of this chapter is to discuss the technologies used for distance education systems and distance education classrooms.

CHAPTER OBJECTIVES

After reading and reviewing this chapter, you should be able to

1. Describe systems for categorizing media used for distance education
2. Explain the technologies used to connect teachers and learners for distance education, including correspondence, audio, video, and desktop systems
3. Explain the configuration of a modern distance education classroom

◆ A TRUE STORY

In the 1980s, the southeast African nation of Zimbabwe was founded from the British Commonwealth country of Rhodesia after a long and painful process. Before the founding of Zimbabwe the educational system of Rhodesia enrolled less than 500,000 learners, and most were located in the major cities and towns of the country. One of the first acts of the new government was to offer free and universal education to the nation's children, no matter where they were located. This meant that the enrollment in the country's schools increased tenfold overnight.

The teacher education faculty at the University of Zimbabwe in Harare and at other institutions of teacher training had to face the immediate problem of preparing the thousands of teachers needed by the many new and enlarged schools of the country. The approach selected was part ingenious and part necessity-based.

It was decided that teachers in training should attend one of the institutions of higher education for their first year of preparation. For their second and third years these teacher education students were assigned to a school where they taught classes of students.

College students functioned as regular educators with two exceptions. First, they were under the guidance of a more experienced colleague, and second they continued their teacher education and higher education coursework at a distance. In other words, they enrolled in a full curriculum of coursework while they also functioned as novice teachers. Their coursework was delivered to them from a distant, higher education institution. For their fourth year they returned to the university or college and completed their degrees.

In Zimbabwe, distance education became the primary technique for preparing the thousands of teachers needed to staff the new country's schools. Interestingly, the technology used to connect professors, such as those of the faculty of education at the University of Zimbabwe, and students located in the many cities, towns, and villages of the country was the postal system. Students received written assignments and printed resources from the university. They used, studied, and interacted with these materials to complete assignments, which then were returned to the faculty of education for evaluation. Follow-up assignments and materials were then posted back to students. This process continued until the second and third years of the bachelor's degree were completed. Periodic visits to the campus occurred, but the majority of the learning events and activities took place at a distance.

This system, born of the necessity of educating millions of students, used the most appropriate technology available—the postal system. Certainly, a major social, political, and ultimately educational problem was solved, even though the approach was not high tech. However, it was efficient and effective. Whatever technology is used, the purpose is to promote communication.

◆ A MODEL OF COMMUNICATION

Communication occurs when two or more individuals wish to share ideas. Communication in a distance education environment happens when learners interact with one another and with their instructor. Communication, including communication for dis-

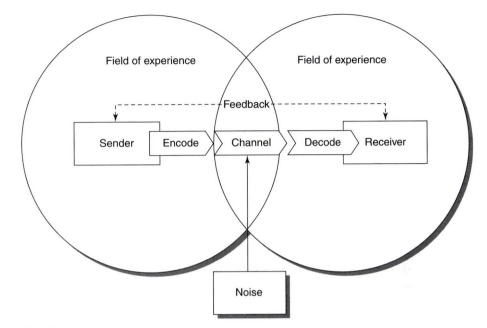

FIGURE 4–1   A model of communication.

tance education, is possible because individuals have overlapping fields of experience. In other words, they have things in common, such as language and culture (Figure 4–1).

Communication must be based on what the senders of messages—distance educators—have in common with the receivers of messages—distant learners. Effective instructional messages are designed according to the situation, experiences, and competencies of learners.

In order to communicate, instructional ideas are encoded into some transmittable form, such as spoken words, pictures, or writing. The instructional message is then sent to the learner over a channel. If the receiver of the message is nearby, such as in the same classroom, the sender—the teacher—may speak or show pictures in order to communicate. If the learner is at a distance, then the instructional message will need to be sent over a wire (e.g., the telephone), hand-delivered (e.g., the mail), or broadcast through the air (e.g., television). In other words, media are used to communicate to distant learners. In fact, media extend the senses, so instructional messages can be sent over long distances, or stored for learning at different times.

When the distant learner receives the message it must be decoded. This means the words spoken must be heard and defined, or the pictures shown must be seen and understood. If communication is successful, the receiver—the learner—will have the same idea or understanding as the sender—the teacher.

Effective communication requires an active audience. The response of the learners who receive messages is called *feedback*. Feedback allows both the sender and receiver, the teacher and learner, to determine if the message was understood correctly. Feedback in distance education systems is often referred to as *interaction*. Feedback permits those involved in communication in a distance education system to evaluate the process.

Noise is also part of the communication process. Any disturbance that interferes with or distorts the transmission of a message is called *noise*. Audible static is one form of noise. Classroom distractions are noise, as is ambiguous or unfamiliar information.

The model of communication has been widely used to describe the interaction between message designers and audiences—teachers and learners. It is also quite relevant for distance education. Specifically, instruction must be designed in a way to capitalize on what learners already know and what they have already experienced—their fields of experience. Then messages should be encoded so they can be effectively transmitted to distant learners.

Channels of communication, the media that connect the teacher and the distant learner, should be appropriate for the learner and the instruction. In other words, the media used to connect the learner, teacher, and learning resources must be capable of conveying all necessary information.

When instruction is designed and when feedback and interaction are planned, efforts should be made to minimize anything that might interfere with the communication process (e.g., noise). One way this can be accomplished is by sending information through multiple channels.

Models of communication provide a general orientation to the process of distance education. The model described in Figure 4–1 contains the elements to be considered when instructional messages are communicated.

◆ THE CONE OF EXPERIENCE

One long-standing method of categorizing the ability of media to convey information is the cone of experience, introduced by Edgar Dale (1946). Dale's "cone of experience" helps organize the media used in distance education systems (Figure 4–2).

Children respond to direct, purposeful experiences, not only because they are young, but because they are learning many new things for the first time. Real experiences have the greatest impact on them because they have fewer previous experiences to look back on and refer to than do older learners. Real experiences provide the foundation for learning.

As learners grow older and have more experiences it is possible for them to understand events that are less realistic and more abstract. This basic idea was first stated by Dale when he introduced his cone of experience. Dale proposed that for students to function and learn from experiences presented abstractly (those at the higher levels of the cone), it was necessary for them to have sufficient and related experiences that were more realistic (those at the lower levels). Learners need to have direct, purposeful experiences to draw upon in order to successfully learn from more abstract events. For example, if children are to look at pictures of flowers and know what they are, they must have first seen, smelled, and touched real flowers.

Media permit the educator to bring sights and sounds of the real world into the learning environment—the classroom. However, when *new* information is presented, it is important that it be as realistic as possible. Similarly, when younger learners are involved, more realistic instruction is needed.

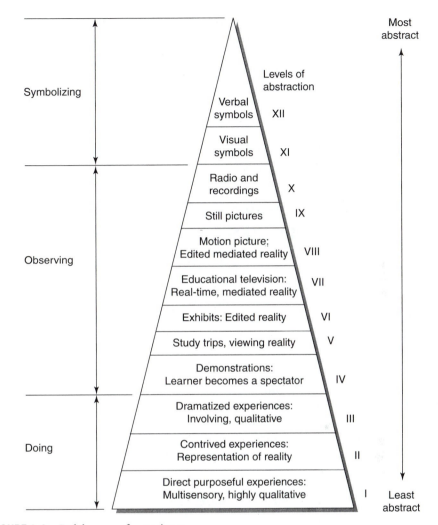

FIGURE 4–2 Dale's cone of experience.

Still, one misunderstanding about the cone of experience is the belief that "more realistic" is always better. This is definitely not true. More realistic forms of learning are considerably less efficient in terms of uses of resources, and are often less effective because of the many distractions of realistic instruction.

The critical job of the educator, especially the designer of distance education materials, is to be only as realistic as needed in order for learning to effectively occur. If instruction is too realistic, it can be inefficient. It may cost too much, it may have too much irrelevant information, or it may be difficult to use. Similarly, learning experiences that are too abstract may be inexpensive, but may not contain enough relevant information and may not be understood.

To clarify the conflict between realistic and abstract experiences, Edgar Dale told a story about the life of a Greek sponge fisherman. The most realistic way to learn about the fisherman's life was to go to Greece and work on a sponge boat. This approach to learning would be very realistic, effective, and authentic. It would also take a long time and cost a great deal, both in money and in learning time. An abstract way to learn about the life of a sponge fisherman would be to read about it in a book. This would take only a few hours and would cost little, even though the experience would not be overly authentic. Today, most would opt for something that is in the middle of Dale's cone, such as a 28-minute video on cable television's Discovery Channel titled "A Day in the Life of a Greek Sponge Fisherman."

◆ A TAXONOMY OF DISTANCE EDUCATION TECHNOLOGIES

In distance education it is imperative that educators think about how communication will occur and how to apply experiences that will promote effective and efficient learning. Most likely, a variety of techniques will be needed to provide equivalent learning experiences for all students (Figure 4–3):

Correspondence
Prerecorded media
Two-way audio
Two-way audio with graphics
One-way live video
Two-way audio, one-way video
Two-way audio/video
Desktop two-way audio/video

◆ CORRESPONDENCE STUDY

The simplest and longest-lived form of distance education is generally considered to be correspondence study. This approach to distance education uses some kind of mail system, such as regular post office mail or electronic mail, to connect the teacher and the learner asynchronously (Figure 4–4). Usually, lessons, readings, and assignments are sent to the student, who then completes the lessons, studies the readings, and works on the assignments, which are mailed to the instructor for grading. For a college-level course worth three credits there are often 10 to 12 units to be completed. Each is finished in turn, and when all are completed satisfactorily, the student receives a grade.

Sophisticated forms of correspondence study have used techniques of programmed instruction to deliver information. Linear programmed instruction is most common, but for a period of time there was an effort by a number of correspondence study organizations to develop print-based branched programmed instruction. Programmed instruction normally has a block of content, followed by questions to be answered. Depending on the answers students give, they move to the next block of text

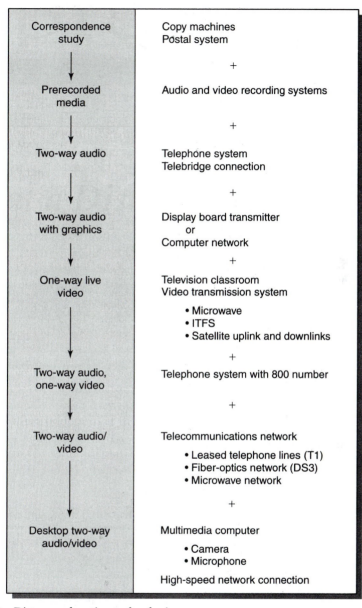

FIGURE 4–3 Distance education technologies.

(linear programmed instruction) or to another section of the programmed text (branched programmed instruction). Sometimes remedial loops of instruction would be provided to help students through difficult content, or content that supposedly had been covered in previous courses or blocks of instruction. Advanced students do not need to study remedial loops. In this manner the rate and route of instruction are varied for students of correspondence courses.

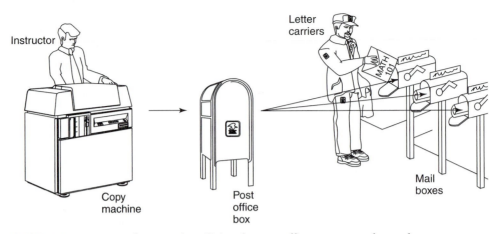

FIGURE 4–4   Correspondence study utilizing the post office to connect the teacher and the learners.

Correspondence study is relatively inexpensive, can be completed almost anywhere, and has been shown to be effective. Correspondence study has been used by millions of learners of all ages since the 19th century.

◆ PRERECORDED MEDIA

The next logical step in the development of distance education technologies, both historically and conceptually, was the incorporation of media other than print media into correspondence study systems. First, pictures and other graphics were added to correspondence study texts. Then, audiotapes and finally videotapes were added to the collection of materials sent to distant learners. Usually, the correspondence study guide would direct the learner to look at, listen to, or view various media, in addition to assigning more traditional readings.

One interesting approach used by distance educators was borrowed from advocates of individualized instruction. This approach used audiotapes to guide the distant learner through a series of learning events, very similar to how a tutor would direct learning. This *audio-tutorial approach* was quite popular for a number of years, and still is used by commercial organizations that present self-help materials for individual study.

◆ TWO-WAY AUDIO

Correspondence study filled a terrific void for those who wanted to learn when they could and wherever they were located. However, many wanted direct, live communication with the teacher, especially for those in precollege schools.

The first widely used live, synchronous form of distance education used two-way audio, with either a telephone hookup, a radio broadcast with telephone call-in, or

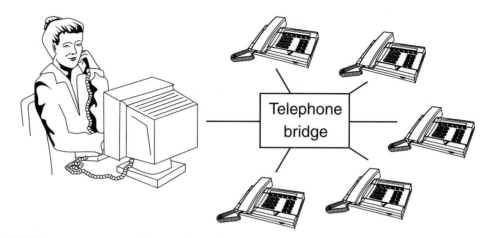

FIGURE 4–5   Two-way audio—audioconferencing.

shortwave radio transmissions (Figure 4–5). In all cases, the distant learner and the instructor are with some form of live, two-way audio connection. Teachers lecture, ask questions, and lead discussions. Learners listen, answer, and participate. Often, print and nonprint materials are sent to distant learners, similar to correspondence study.

The key to this approach is the participation of the teacher and learners in a class session at a regularly scheduled time, or a set period of time, over a predetermined number of weeks or months, such as a semester. For example, a high school class in French might be offered by telephone, radio station broadcast, or shortwave signal every weekday from 10:00 a.m. until 10:50 for nine weeks. Students would tune in at home, and assignments would be made and activities completed. In other words, this form of distance education models the traditional classroom, except the teacher and learners can only hear one another. They cannot see each other.

◆ TWO-WAY AUDIO WITH GRAPHICS

Recently, an embellishment of the two-way audio form of distance education has incorporated electronic methods of sending graphics information synchronously to distant learners. Two general approaches are used. The first incorporates a special display board that looks like a chalkboard but that actually transmits whatever is drawn on it to a similar display board at a distant site. Since the electronic boards are connected to one another, whatever the students at the distant site draw is also seen by the instructor. The main disadvantage of this approach is the limited visual capability of the system and the difficulty in connecting more than two locations.

A modification of this approach uses personal computers that are connected to one another, either through a central bridge computer or by using special software. For these systems, the instructor sends graphics, visuals, pictures, and even short video clips to desktop computers located at distant sites. Members of the class are connected by telephone or some other two-way audio system, so they can discuss the visual information being sent via the computer.

This approach is relatively inexpensive and permits the visualization of the tele-class. The major problem is the availability of powerful, networked computers at distant learning sites.

◆ ONE-WAY LIVE VIDEO

This approach is often referred to as broadcast distance education, popularized in the 1950s by programs such as *Sunrise Semester,* which was broadcast over commercial television stations. Presently, most broadcast television approaches to distance education are offered by public television stations or are broadcast in the early morning hours by commercial stations (Figure 4–6).

Programs are broadcast in installments over a 12 to 15 week period. Often, each program is about 60 minutes in length and is accompanied by packets of printed materials and readings. Sometimes, instructors are available for telephone office hours, but most commonly students watch the programs on television and respond to assignments that are described in the course packet. Completion of the assignments depends on viewing each television program, which is often broadcast several times. For those

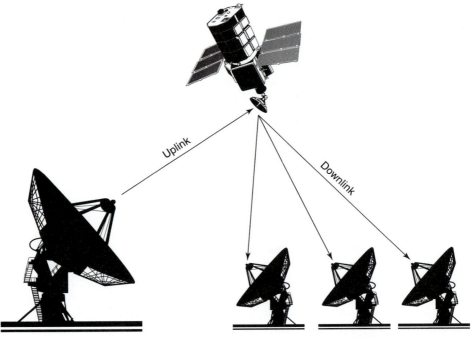

Receive sites

FIGURE 4–6 Satellite transmission—one-way audio, one-way video.

students who miss a broadcast, videotape versions are available, or students can tape the program with their own videocassette recorder.

One advantage of this approach is the relatively high quality of the video broadcasts. Public television stations offer excellent productions of important historical, political, and social events. These broadcasts are used by educational institutions as the basis for high school and college courses related to the topics of the television shows. The Civil War series and the Lewis and Clark series are examples of public television programming that was modified into distance education courses.

◆ TWO-WAY AUDIO, ONE-WAY VIDEO

In the last few decades a number of organizations have begun to use live television to broadcast high school and college courses. Initially, this approach used microwave transmission systems, instructional television fixed service (ITFS), or community cable television networks (Figures 4–7 and 4–8). Recently, satellite communications systems have become widely available (Figure 4–9).

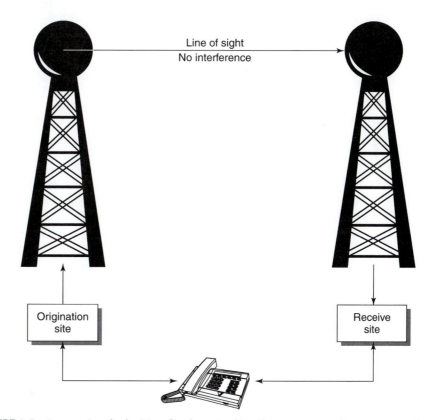

FIGURE 4–7   Instructional television fixed service (ITFS)—two-way audio, one-way video.

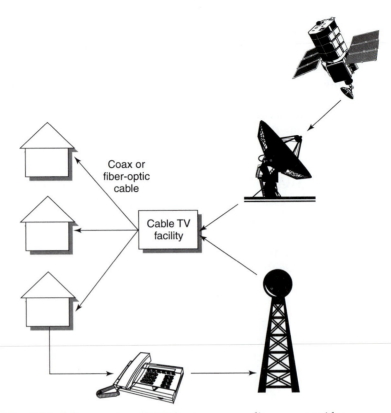

FIGURE 4–8   Cable delivery system (CATV)—two-way audio, one-way video.

In these systems, the courses are offered synchronously (e.g., live) to students in as few as two to as many as hundreds of locations. Students are given a toll-free telephone number to call to ask questions of the instructor both during class and after class. Normally, students have a packet of instructional materials, including interactive study guides, that they use and complete during the class presentation. Interaction between instructor and students is stressed in these kinds of courses, even ones where hundreds of students are enrolled.

In the last decade as satellite uplinks and downlinks have become more prevalent, the concept of the teleconference has become popular. Teleconferences are short courses on specialty topics such as copyright, classroom discipline, sexual harassment, due process, or funding strategies that are offered by an organization to individuals or small groups spread throughout a wide geographic area. Since one satellite in geosynchronous orbit in the Clarke Belt above the equator can transmit a video signal to nearly one-third of the earth's surface, it is possible to offer satellite programming to literally thousands of learners.

A number of educational organizations have used satellite broadcast coursework to offer entire high school and college curricula. The TI-IN Network from San Antonio, Texas, offers an entire high school curriculum, and has so since the mid-1980s.

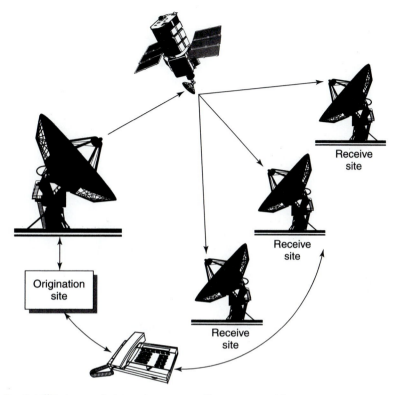

FIGURE 4–9   Satellite transmission—two-way audio, one-way video.

◆ TWO-WAY AUDIO/VIDEO

Recently, especially in the United States, distance education is being widely practiced using live, synchronous television employing one of several technologies. The prevalent technology is called compressed video (Figure 4–10). This approach, commonly applied in corporate training, uses regular telephone lines to send and receive audio and video signals. The approach is called *compressed* video because fewer than the normal number of 30 video frames per second are transmitted between the sites. In the compressed video form, usually 15 video frames per second are transmitted using what is called a T-1 connection. This level of quality is quite acceptable for most instruction, except when some kind of rapid motion or movement is part of instruction.

Compressed video systems are often used in teleconferences for corporate training. Increasingly, schools and colleges are installing compressed video networks. For this approach, a special classroom is needed that has video and audio equipment to capture the sights and sounds of instruction. The video and audio signals are manipulated by a device called a CODEC (coder/decoder) that removes redundant information for transmission to the distant site. At the receive site another CODEC converts the compressed information

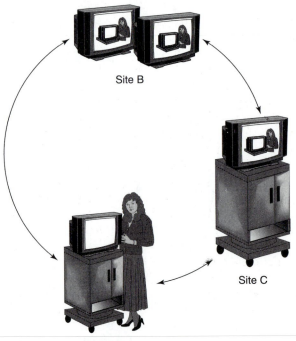

FIGURE 4–10   Two-way audio/video—compressed videoconferencing system.

back into video and audio signals. Camera control information is also transmitted between sites, so it is possible for the instructor to pan, tilt, and zoom cameras.

One major advantage of compressed video systems is their portability. Many systems are installed in movable carts that can be set up in almost any classroom or training site where there is a telephone connection.

A second, more sophisticated, approach to two way audio/video instruction uses fiber-optics cable to connect sites. Fiber optics cable is the telecommunications medium of choice for new and updated telephone, video, and computer networking. Fiber's cost inhibits its installation in all situations, but fiber's high capacity makes it possible for one fiber (sometimes called a DS-3 connection) to carry full-motion video signals, in addition to high-quality audio signals and almost unlimited amounts of other voice and data information. One exemplary use of fiber optics for distance education is Iowa's publicly owned Iowa Communications Network.

An Example: Two-Way Audio/Video in Iowa

In Iowa, distance education is being redefined on a statewide basis. Iowa's approach to distance education is based on the belief that live, two-way interaction is fundamental to effective learning. High-quality interaction is made possible in the state by the Iowa

Special "distance learning" carts are sometimes used. These carts can be wheeled into any classroom or office.

Visual presenters permit the transmission of flat visuals such as book pages, pictures, and drawings.

Communications Network (ICN). The ICN is a statewide, two-way, full-motion interactive fiber-optic telecommunications network with hundreds of connected classrooms. It is designed to be used by teachers and students in learning situations where they can and expect to see and hear each other. Distant and local students function together and learn from and with one another.

A key to Iowa's successful distance education system is the concept of sharing. Iowa's vision for distance education is being built around the development of partnerships of schools that share courses and activities. For example, a physics class originating in Jefferson, a small town in west central Iowa, may have students in Sac City and Rockwell City, schools in two other counties. French students in Sac City have distant classmates in Jefferson and Rockwell City, and a calculus class that originates in Rockwell City is shared with students in Sac City and Jefferson. All three schools provide courses to partner schools and receive instruction from neighbors. Classes are small, with enrollments of 30 to 35 or less, and are taught by teachers prepared in the skills needed by distance educators.

The use of fiber-optic technology, because of its extensive capacities and flexibility of use, provides unique opportunities for augmenting the instructional process beyond what is possible with other distance delivery technologies. The Iowa approach demonstrates the use of a system that emphasizes

◆ Local control of the distance education curriculum
◆ Active involvement by educators from local school districts
◆ Interactive instruction
◆ Statewide alliances and regional partnerships
◆ Preservice, in-service, and staff development activities to support teachers
◆ Implementation using existing organizations and expertise
◆ Research-based instructional decision making

The Iowa Communications Network

Central to distance education in Iowa is the Iowa Communications Network. The ICN is a statewide, two-way, full-motion interactive fiber-optic telecommunications network with at least one point of presence in each of Iowa's 99 counties. The ICN links colleges, universities, and secondary schools throughout the state and was constructed entirely with state and local funds. Part 1 of the Iowa Communications Network connected Iowa Public Television, Iowa's 3 public universities, and Iowa's 15 community colleges to the network. Part 2 connected at least one site in each of Iowa's 99 counties. Most Part 2 sites were high schools. Part 3 of the system is under construction and connects an additional 700 schools, libraries, armories, area education agencies, and hospitals.

The plan for the ICN was completed and adopted by the Iowa legislature in 1987. Construction of Parts 1 and 2 of the network was completed during 1993. In addition to the capability of transmitting up to 48 simultaneous video channels, the ICN carries data and voice traffic; and as demand increases, the system is easily expandable without the need for "opening the trench" to lay more fiber.

In Iowa, and in many other states and regions, traditional education works. Iowa educators adopted distance education, but wanted to preserve their beliefs about effective education. The fiber-optics-based Iowa Communications Network permitted this since the ICN is a live, two-way audio/video network

◆ DESKTOP TWO-WAY AUDIO/VIDEO

One disadvantage of the video telecommunications systems described in this chapter is their cost and their cumbersomeness. In order to provide video-based distance education, special electronic devices are needed, satellite or telephone network time must be reserved, and equipped classrooms are required. Desktop systems often reduce the need for special high-cost equipment or special networking. Desktop systems use personal computers and the Internet to connect local and distant learners (Figure 4–11). Increasingly, the Internet and Internet II have the capacity to connect personal computers for the sharing of video and audio information. Inexpensive servers that function as reflector sites for connecting multiple sites are also available.

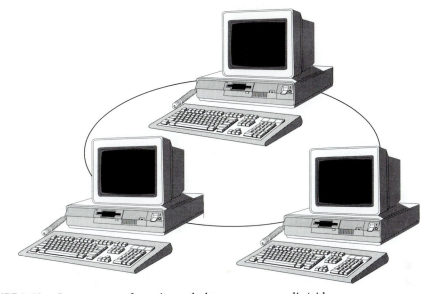

FIGURE 4–11   Computer conferencing—desktop two-way audio/video.

Early systems used CU/SeeMe technology that was free and used very inexpensive video cameras. These systems permitted two sites to connect and to share video and audio. Multiple sites could be connected if a reflector computer was available. The CU/SeeMe approach was relatively low quality and was used mostly for conferencing and meetings. However, it pioneered the use of desktop systems. Now higher quality cameras and even complete classrooms can be connected to a personal computer for transmission of instruction to distant learners. Certainly the desktop personal computer will be the telecommunications tool of the future.

There are four categories of desktop video/audio systems: analog, high speed, medium speed, and low speed. These systems permit sharing of video and audio from the instructor's computer to a student's computer.

Analog systems use existing telephone wiring in buildings, commonly called twisted-pair wires. The major advantage of this approach is the high quality of the video and audio. Since existing wiring is used, connections are limited to relatively short distances—several thousand feet. Analog systems are limited to a campus, or a building, which significantly reduces this application in distance education.

High-speed videoconferencing sends video at millions of bits per second. Even at this high rate, the video signal is compressed using a compression protocol such as MPEG or motion JPEG. The H.310 protocol is used for high-speed desktop videoconferencing. Currently, high-speed videoconferencing is used primarily with dedicated networks within individual schools or businesses.

Medium-speed desktop videoconferencing is currently the primary approach used today. This type of desktop video transmits at speeds of 128,000 or 256,000 bits per second. The video signal is compressed so it can be transmitted over the Internet (H.323

A computer board is just about all that is
necessary to convert a computer into a desk top
teleconferencing system.

protocol). There are both hardware and software methods to compress and decompress
the video signal. Since the Internet is used, medium-speed systems have considerable
promise for distance education.

Low-speed desktop video includes all systems that transmit at speeds lower than
56,000 bits per second (56 kbps). This category permits conferencing using the
Internet and modems at speeds of 28.8 kbps. A V32 model modem with v.80 extension is generally what is needed for low-speed desktop video. Once again H.323 protocols are used, and software and hardware compression systems are available. Very
inexpensive systems are currently in use. However, the quality is quite poor and the
video signal is usually limited to a small window on the computer screen. Low-speed
systems are widely used for limited types of instructor/student conferencing, rather
than for course delivery.

When the Internet is used, rather than a special or dedicated network, the H.323
standard is used. The primary problem with desktop videoconferencing using the
Internet is the poor quality of the video and the limited capacity of the Internet to carry
video signals. Since the Internet is a "packet-switched" network, a video signal is broken into packets that are disassembled and then sent to the distant site where the packets are reassembled into a signal. Obviously, this approach is a limiting factor when live,
interactive video is sent.

Desktop videoconferenceing is a critical area for growth in distance education.
Increasingly, the Internet will be used to connect learners for sharing of video, in addition to data (text and graphics). Before this happens, however, advances in compression
standards, network protocols, and transmission media will need to be made.

DISTANCE EDUCATION CLASSROOMS

Video-based distance education requires a classroom or studio that is equipped with
the technology needed for recording and displaying video and listening to sound.
Initially, studios were used as distance education classrooms. Then as distance educa-

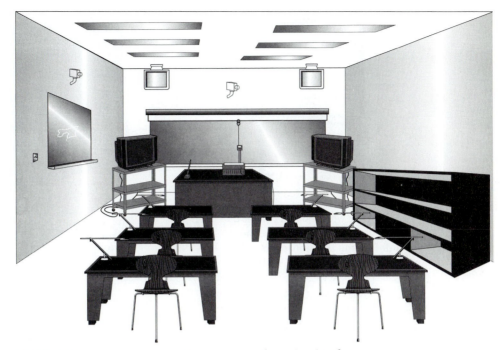

FIGURE 4–12   Distance learning classroom—teaching site view from rear.

tion became more widespread, regular classrooms were converted into distance education receive and send sites (Figure 4–12).

Video classrooms need recording, instruction, and display equipment. Recording equipment includes video cameras—usually three—one that shows the instructor, one for the students, and an overhead camera mounted above the instructor console to display printed graphics materials. A switching system is needed to permit the instructor to switch between cameras and instructional equipment, such as a computer, a videocassette recorder, and a video slide projector. Several companies offer devices that attach to video cameras and cause them to follow the action in the classroom. For example, when its activation button is pushed, the student camera automatically pans and zooms to the appropriate microphone location to show the student who is talking. Also, the instructor camera has sensing devices that, when activated, automatically direct the camera to follow the instructor's movements in the classroom.

Additionally, audio equipment is needed. Audio tends to cause more problems than video in distance education classrooms. Early classrooms used voice-activated microphones, but currently push-to-talk microphones are found most often.

Instructional media often found in distance education classrooms include a computer, a videocassette recorder, and a video slide projector. Laser disk players are sometimes supplied. Student equipment includes desktop computers that are networked and that can be displayed for others to see both in the local classroom and at remote sites.

Electronic white boards permit the instructor to write and have the information transmitted to a computer screen at the distant site.

The "Cameraman" can be used with sensors that automatically follow the instructor as she or he move about in the classroom.

Cameras for computer desktop systems are small, high quality, and relatively inexpensive.

Distance education classrooms are configured in a variety of ways, depending on how they are used.

Push-to-talk microphones are used most often in distance learning classrooms.

A simple teleconferencing system.

Video cameras are normally included as part of video teleconferencing systems.

Self-contained teleconferencing systems such as this one from VTEL Corporation are often used by businesses and in higher education settings.

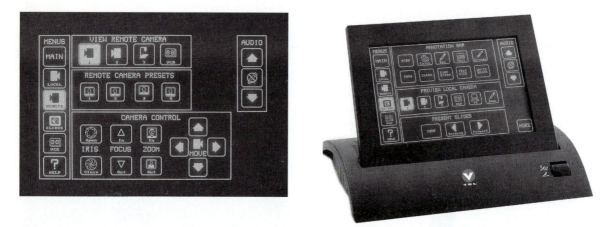

Touch panels and control systems make it easy for the classroom teacher to control a sophisticated distance education sytem.

Display equipment includes large television monitors and audio speakers. Most often three display monitors are mounted in a classroom—two in the front of the room for students to view and one in the rear for the instructor. Audio speakers are connected to a volume control.

Sometimes classrooms are connected to a control room where technicians can monitor action and even control the recording and display equipment. Increasingly, however, classrooms are teacher- and student-controlled. In other words, the teacher is responsible for equipment operation and use, or students in the class are assigned these responsibilities.

◆ SUMMARY

The technologies used for distance education fall into two categories: telecommunications technologies that connect instructors to distant learners and classroom technologies that record, present, and display instructional information. Increasingly, video-and computer-based systems are being used.

Most often, teachers and students use classrooms that have been designed and installed by others. However, the effective utilization of distance education classrooms requires a new set of skills for most educators and learners. Teaching with technology to learners who are not physically located in the same site where instruction is taking place requires a different set of skills and competencies than traditional education. Technologies are tools that must be mastered to be effective.

Self-Test Questions

1. True/False. Abstract learning is possible because an individual can draw upon and relate to previously acquired realistic experiences. Discuss why abstract learning experiences are sometimes better than more realistic experiences.

2. According to Dale's cone of experience, which is most realistic, a video or a field trip? Why are both appropriate instructional strategies?

3. Define *noise*. Explain how noise is overcome by the teacher.

4. Why must communication be based on the overlapping fields of experience between teacher and learner? Discuss what happens when the fields of experience of the teacher and learner do not share elements in common.

5. True/False. According to Dale, realistic instruction is almost always better. Discuss why some think realism is better for younger learners.

6. What is the most traditional and longest-used form of technology in distance education? Discuss why this approach is still important.

7. What does a CODEC do? Why is it important for educators to know about devices such as CODECs?

8. Describe the Iowa Communications Network. In your opinion, is this system a model for other states?

9. What is CU/SeeMe? Why is this technology important?

10. True/False. Increasingly, regular classrooms in schools are being equipped to be distance education classrooms. Discuss why you feel this trend will continue or not continue.

Answers to Self-Test Questions

1. True.

2. A field trip.

3. Noise is anything that interferes with communication.

4. Overlapping fields of experience are what the teacher and student have in common. Communication—teaching—must be based on what the two individuals who are attempting to communicate have as similar experiences, such as language or ability to understand meaning from visuals. If communication is not based on what is shared in common, then it is difficult, even impossible, for the receiver of the message to draw meaning from the transmitted message. As learners grow older, their level of experience increases, and it is possible for them to understand information, even construct meaning, from abstract messages.

5. False.

6. Printed materials made available by correspondence.

7. A CODEC is a device that codes and decodes information that is sent over telecommunications media such as fiber-optics cable. The CODEC codes the video and audio information generated in a distance education classroom for transmission to a receive classroom where another CODEC decodes the information for display.

8. The ICN is a 3,000-mile statewide, two-way, full-motion, interactive fiber-optics telecommunications network used for transmission of video, audio, and data in distance education. The ICN has over 700 classrooms connected to its fiber-optics backbone network.

9. A CU/SeeMe is a simple, inexpensive desktop video/audio system that permits the sending and receiving of video and audio information using a desktop computer and computer network, such as the Internet.

10. True.

Reference

Dale, E. (1946). *Audiovisual methods in teaching.* Hinsdale, IL: Dryden Press.

Additional Readings

Baumgarn, K. (1995). *Classrooms of the Iowa Communications Network.* Ames, IA: Research Institute for Studies in Education.

Cyrs, T. (1997). *Teaching at a distance with the merging technologies.* Las Cruces, NM: Center for Educational Development.

Kemp, J., & Smellie, D. (1994). *Planning, producing, and using instructional technologies,* 7th ed. New York: HarperCollins.

Moore, M., & Kearsley, G. (1996). *Distance education: A systems view.* Belmont, CA: Wadsworth.

Richardson, A. (1992). *Corporate and organizational video.* New York: McGraw-Hill.

Simonson, M., & Volker, R. (1984). *Media planning and production.* Columbus, OH: Merrill.

Zettl, H. (1995). *Video basics.* Belmont, CA: Wadsworth.

URL for Information About Distance Education Classrooms

http://www3.iptv.org/iowa_database/ICN/icnsites/prices/contents.html

PART II

APPLICATIONS

chapter 5

Copyright and Distance Education

CHAPTER GOAL

The purpose of this chapter is to discuss the implications of U.S. copyright law for teaching in distance education environments.

CHAPTER OBJECTIVES

After reading and reviewing this chapter, you should be able to

1. Differentiate between myth and fact related to copyright applications in distance education.
2. Recognize the exclusive rights granted to copyright holders by U.S. copyright law.
3. Apply the four essential fair use criteria and published guidelines to determine whether use of copyrighted materials requires permission from rights holders.
4. Determine whether use of instructional media materials in a video-based distance education course falls under the criteria of Section 110 or existing guidelines or requires permission.
5. Recognize what materials may be placed on the Internet without permission and what requires rights holder approval.
6. Recognize the circumstances under which Internet materials copyrighted by others may be forwarded, downloaded, and printed.
7. Follow appropriate procedures for obtaining permission from rights holders to use copyrighted materials in a distance education course.
8. Recognize the potential consequences of copyright infringement.

◆ COPYRIGHT—MYTHS

Not long ago, an instructional developer at a large university received a telephone call from a faculty member developing an on-line course. The professor planned to digitize a number of journal articles and book chapters and place them on the course Web site so students would not have to buy coursepacks, and he wondered where he could gain access to a scanner. Astonished, the instructional developer asked if the professor had obtained permission from the rights holders to put their publications on the Internet. No, came the reply, but that was irrelevant because the site was going to be password-protected and so only the students could gain access.

This example represents the kind of mythology that has evolved as educators try to determine what is copyrighted and what is not, and what can be used in a course and what cannot, at least without permission, and how it can be used. Misinterpretations of copyright are commonplace:

Myth 1. A work has to be published and registered with the U.S. Copyright Office to receive copyright protection. Any work, published or unpublished, meeting the criteria specified in the copyright law receives protection as soon as it is fixed in a tangible medium of expression. For example, an original manuscript prepared on a word processor is protected as soon as the file is saved to disk or printed. Copyright covers a slide as soon as the image is recorded on film. Registration with the Copyright Office is optional, not a requirement. However, a work must be registered before a plaintiff can collect statutory damages in the event of an infringement.

Myth 2. If it does not have a copyright notice, it is public domain. As of March 1, 1989, when the U.S. adopted the Berne Convention international copyright treaty, a work is no longer required to include a copyright notice in order to receive protection. If a notice does appear, it may include either the familiar © symbol or the word *copyright.*

Myth 3. Anything on the Internet is public domain. Nothing could be further from the truth. Original works of authorship placed on the Internet are entitled to protection just like any other works meeting the law's criteria. However, the Internet has made possible copyright infringements on a global scale.

Myth 4. A work copyrighted in another country is public domain in the United States. This myth seems to arise when instructors want to use videotapes or publications from another nation in a U.S. distance education course. The Berne Convention treaty specifies that the copyright laws of any signatory country apply within that country to a work copyrighted in another signatory country. In other words, within the United States, any work copyrighted in any other Berne Convention nation (i.e., most nations) receives the same protection as a work copyrighted in the United States.

Myth 5. The doctrine of "fair use" means that copyrighted materials can be used in an educational setting without permission. As a blanket statement, this is perhaps the biggest myth of all. Education is one of the purposes for which fair use *may* apply, but fair use can be determined only after careful consideration of four rather complex criteria. Many educational applications are completely beyond fair use and require permission—for example, the development of most coursepacks.

Myth 6. A teacher can use a videotape in a distance education course under "fair use." This myth is incorrect on two counts. First, fair use applies to the *reproduction* of copyrighted materials, not public display or performance. Second, the "face-to-face teaching exemption" described in the law specifically *excludes* videotapes and other "audiovisual" materials from use in "transmitted" distance education courses without a license or other form of permission.

◆ COPYRIGHT ESSENTIALS

Copyright is hardly a new concept. The first forms of legal copyright protection appeared in 15th-century Venice shortly after Gutenberg invented the printing press (Zobel, 1997). In 1557, Queen Mary chartered the Stationer's Company to "enlist the covetous self-interests of the very printers and booksellers," as a means of imposing censorship during a time of political and religious turmoil in England (Kaplan, cited in Miller, 1975). Registration of a book with the Stationer's Company provided the printer exclusive rights to print copies of the book and sell them.

The statute of Anne, passed by Parliament in 1714, contained features similar to some of those found in our copyright law today. Existing books were entitled to 21 years of copyright protection. Books published subsequent to the statute were copyrighted for 14 years, with the copyright assigned to the author. If the author were still living at the end of this period, the copyright could be renewed for another 14 years. The law provided for the payment of fines for copyright infringements (one penny per page—a substantial amount in the early 18th century), with the penalties split evenly between the copyright holder and the Crown. Such protection was not extended to books that had not been registered with the Stationer's Company (Miller, 1975).

The first copyright legislation in the United States was enacted by Congress in 1790, a bill modeled after the statute of Anne. The law, Title 17 of the U.S. Code, has undergone several major revisions, the latest in 1976 as Public Law 94-553. Section 102 specifies that copyright protection subsists *in original works of authorship fixed in a tangible medium of expression, now known or later developed, from which they can be perceived, reproduced, or otherwise communicated, either directly or with the aid of a machine or device.*

Two critical conditions thus exist before a work is eligible for copyright protection. First, copyright applies to *works of authorship* representing the tangible expression of ideas, requiring originality and some degree of creativity. Copyrighted works of authorship in a distance education course may include the instructor's lecture notes, electronic-mail messages, graphic images in a course Web page, videotapes and photographic slides, presentation graphics, literature that is read aloud, sound recordings, and printed materials reproduced for student study. Copyright protection does not extend to facts, titles, names, familiar symbols, standard forms, procedures, and works consisting of common property, although some items in these categories may be eligible for patent or trademark protection. (Congress has been considering expanding the scope of copyright protection to include some works of authorship currently in these categories.)

Second, the work *must be fixed in a tangible medium of expression.* The examples above are self-evident because they *can be perceived, reproduced, or otherwise communicated.* Copyright would *not* apply to comments made in a live classroom discussion unless the interaction were recorded or otherwise transcribed. Courses themselves are eligible for copyright protection if they are videotaped or offered on-line via an Internet server.

◆ EXCLUSIVE RIGHTS OF COPYRIGHT HOLDERS

The law grants to copyright owners exclusive rights to do, or to authorize others to do, any of the following:

- ◆ Reproduce the copyrighted work.
- ◆ Prepare derivative works based on the copyrighted original.
- ◆ Distribute copies of the copyrighted work.
- ◆ Perform the copyrighted work.
- ◆ Display the copyrighted work publicly.

Fortunately, Congress recognized that *under certain circumstances* the use of protected materials could be acceptable without permission from the copyright holder. In fact, limitations on exclusive rights consume the majority of Chapter 1 of Title 17. Two sections are of particular importance to distance educators. Section 107 provides the criteria for "fair use," while Section 110 addresses public performance and display.

◆ FAIR USE

According to Section 107, "the fair use of a copyrighted work. . . . for purposes such as criticism, comment, news reporting, teaching (including multiple copies for classroom use), scholarship, or research, is not an infringement." The legislative history of the law (House of Representatives Report No. 94-1476) noted that no adequate definition of the concept of fair use had emerged, and that no generally applicable definition was possible. Rather, the doctrine should be viewed as "an equitable rule of reason," with each case to be decided on its own merits against the criteria provided in the law.

The phrasing here is critically important. Section 107 does not grant educators wholesale permission to use copyrighted materials simply because they work in schools or colleges. Only a *fair use* is legal, and fair use cannot be determined until four essential criteria have been considered. Congress deliberately wrote the criteria in broad, general terms to provide a flexible structure that could be applied across a multitude of potential fair use scenarios without the need for constant revisions to the law. No single criterion is enough to deny fair use. Even if one criterion weighs against, the use may still be legal if the other three criteria weigh in favor. The criteria include the following:

◆ *The purpose and character of the use, including whether such use is of a commercial nature or is for nonprofit educational purposes...* Uses in a nonprofit, educational setting are more likely to be fair use than those in a corporate training or proprietary college setting. Reproduction for purposes of criticism or commentary may be considered more favorably, even if for commercial purposes.

◆ *The nature of the copyrighted work...* Nonfiction works are more likely to be considered fair use than fictional or artistic works containing a higher degree of creative expression. Published works are generally favored by courts more than unpublished materials, and printed works more than audiovisual materials. Publications designed to be consumable, such as workbook pages or standardized test forms, should never be reproduced without permission.

◆ *The amount and substantiality of the portion used in relation to the copyrighted work as a whole...* The law itself does not provide specific limits or percentages, although criteria have been set in negotiated guidelines that will be discussed below. In many cases with printed materials, the entire copyrighted work is desired, such as a journal article, illustration, or photograph. The case for fair use can be enhanced if no more of the published original is taken than is necessary to meet the user's needs. This criterion also has a qualitative component in that reproduction of even a small proportion of a work may exceed fair use if that portion contains the heart or essence of the original.

◆ *The effect of the use upon the potential market for or value of the copyrighted work...* In infringement suits, the courts consider whether it was reasonable to expect the ultimate recipient of a reproduction to have purchased that copy or paid a licensing fee. Courts also consider effect in the context of the potential financial harm to the copyright holder if the act in question were a widespread practice. This factor has particular implications for video-based distance education courses. Under the current law, audiovisual materials cannot be transmitted without permission, partly because of fears of copyright owners that the transmissions will be recorded and reused at receive sites, resulting in a potential loss of sales.

◆ DURATION OF COPYRIGHT

Several formulas have been devised to help determine when works pass into the public domain. Terms of protection vary according to what the date of creation was, whether the work was published, whether ownership resides with an individual or an employer or other legal entity, and whether the original copyright on an older work was renewed. Table 5–1 provides a general guide. In summary:

◆ A work published more than 75 years ago is now in the public domain.

◆ A work created on or after January 1, 1978, is protected for the lifetime of the author plus 50 years, or if of corporate authorship, 75 years from publication. In other words, the earliest such a work could fall into the public domain is January 2028.

◆ A work published between 1964 and 1977 cannot fall into the public domain until at least 2039.

TABLE 5–1 ◆ *Duration of Copyright Under U.S. Law*

Status of Work	Term of Copyright	Earliest Public Domain Date
Published over 75 years ago	None	Now in public domain
Published between 1922 and 1963	28 years, renewable for 47 years	If not renewed, in public domain; if renewed, 75 years from publication date
Published between 1964 and 1977	75 years	2039
Created before 1978 but not published	Lifetime of author plus 50 years, or until 12/31/2002, whichever is later	2003, but only for author who became deceased before 1953
Created after 1/1/1978, personal authorship	Lifetime of author plus 50 years	2028
Created after 1/1/1978, corporate authorship	75 years from publication or 100 years from creation, whichever occurs first	2053

◆ A work created before January 1, 1978, but not published is protected for the lifetime of the author plus 50 years, or until December 31, 2002, whichever is later.

Efforts have been under way in Congress to extend these terms of protection to become consistent with those of other nations. Current information is available at the U.S. Copyright Office Web site (http://lcweb.loc.gov/copyright/). The task of determining the term of copyright is compounded by the layers of protection that may exist for a given work. For example, Mozart's symphonies are long since in the public domain, but a 1994 recording of the Symphony no. 41 will receive protection until long after the playback device has become hopelessly obsolete. A textbook photo of an artwork may be copyrighted at several levels: by the publisher, the photographer, the owner of the original work, and perhaps even the owner of another intermediate stage, such as a digitized image taken from the photographer's slide.

◆ PUBLIC DOMAIN

Any work in the public domain may be used freely in a distance education course. Works may enter the public domain several ways, most often through simple expiration of copyright protection. Most materials published by the U.S. government are specifically excluded from copyright protection by Section 105 and are in the public domain from the date of creation. However, audiovisual works produced for federal agencies by independent contractors *are* eligible for copyright protection and must be treated in distance education courses like any other audiovisual work. Also, restrictions on the federal government do not apply to states. Works developed by or for state agencies, including videotapes and other audiovisual materials, may be declared public domain according to the state's policies but are likely to be copyrighted.

The third means by which works enter the public domain is for owners to abandon their copyrights. For example, as Myth 3 previously illustrated, a popular and widespread misconception holds that materials posted to the Internet become public domain because the Internet is such a public and uncontrolled medium. Abandonment of copyright actually requires an explicit and overt statement from the copyright holder, and rarely occurs.

◆ GUIDELINES

As the copyright law was undergoing revision in the mid-1970s, Congress recognized that the nonprofit educational community could benefit from guidelines that help define acceptable practices under fair use. The House report contained guidelines for classroom copying and educational uses of music that had been negotiated by educator and publisher groups. A third set of guidelines was approved in 1979 to cover off-air recording of broadcast programming for educational purposes.

Although the authors of the law tried to accommodate future technological developments with vague terminology such as "fixed in a tangible medium of expression, now known or later developed" and "with the aid of a machine or device," they had no way of anticipating the phenomenal growth of computing, software capabilities, digitization, and video and data networks. As a result, application of a 1976 statute to 1990s technology has become a source of considerable frustration and confusion. In September 1994, the U.S. Department of Commerce convened the Conference on Fair Use (CONFU), bringing together information proprietors and user groups in an attempt to develop fair use guidelines addressing new technologies. Over a 2½-year period, representatives of more than 100 organizations met as a whole and in smaller work groups to draft guidelines for distance learning, image collections, multimedia, electronic reserves, and interlibrary loan. By May 1997, only the first three work groups had developed formal proposals, and none of the three garnered widespread support in the education community. Ultimately, CONFU elected neither to endorse nor to reject any of the proposals but to continue the negotiation processes. Table 5–2 summarizes the seven sets of fair use guidelines that have thus far been accepted by the U.S. Congress or have appeared in draft form under CONFU.

The draft Educational Fair Use Guidelines for Distance Learning and the other guidelines may be found on the World Wide Web. (See the list of Web sites at the end of the chapter.) The work group agreed not to address on-line learning technologies in the proposal. Members felt the technologies were evolving too quickly and that the delivery of courses by educational institutions via the Internet was still in the experimental stage. The guidelines thus focused almost exclusively on video-based delivery systems. The greatest resistance to the guidelines came from K–12, higher education, and library groups, which felt the criteria were too restrictive. The lack of attention to on-line courses was also seen as a major shortcoming.

TABLE 5–2 ◆ *Status of Fair Use Guidelines of Interest to Distance Educators*

Guidelines	Applies to	Status
Guidelines for Classroom Copying in Not-for-Profit Educational Institutions	Text and other resources (e.g., photographs, illustrations) in printed publications	Accepted by Congress
Guidelines for Educational Uses of Music	Published music and sound recordings used in music classes	Accepted by Congress
Guidelines for Off-Air Recording of Broadcast Programming for Educational Purposes	Broadcast programming taped off-air (excludes cable channel programs)	Accepted by Congress
Fair Use Guidelines for Educational Multimedia	Copyrighted materials incorporated into multimedia works (includes use in distance education)	Accepted by Congress
Guidelines for the Educational Use of Digital Images	Digitized versions by visual images such as photographs, illustrations, and works of art	CONFU draft; not widely endorsed
Educational Fair Use Guidelines for Distance Learning	Audiovisual works used in video-based distance education (excludes asynchronous delivery)	CONFU draft; not widely endorsed
Fair Use Guidelines for Electronic Reserve Systems	Digitized publications maintained on-line as counterpart to library reserve system for printed materials	Draft prepared as part of CONFU process but not submitted for consideration

◆ COPYRIGHT APPLICATIONS IN DISTANCE EDUCATION

What then are the major implications of U.S. copyright law for distance education? For the purpose of this chapter, issues are grouped by video- and Internet-based delivery systems.

Printed Materials

Regardless of the delivery vehicle, teachers of distance education courses may want their students to have copyrighted articles and other printed materials in hand for study purposes. The Guidelines for Classroom Copying in Not-for-Profit Educational Institutions permit limited reproduction and distribution of copyrighted materials (no more than one copy per student in the course), *as long as the tests of brevity and spontaneity and the cumulative effects test are met.* A discussion of numerical limitations is beyond the scope of this chapter. Readers are referred to the guidelines for limits from a single author or publication. The test of spontaneity requires that the inspiration to use the work and the moment in time of actual use in the course do not allow for a reasonable attempt to obtain permission. This test effectively prohibits use of the same materials in subsequent academic terms without the copyright holder's approval. The cumulative effects test caps the number of items copied for a single course at nine per academic term.

The criteria specified in the guidelines help to determine what can be reproduced without the need to seek permission. The development of coursepacks, particularly those including the same materials term after term, normally requires licensing and the payment of fees. The licensing of printed materials is not an overwhelming task. The Copyright Clearance Center (CCC) (http://www.copyright.com/) has been established as the reproduction rights organization (RRO) for the United States and serves this clearinghouse function. The CCC can license the reproduction of any of over 1.7 million titles already preauthorized by rights holders and collects and distributes royalties. Many copy centers and bookstores serving academic institutions maintain accounts with the CCC, provide liaison on the instructor's behalf, and then duplicate and sell the coursepacks. Some 30 RROs exist worldwide, providing similar services to faculty in other countries.

Audiovisual Materials

In conventional classroom settings, Section 110 permits the performance or display of a copyrighted work under what is termed the "face-to-face teaching exemption," provided that the activities take place in a classroom or similar place devoted to instruction, in a nonprofit educational institution, with a lawfully made copy (if applicable). For example, the law allows classroom activities to include the reading aloud of literature, performance of dramatic works and musical compositions by instructors and students enrolled in the course, and display of videotapes and other audiovisual materials. However, in the case of courses that are "transmitted" to remote sites, the law permits performance of musical and nondramatic literary works *but specifically excludes dramatic works and audiovisual materials.*

Section 101 defines "audiovisual materials" as "works that consist of a series of related images which are intrinsically intended to be shown by the use of machines or devices such as projectors, viewers, or electronic equipment. . . ." Allowable activities in a distance education course would thus include the display of photographs, illustrations, maps, and other printed materials, still images from videotapes, and 35-mm slides as long as they are not shown in sequence from a copyrighted program. A course that is transmitted cannot include a videotape, videodisk, 16-mm film, or consecutive images from a photographic series without the copyright holder's permission.

The same criteria would also apply to the display of digitized images downloaded from a server and then incorporated into a transmitted course, although the legality of digitizing third-party images and placing them on a server for faculty and student access represents a different copyright issue. The guidelines proposed to CONFU in 1997 by the digital images work group permitted the digitization and storage of images not already commercially available at a fair price, provided that the images were accessed through a secure network and available only to faculty and students associated with the course. Furthermore, the guidelines restricted use to a maximum of one academic term if the rights holder is known; thereafter, permission must be obtained. Educators should be aware that the digital images guidelines were not widely endorsed and may or may not be considered by the courts in deciding infringement suits.

The CONFU Fair Use Guidelines for Educational Multimedia provide numerical limits on the amount of copyrighted material that can be incorporated in a multimedia development project without permission and also permit the use of the completed products on a controlled access distance education network. Development of the multimedia guidelines was already well under way before CONFU was convened and took place largely outside the CONFU process. The completed draft was endorsed by more than 30 organizations, including the U.S. Copyright Office, and was recognized by Congress. As a result, the multimedia guidelines are likely to carry more weight in the courts than the other CONFU drafts. Resistance within CONFU came primarily from education and academic library organizations, which felt the guidelines were too restrictive.

The constraints on the use of audiovisual materials in a transmitted distance education course place an extraordinary burden on faculty accustomed to using instructional technology in their teaching. While the Copyright Clearance Center provides licensing services for printed materials, no such clearinghouse yet exists for audiovisual works. Each copyright holder must be located and permission obtained. Often this is not an easy task. McKay (1995) described a litany of frustration—including endless voice mail messages, mail responses that did not address his request, operators in other countries who did not speak English, and terse rejections—during his attempts to gain permission to use videotapes in course lectures shown on a local cable television channel. As a result, students were required to drive to campus to view the tapes in the college library, hardly "distance education."

The CONFU guidelines for distance learning provide an indication of the degree to which some rights holders seem willing to bend. The guidelines require that the transmission be over a secure system with limited access and would not apply to courses broadcast via television stations or cable systems. Performance of an entire copyrighted work or large portion thereof would be permitted just one time for a distance learning course; permission would be required if the course is offered in a subsequent academic term. Receiving sites would be permitted to record the class sessions containing the copyrighted materials and make the tapes available for student viewing, but the tapes must be viewed only in a controlled-access environment and must be erased after 15 working days, and the playback system must prevent further reproduction of the portion of the class tape including the copyrighted material. As with the guidelines for digital images, it is unknown whether a court would consider these criteria the upper limits of fair use in a distance education course, because no case law yet exists on the topic. The safest alternatives are (1) seek permission and (2) use locally produced materials for which the copyright rests with the instructor's own institution. These would include not only videotapes but photographs, graphics, and digitized images as well.

Computer-Based Distance Education

The Internet is rapidly becoming the medium of choice for distance educators in a wide variety of academic, corporate, and government settings. The CONFU work group's reluctance to address on-line learning environments has left educators without fair use guidelines in this area, although the multimedia and digital images guidelines are equally applicable to video and computer networks.

Materials placed on the Internet, whether electronic-mail messages, postings to mailing lists (often inappropriately referred to as "listservs") or Usenet newsgroups, files and images that make up World Wide Web pages, Gopher pages, or documents placed in FTP archives, represent intellectual property fixed in a tangible medium of expression and are entitled to copyright protection just like any other work of authorship. From a legal perspective, placement of the material on the Internet is no different from any other form of distribution, except that access and the potential for abuse are both greatly expanded. While some persons contend that such action implies an abandonment of copyright, clearly this is not the case without an explicit statement to that effect on the part of the copyright holder (which often is someone other than the individual who posted the material) (Templeton, 1997).

Many distance education courses are conducted via electronic mail and on-line discussion groups. The author of an e-mail message, whether sent to an individual or a list or newsgroup, retains ownership of the intellectual property that message contains. Under the concept of "implied license," a recipient can save the message, print it, and forward it to a limited number of individuals interested in the same topic without the originator's permission, but a person-to-person message should never be posted to a mailing list or newsgroup without permission. O'Mahoney (1997) suggests that forwarding a message from one list or newsgroup to another without permission may also extend beyond the boundaries of implied license, particularly if the forwarded message reaches essentially a different audience or is sent through a different distribution system.

Courses offered via the World Wide Web provide excellent opportunities for copyright abuse. Course Web page developers must be careful that all page components either are original or have the necessary clearances. For example, attractive buttons, bars, bullets, backgrounds, icons, clip art, and other graphics are available for downloading from dozens of Web sites. Most of these locations specify their copyright policies within the site. Some offer their graphics freely with no restrictions, others require notification of use and/or reciprocal links, while others charge fees. Under no circumstances should a text document be copied and put on a course Web site without permission.

The presence of Print and Save buttons on browser toolbars may imply that documents on the Web are fair game. On the contrary, unless they are specifically dedicated to the public domain or grant downloading privileges, Web documents are entitled to full copyright protection. A fair use handbook published by the Consortium for Educational Technology for University Systems (CETUS, 1995) suggests that copying a short Internet document for personal study or research likely falls within fair use but recommends that the four-factor fair use analysis be applied. Saving or printing from sites that have restricted access or contain documents that are commercially available may be more difficult to justify as fair use. Many Web sites include copyright policies that provide the site sponsor's positions on downloading. Care must be taken to confirm that the site sponsor actually is the rights holder of the desired document.

Is it necessary to obtain permission before linking to someone else's Web site? In 1996, the Georgia legislature made it a crime to link to another site without permission (Cook, 1997). However, the law offices of Oppedahl & Larson (1996) proposed that freely linking to the Web sites of others not only is legal but is encouraged, and that those who object to setting up hyperlinks are "missing the point of the World Wide Web." Even if permission is not a legal requirement (except perhaps in Georgia), "netiquette" dictates that the Web master be notified that a link has been established and be given the opportunity to ask that it be removed.

Many courses, particularly in higher education and corporate training settings, are now offered via some form of Internet conferencing, groupware, or Web course software. Some of the more advanced provide sophisticated communication tools, featuring one-to-one e-mail and threaded large- and small-group discussions, and content presentation via Web pages. The copyright implications described above are equally applicable in these settings, even though most of these systems require special client software and/or passwords that restrict access to the participants.

Obtaining Permission

If guidelines are not applicable and fair use cannot be determined, distance educators should obtain permission from rights holders before using copyrighted materials in their courses, as challenging as that task may seem. Begin by contacting the publisher or distributor. If no address or telephone number is provided, check catalogs or ask a reference librarian for assistance. In the case of printed publications, the Copyright Clearance Center is a potential source. As a last resort, a plea for help sent to appropriate Internet mailing lists almost invariably delivers the desired information.

The first contact with the rights holder should be made by telephone to confirm precisely to whom the request should be addressed. A phone call also provides an opportunity to discuss the circumstances of the request and negotiate fees. Ultimately, the rights holder will likely ask for a written copy of the request, by either mail or fax, for record purposes and to minimize misunderstandings. See Figure 5–1 for a sample request letter. At a minimum, the rights holder will need the following information:

◆ Name, position, institution, mailing address, and phone and fax numbers for the person making the request.
◆ Identification of the item to be used, including title, author or producer, publication title and date in the case of periodicals, and amount desired.
◆ Complete description of the intended use, including purpose, course name, number of copies, means of distribution, intended dates of use, description of recipients, and precautions anticipated to prevent further reproductions (if applicable).
◆ Date by which permission is requested. (Allow at least six weeks.)

While approval can be granted over the telephone, for record purposes written permission is strongly recommended, preferably on the copyright holder's letterhead paper. This provides tangible evidence confirming exactly who provided permission for what, and when.

Department of English
328 Loess Hall
University of Western Iowa
Council Bluffs, Iowa 51508

July 16, 20XX

Mrs. Caroline B. Day
Manager of Permissions
American Heritage Productions
2877 Revere Highway
Boston, MA 02226

Dear Mrs. Day:

As a follow-up to our telephone conversation this morning, I am hereby requesting permission to show your excellent videotape, *The Life of Edgar Allen Poe,* in my distance education course this fall. Our department purchased this tape from your company in 1999 but did not obtain the transmission rights at that time.

The course is entitled "Early American Literature" and is expected to enroll around 25 students, including about 10 participating at off-campus locations. The course will be transmitted to four receive sites (in Sioux City, Clear Lake, Waterloo, and Ottumwa) via the Iowa Communications Network, a closed-access, statewide telecommunications system. The transmission will be received only in these four specially equipped ICN classrooms, and no local recordings will be permitted. A backup recording of the entire class period will be made at the origination site and made available to students who were not present. This tape will be provided for viewing only in a controlled access environment with no reproduction equipment accessible. The tape will be erased after two weeks.

The anticipated date of use is November 17, 20XX. I would appreciate your response by November 1 if possible so I can make alternative course plans if necessary. I do hope you will honor this request, however, because your tape is a highly informative reconstruction of Poe's life and is extremely valuable to my students.

Thank you very much for your consideration. Please contact me directly if I can provide further information.

Sincerely,

Michael T. James

Associate Professor English

Phone: (712) 555-2838
Fax: (712) 555-2840
E-Mail: mtjames@westiowa.edu

FIGURE 5–1   Sample permission letter

Current Issues

As the digital age progresses, the shortcomings of the current copyright law become more and more apparent. In 1995, the Working Group on Intellectual Property Rights, convened by the Clinton administration under the U.S. Department of Commerce to explore the implications of new technologies, concluded that the law needed only "fine tuning" in the form of minor amendments "to maintain the balance of the law in the face of onrushing technology" (Lehman, 1995). These amendments have yet to materialize, and the CONFU process has found the participants from education and proprietary groups so far apart that common ground has been difficult to locate.

Since permission from rights holders is required before audiovisual materials can be used in transmitted distance education courses, a clearinghouse to process clearances and fee collection and distribution is urgently needed for these works. McKay (1995) observed that in the present system, "getting written permission is analogous to pushing your way through coils of barbed wire." Unless the law is changed or a clearinghouse is established, the agonies faced by course developers in obtaining copyright clearances will ensure that (1) the law will be subject to abuses even more flagrant than those we see today, or (2) instructors will teach without embedded technology, or (3) both, and none of these options is desirable.

Congress passed the Copyright Remedy Clarification Act in 1990, one provision of which removed the sovereign immunity enjoyed by governmental agencies and their employees. As the result, schools, colleges, and other agencies supported by state funding, as well as their faculty and staff members, can be sued for copyright infringement (Bruwelheide, 1994). Thus, the development and implementation of firm copyright policies and employee training should be a high priority for institutions operating distance education programs. Faculty and staff who commit infringements in violation of institutional policies may find themselves completely responsible for their own defense.

◆ SUMMARY

Somewhere in the not too distant future, our homes, workplaces, and schools will be equipped with advanced telecommunications systems integrating what is known today as telephone services, Internet access, on-line financial and news services, and cable television, probably with many other features not yet conceived. Distance education will play a central role in that future, as multimedia-based curricula will be offered by educational institutions and private corporations on a global basis to anyone, anywhere, at any time. Despite the assessment of the Working Group on Intellectual Property Rights, the current copyright law will likely be unable to deal with the enormous complexity of protecting intellectual property rights while providing legal access in this international information marketplace and will require a major overhaul. The basic concepts of copyright and fair use may need to be reconsidered. However, a more probable intermediate solution is the development of technologies that prevent reproduction of copyrighted materials from networked sources.

Meanwhile, the present law may be inadequate, but educators must abide by its provisions or face the consequences. For the most part, the copyright statute is civil law, not criminal law. Unless violators have made a business out of infringements, they are likely to be sued, not sent to prison. The penalties can be severe—statutory damages of up to $100,000 per instance, plus payment of the plaintiff's legal fees, which can be substantial. Distance educators have not only a legal and ethical obligation to "practice safe copyright" but monetary incentives as well.

Self-Test Questions

1. True/False. If a printed document has not been published and does not include a copyright notice, it can legally be reproduced and distributed to distance education students without the author's permission. What should the instructor do with this material in order to use it?
2. What are the two critical conditions that determine whether a work is eligible for copyright protection?
3. What are the five exclusive rights granted to copyright holders by U.S. Copyright law?
4. True/False. As long as the use of copyrighted materials is in a nonprofit, educational setting, and the first "fair use" criterion is satisfied, the other three criteria can be ignored. Why?
5. Which of the following may be used for the first time without the permission of the copyright holder in a distance education course delivered via a controlled-access statewide network—a newspaper photograph shown on a document camera, a videotape obtained from the media center, a contemporary short story read aloud by students, a single digitized image taken from a commercially produced slide set, the entire slide set, a contemporary play read aloud by students, and a newly published journal article reproduced and distributed to students?
6. Which of the items in question 5 could legally be used without permission if the course were offered via the same system in a subsequent academic term?
7. True/False. In a distance education course offered via the World Wide Web, it is legal to link to a third party Web site as a course resource without the permission of that site's copyright holder.
8. What are the four key information elements that should be included in a letter requesting permission to use copyrighted materials in a distance education course?

Answers to Self-Test Questions

1. False. Unpublished materials are eligible for copyright protection. The copyright notice is recommended but not required. The presence of a copyright notice on a work prevents the defendant in a civil suit from claiming "innocent infringement."

2. The law applies to an *original work of authorship* that is *fixed in a tangible medium of expression.*

3. The rights of reproduction, preparation of derivative works based on the copyrighted original, distribution, public performance, and public display.

4. False. All four criteria are equally important and must be considered for all uses, including those in education. No single criterion is sufficient to determine whether a use does or does not fall under fair use.

5. Legal without question: the photograph, the short story, the single digitized slide image, and the journal article (as long as the cumulative effect test is met); possibly legal under guidelines that have not been widely endorsed: the videotape; illegal without question: the entire slide set and the contemporary play.

6. The photograph, short story, and single slide image could be used. The journal article and videotape would require permission the second time the course is offered. The slide should be used in its original photographic form. The digitized version may require permission.

7. Generally true. Depending upon state or local laws that may apply, linking to other sites is not only legal but encouraged. Those site managers should be notified as a courtesy and given the opportunity to ask that the link be removed.

8. Identification and contact information for the person making the request, complete identification of the item(s) to be used, complete description of the intended use, and date by which permission is requested.

References

Bruwelheide, J. H. (1994). Distance education: Copyright issues. In B. Willis (Ed.), *Distance education strategies and tools* (pp. 233–244). Englewood Cliffs, NJ: Educational Technology Publications.

Consortium for Educational Technology for University Systems (1995). *Fair use of copyrighted works.* Seal Beach, CA: California State University Chancellor's Office.

Cook, R. (1997, June 1). It's OK to put a link to another site on my page, right? Maybe not. *Netscape World* [On-line], June 1, 1997. Available: http://www.netscapeworld.com/netscapeworld/nw-06-1997/nw-06-bestpract.html.

Lehman, B. A. (1995). *Intellectual property and the national information infrastructure: The report of the Working Group on Intellectual Property Rights.* Washington, DC: U.S. Department of Commerce.

McKay, G. (1995). *Copyright in the pipeline: An examination of distance learning issues and possible solutions.* Paper presented at the 1995 conference of the Council for Higher Education Computing Services, Roswell, NM, November 1995. (ERIC Document Reproduction Service ED 398 913)

Miller, J. K. (1975). A brief history of copyright. *Audiovisual Instruction, 20*(10), 44.

O'Mahoney, B. (1997, May 1). *Newsgroups* [On-line]. Available: http://www.benedict.com.

Oppedahl & Larson Law Offices (1996, October 29). *Web law FAQ* [On-line].
Available: http://www.patents.com/weblaw.sht.
Templeton, B. (1997, May 19). *10 big myths about copyright explained* [On-line].
Available: http://www.clari.net/brad/copymyths.html.
Zobel, S. M. (1997). Legal implications of intellectual property and the World Wide
Web. In B. H. Khan (Ed.), *Web-based instruction* (pp. 337–340). Englewood Cliffs,
NJ: Educational Technology Publications.

Additional Reading

Gasaway, L. (1996, December 3). *When works pass into the public domain* [On-line].
Available: http://library.law.unc.edu/faq/chart.shtml.

Sources of Information

Conference on Fair Use Homepage

http://www.uspto.gov/web/offices/dcom/olia/confu/
Activities and reports of the Conference on Fair Use (CONFU)

Copyright and Fair Use

http://fairuse.stanford.edu
Comprehensive fair use information site maintained by Stanford University
Libraries

Copyright and Intellectual Property

http://www.public.iastate.edu/~mikealbr/links/copyright.html
Copyright site links maintained by Mike Albright; includes links to fair use
guidelines

Copyright and Intellectual Property Resources

http://www.nlc-bnc.ca/ifla/II/cpyright.htm (II = two capital I's)
Voluminous amount of copyright information from all parts of the world,
including full text of numerous articles and papers

Copyright Clearance Center

http://www.copyright.com
Web site for the reproduction rights organization serving the United States

Copyright Law Materials

http://www.law.cornell.edu:80/topics/copyright.html
Site maintained by the Cornell University Law School, providing full text of the
copyright law and copyright treaties, court decisions, and other resources

Copyright Resource Page

http://www.aimnet.com/~carroll/copyright/faq-home.html
> Site of Terry Carroll's popular Copyright FAQ (frequently asked questions) and other resources

Copyright Web Site

http://www.benedict.com
> Comprehensive source of copyright information maintained by intellectual property attorney Benedict O'Mahoney

U.S. Copyright Office

http://lcweb.loc.gov/copyright/
> On-line source of Copyright Office publications, forms, and other information, including status of pending copyright legislation

Other Web Sites

Counterfactual Research News

How might your life have unfolded differently? This web site contains a bibliography of counterfactual publications, in press articles, and cartoons.

Social Cognition Paper Archive and Information Center

This web page, maintained at Purdue University, archives various abstracts of social cognition articles in such areas as stereotyping, and person memory.

chapter 6

Instructional Design for Distance Education

CHAPTER GOAL

The purpose of this chapter is to present a process for designing instruction at a distance.

CHAPTER OBJECTIVES

After reading and reviewing this chapter, you should be able to

1. Explain why it is important to plan ahead when teaching at a distance.
2. Describe the systematic design process for instructional design.
3. Describe the types of learner information to be collected for planning.
4. Explain the decisions about content that need to be made.
5. Explain why it is important to examine teaching strategies and media.
6. Discuss how technology and resources influence the distance learning environment.
7. Describe the process for planning to evaluate instruction.

◆ WHY PLAN FOR TEACHING AT A DISTANCE

Just like other kinds of teaching, teaching at a distance requires planning and organizing. However, teaching at a distance, whether synchronous or asynchronous, requires that greater emphasis be placed on the initial planning phase.

Instructional design should consider all aspects of the instructional environment, following a well-organized procedure that provides guidance to even the novice distance instructor. (See, for example, Figure 6–1.) The instructional environment should be viewed as a system, a relationship among and between all the components of that system—the instructor, the learners, the material, and the technology. Especially when planning for distance education, the instructor must make decisions that will affect all aspects of the system (Moore & Kearsley, 1996).

This chapter presents an organized and systematic way to go about planning instruction. This design process allows the instructor to consider elements such as the content, the nature of the learner, the process by which the learning will take place (methodology), and the means for assessing the learning experience. By following through with this process, the instructor will find that teaching at a distance is an exciting and dynamic experience, one that will be welcomed by both the instructor and the learners.

◆ PRINCIPLES OF INSTRUCTIONAL DESIGN SYSTEMS

Systematic Process

The process of systematic planning for instruction is the outcome of many years of research (Dick & Carey, 1996). An analysis of the application of this process indicates that when instruction is designed within a system, learning occurs.

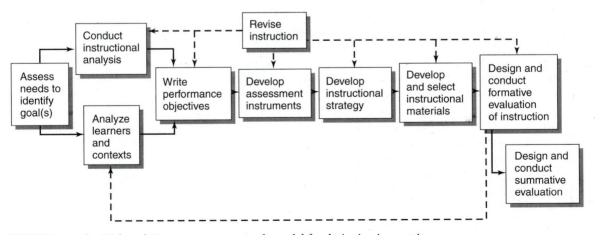

FIGURE 6–1   The Dick and Carey systems approach model for designing instruction.

A critical part of the process is to consider the components of a successful learning system (Dick & Carey, 1996). These components are the learners, the content, the method and materials, and the environment, including the technology. The interaction of these components creates the type of learning experience necessary for student learning.

The components must interact both efficiently and effectively to produce quality learning experiences. There should be a balance among the components—none can take on a higher position than the others. The attempt to keep the components equally balanced while maintaining their interaction effect is essential to planning quality instruction. Simply stated, a series of activities alone cannot lead to learning; it is only with the careful planning for their balance and interface that learning is the result.

Another critical part of the process is evaluation. For successful learning to take place it is vital to determine what works and what needs to be improved. Evaluation leads to revision of instruction, and revision of instruction helps secure the final outcome of helping students learn (Heinich, Molenda, Russell, & Smaldino, 1996). Because of an emphasis on planning and revising, well-designed instruction is repeatable. This means that the instruction can be applied again in another class. For example, instruction designed for a televised, multisite class can be used again with a new group of students at different sites. Because it is "reusable," the considerable initial effort is well worth the time and energy.

Planning for Instruction at a Distance

The process of planning and organizing for a distance education course is multifaceted and must occur well in advance of the scheduled instruction. To eliminate trial-and-error preparation, distance learning faculty should

◆ Keep in mind that courses previously taught in traditional classrooms may need to be retooled. The focus of the instruction shifts to visual presentations, engaged learners, and careful timing of presentations of information.

◆ In revising traditional classroom materials, consider ways to illustrate key concepts, or topics, using tables, figures, and other visual representations.

◆ Plan activities that encourage interactivity at all the sites. It is a common pitfall to focus on only one site during the process of managing the class and operating technology. Planning for interactivity reduces this problem and helps learners. Not only does the instructor have to plan for interaction, but students may require training to participate actively in these types of activities.

◆ Plan activities that allow for student group work. This helps construct a supportive social environment. For example, the instructor could present case studies related to theories and concepts covered in the course, and then groups of students, perhaps in different sites, could discuss case study questions and reach consensus on a solution to the problem.

◆ Be prepared in the event that technical problems occur. If the equipment fails, it is important for students to have projects and assignments independent of the instructor and alternative means of communication (e.g., fax, phone, e-mail). Discussing with students ahead of time alternative plans in case there is a technological problem will eliminate confusion and loss of productive class time when a problem occurs (Herring & Smaldino, 1997).

In addition to considerations related to planning for instruction, there is also a need to examine issues associated with the separation of instructor and some or all of the students. Time constraints for class delivery, lack of eye contact, visualization of the materials, and planning for interaction require a reconsideration of classroom dynamics. Often instructors use visual cues, such as student facial expressions, within the traditional classroom and conversations with students after class to decide quickly to adjust the instructional approach for a course. These cues give instructors insights that help them personalize the instruction for the students and ensure a quality learning experience for all. Teaching at a distance eliminates many of these cues. Alternative approaches to ongoing evaluation of instruction must be incorporated. If instructors ignore this area of preparation, planning to teach as they always have, they will feel frustrated. Likewise, students may feel alienated and will begin to tune out the instructor. The instructional development process must be based on the unique characteristics and needs of students, meshed with the teaching style of the instructor and the course goals and content. Interaction must be maximized, the visual potential of the medium must be explored, and time constraints must be addressed.

◆ ISSUES TO ADDRESS IN THE PLANNING PROCESS

Who Are the Learners?

There are several reasons for bringing students together in a distance learning setting. Students can be pooled into classes of sufficient size to create a critical mass (Dede, 1990). Students can aggregate for advanced courses in subjects that might not otherwise be available on-site. Distance education can be an important approach to responding to the growing pluralism of learners' backgrounds, characteristics, or unusual learning needs that may require or benefit from specialized instruction.

Taking the time to learn about the learners in the class yields a more productive learning environment. Knowledge of general learner characteristics can inform the instructor of the nature of the students at origination and distance sites. This knowledge can aid the distance education instructor in overcoming the separation of instructor and students.

Along with the general information about the learners, an instructor needs to know the number of students in the class. Knowing how many students there are at each site and the number of sites involved in a face-to-face class can influence the level of interactivity. For example, in an Internet-based class (e.g., on the Web) with a large number of participants, it is likely that some students will fail to interact in discussions. Thus, an instructor needs to know how many students are enrolled, how many sites there are, and what technologies are available to them to plan effectively for interactive learning.

Also, it is essential to know the nature of the audience. Are students from an urban area? A rural area? What is their age range, grade range, and educational background? All this can have a marked impact on the levels of interaction among students. The instructor may have to plan more carefully for the types and levels of interaction to ensure a quality learning experience for all members of the class.

The cultural, social, and economic backgrounds of the students also constitute important information for the instructor (Willis, 1994). In addition, educational expectations of learners can also influence the quality of the learning experience. The attitudes and interests students bring to the class will impact the learning environment. Thus, an instructor who wants to create a quality learning experience for all members of the class, with the ultimate goal of learning as the outcome, will be certain to account for these variables in planning.

Analyze the General Abilities of the Class.

Analysis of the cognitive abilities of the class allows the instructor to observe how students relate to the content of the lesson. Such issues as clearly defining the prerequisite knowledge or skills for the specific learning experience are important to ensure a successful learning experience. The students' prior experience with similar types of cognitive tasks is important.

Further, learning styles have once again become an important area of consideration. With the introduction of Gardner's multiple intelligences has come the resurgence of an examination of learning styles (Gardner, 1993). How students approach learning is as important as how well they can function in the classroom. So knowing more about how students interact with information is important in creating a valuable learning environment.

There are a number of ways in which an instructor can determine students' general knowledge and ability. Pretests and portfolio reviews can provide information about learners' abilities. Because students are coming to the class from a variety of backgrounds and learning experiences, they may be underprepared for the content intended for a particular course, and thus will be frustrated and even unsuccessful in the learning experience. Or, conversely, they may already be familiar with the content and will be bored and uninterested in participating in the class.

By knowing more about students the instructor can develop supporting materials to individualize instruction. Varying the presentation of materials to match different learning styles (e.g., animation, text, verbal descriptions, visual messages) can also ensure the greatest potential for reaching all learners.

The instructor can present complex cognitive content in ways that give learners various tags for understanding the fundamental concepts, and thereby reach a wider range of individuals. People can remember complex material better if chunks of information are grouped into spatially related locations. Placing similar ideas in a logical sequence can aid retrieval of information at a later date.

Analyze Potential for Learner Interactivity.

Students who are less social may find the distance education environment more comfortable for them. Students may become more expressive because of the perception of privacy and the informative nature of mediated communication. They may perceive the increased and varied interactivity and immediate feedback as a positive input to their interface with the learning experience.

Additionally, students can benefit from a wider range of cognitive, linguistic, cultural, and affective styles they would not encounter in a self-contained classroom. The emphasis should not be on the inherent efficiency of the distance learning, but on the values and services offered to students through their exposure to others (Herring & Smaldino, 1997). Relationships can be fostered, values can be expanded, and shared purposes or goals can be developed. Distance learning experiences can serve as windows to the world by providing extended learning experiences.

When special efforts are made, distance education actually can enhance learning experiences, expand horizons, and facilitate group collaboration (Dede, 1990). Students can have more direct experiences with the information; e.g., close-up viewing of an experiment is possible. Time for reflection is possible before responding to the prompts presented. And the ability to work with peers or experts enhances the potential for learning.

Understand Learner Characteristics.   To be effective, it is necessary to understand the learners in the target audience. Willis (1994) suggested the following questions be asked prior to development of distance learning environments:

◆ What are students' ages, cultural backgrounds, interests, and educational levels?
◆ What is the level of familiarity of the students with the instructional methods and technological delivery systems under consideration?
◆ How will the students apply the knowledge gained in the course, and how is this course sequenced with other courses?
◆ Can the class be categorized into several broad subgroups, each with different characteristics?

These questions are not easy ones to answer. An instructor should attempt to find the answers prior to the first class meeting. Asking a few well-chosen questions of individual students will help the instructor understand their needs, backgrounds, and expectations. Additionally, students will feel they are important to the instructor. It may also be beneficial to discuss the learners with the remote-site facilitator.

What Is the Essential Content?

The content of a course needs to reflect where this content relates to the rest of the curriculum. It is essential to examine the nature of the content, as well as the sequence of information. In any distance learning environment, one particular issue, that of time constraints, impacts other planning areas. Time constraints refer to the actual on-line time for delivery, which is often limited and inflexible. The issue of limited time makes it necessary to closely examine the essential elements of the course content. The instructor needs to balance content with the limited time for learning activities and possibly remove extraneous, nonessential information.

Generally speaking, the scope of the content for a course needs to be sufficient to ensure the entire learning experience will lead to the desired outcomes. Concepts, knowledge, and specific skills need to be identified (Dick & Carey, 1996). Supporting information or knowledge is important to the scope of content analysis. Follow-up and applications of the content should be considered.

The instructor's time is best spent on content analysis if the content is organized within a hierarchy. Starting with the general goals, followed by more specific goals and objectives, the nature of the structure of the content can be made to fall into place. The resulting framework of information about content helps the instructor decide the value and importance of specific information to the total instructional package. It is important to remember that no matter which technological formats are used in distance education, the trend is to reduce the "amount" of information delivered and to increase the "interactive value" of the learning experience (Herring & Smaldino, 1997). Thus, the instructor may need to throw out content that had been included in a traditional presentation of a course. Or the instructor may need to consider delivering information through alternative means, such as additional readings or booklets designed specifically for the tasks.

The instructor also needs to examine the sequencing of information. A number of variables, e.g., characteristics of the learners, their prior knowledge, content, time, and number of sites involved, are critical when deciding the order of presentation of information. Because the instructor and some or all of the members of the class are separated, the material must be sequenced in a logical fashion for the students.

Goals and Objectives for Instruction.   The challenge of education is to match the content of the subject to the needs of the learners. Broadly stated goals are a helpful starting place for the instructor. The instructor must decide what is appropriate for a group of students and for the individuals within that group. Each instructor constantly must face the challenge of adapting instruction to the student who is expected to learn it. While content is important, instructors must remember their focus is on the students. This is critical when establishing goals for any course.

The traditional approach for writing objectives is also effective for distance education courses. Specifically, objectives should state the conditions under which learning should occur, the performance expected of the learner, and the standard to which the performance will be matched.

One way to write objectives is as follows:

Given:	*the conditions under which learning occurs*
the learner will:	*the performance*
according to:	*a minimum standard*

The objectives of a particular lesson may not necessarily change simply because one teaches at a distance. Good instructional goals should form the basis for instruction, regardless of the medium used. Instructional goals and objectives always should be shared with the students, helping both the origination and remote-site students to focus on the parameters of the instruction. This information may be included in course outlines, presentation handouts, or materials presented at the beginning of the course.

What Teaching Strategies and Media Should Be Used?

Students can provide insight into the design of the learning experience. They can give feedback in lesson design and instruction delivery. Using a simple feedback form, students can describe or indicate in some other way their expectations and perceptions of the class structure and the delivery mode. The instructor can examine the information from both origination and remote-site students to determine if the mode of presentation was effective for both types of locations. Evaluating these responses, the instructor can gain an understanding of how the learners perceived the class experience.

An instructor's personal philosophy will influence the approach to teaching at a distance. An individual's philosophical belief will affect selection of goals and curricular emphases, and influence how one views oneself as a classroom instructor. The instructor who believes in the philosophical arena of realism, idealism, essentialism, or perennialism will see the instructor as the central figure in the classroom, delivering knowledge and modeling to the student, an instructor-centered approach. On the other hand, the instructor who believes in the philosophies of pragmatism, existentialism, progressivism, constructivism, or social reconstructionism believes that the student is the central figure in the classroom (Herring & Smaldino, 1997). The instructor is viewed as the facilitator of learning by guiding, rather than directing, the students, thus modeling a student-centered approach.

While the dynamics of a philosophy will not predict an instructor's success in the distance education classroom, successful teaching at a distance places the recipients' needs before organizational convenience and at the center of planning and decision making. The individual needs of the learners are brought to the forefront in education that uses electronic technology, because separation of learners from the instructor requires students to take more responsibility for learning. Consequently, the learner's opinions and needs play a more important role in decision making than is usual in an instructor-centered environment (Macfarlane & Smaldino, 1997).

It is oversimplified to suggest that there is one best way to teach at a distance. In any given content area there are several potential ways of providing a quality learning experience for the students (Heinich et al., 1996). However, the one thing that has been repeatedly demonstrated through research is that lecture, or the "talking head" approach, is the least successful strategy to employ in distance education (Schlosser & Anderson, 1996). What is essential in deciding which strategy or strategies to employ is the issue of engaging the learner.

The instructor needs to focus on selecting instructional strategies that engage all the learners in active learning. To do this, the instructor may need to de-emphasize the "informative" part of the instruction for more "discovery" of information. The emphasis on keeping the learners engaged in learning ensures that students will be in tune with the class.

Media Selection.   Several models are often used in selecting media (Dick & Carey, 1996). The common theme among these models is the learning context, which is the content, the intended outcome, and the nature of the students. Practical considerations such as available resources for creating media and the technologies for delivery of instruction also play a hand in the selection process. Mainly, though, the goals and objectives will influence the selection of media.

McAlpine and Weston (1994) have come up with a set of criteria for selecting media, whether they are commercial media or media developed specifically for a particular course. The first criterion is to match the medium to the curriculum or content. Other criteria include the accuracy of information, motivational quality, engagement quality, technical quality, and unbiased nature of material. These should be considered in selecting media in order to match student needs to the strategies employed.

Media that are "off the shelf" are often considered sufficient for a quality learning experience in the traditional classroom (Heinich et al., 1996). However, in a distance learning environment, the "ready-made" materials may need to be adapted or modified to accommodate the technologies involved. Some materials may need to be enlarged or enhanced to be seen by students at a distance. With others the format may need to be changed to allow access.

Because of the nature of distance learning and the separation of the instructor from the students, it is essential that the instructor begin to think visually. Too often, instructors do not place enough emphasis on designing and using quality visual materials. Taking the time to develop good visual media will enhance the quality of the learning experience (Heinich et al., 1996).

Visualizing Information.   Visuals provide a concrete reference point for students, especially when they are engaged in a nontelevised learning experience. Even if the visuals are just lists of concepts and ideas, they can help students. Visuals also help learners by simplifying information. Diagrams and charts often can make it easier to understand complex ideas. A visual that breaks down a complex idea into its components can show relationships that might be otherwise confusing to students. Also, visuals that serve as mnemonics can assist student understanding. And visuals help students in their study. They can use the visuals to prepare for tests and other means of assessing their learning.

When creating visuals, the instructor needs to keep certain things in mind (Herring & Smaldino, 1997). First is legibility. In a televised distance learning environment, even with the close-up capabilities of the cameras, the choice of font and size can influence how easily students can read the text. Several "rules of thumb" should be applied:

◆ Use a large font, e.g., 24 or 36 point.
◆ Use a sans serif font, e.g., Helvetica.
◆ Use just a few words per line of text, e.g., six words per line maximum.
◆ Use only a few lines of text per visual, e.g., six lines per visual.
◆ Use a combination of both uppercase and lowercase letters; all uppercase is difficult to read.
◆ Use plenty of "white space" to enhance the readability.

Color can also play an important role in designing visuals (Herring & Smaldino, 1997). Color can increase the readability of text or graphics. However, the key to good use of color is in the contrast. Use a dark background and light lettering, or vice versa. Make certain to select colors that will not be compromised by the technology used for transmission; e.g., red vibrates in a televised environment. Further, select colors that will not be a problem for students who might be color-blind. More will be discussed on the use of media in Chapter 8, "Teaching at a Distance."

There are two other very important issues to be raised. First is that of copyright. No matter what technologies are incorporated in the distance environment, the instructor needs to respect the copyright restrictions that might apply. For example, in a televised class, the instructor may not be able to use a video without first obtaining permission to display it to the class. In a Web-based class, the instructor may have to have permission to post a journal article. An instructor needs to be responsible in obtaining copyright permissions where appropriate.

The second issue is that of access. The instructor cannot assume that all students at a distance have equal access to resources. Students may not have the technologies available. Also, students may not have the facilities at hand. The instructor needs to be certain that all students have similar learning experiences, including access to the materials. For example, if the instructor wishes students to use certain books or journals for outside reading, it is important to check with local libraries to be sure these materials are available.

What Is the Learning Environment?

Educators are familiar with classroom settings. They are comfortable with using the space available to enable learning to take place. It is when the classroom shifts into a distance learning setting that the environment often becomes a challenge to the instructor. There are several important elements to address within the distance learning environment.

Technology.   The type of setting, be it place- or time-shifted, will influence planning decisions. Environments that are place-shifted are those that are synchronous but are not in the same location (e.g., a live video-based distance class). Those that are time-shifted are asynchronous, where students access the class at different times. Assessing the use of technology in a distant setting is essential. In any distance learning environment the technology becomes the element of most concern for the instructor. The instructor must become familiar with the hardware and the nuances of the technology to use them effectively. The instructor needs to balance concern for the operation of the equipment with effective teaching. Once the technology becomes transparent in the educational setting, the instructor can reflect on the lesson quality, the outcomes, and the plans for subsequent lessons.

Several issues are associated with technology when teaching in a distance learning mode. First is the basic operation of the equipment. In a televised distance learning setting, switching between sites is usually a simple procedure, but it does require time to acquire the finesse to operate the switching buttons smoothly. Second, using additional cameras in the classroom can create some concern for the instructor. The overhead camera needs to be focused and materials lined up to ensure that learners in all sites can see the material. Third, the instructor should always consider what the student should be viewing during the lesson. Is it better to see the instructor, the visuals, or other students? When an instructor has had experience teaching with the equipment, these decisions become automatic, making learning the foundation for the decisions made (Herring & Smaldino, 1997).

In an Internet-based learning environment, the instructor needs to be concerned with the layout of the courseware and the types of resources available to the students at the distant sites. The instructor needs to be certain the material is designed in a way that is intuitive for the various types of learners who may be interacting with it. Further, the instructor needs to be concerned about student access to the appropriate hardware and software to be successful in connecting to the courseware. And the instructor needs to be concerned that the students can complete the tasks expected of them. Finally, the instructor needs to be certain that the students understand the terminology being used.

It is essential the instructor be prepared with alternatives for each lesson in case of system problems. What will the students do during the lesson time if the technology is not operating properly—or at all? Preplanned contingencies should continue the learning process even though the technology is malfunctioning. Alternative lessons must always be ready, but, it is hoped, never needed. And students need to be prepared to know what to do with those materials. The materials must be designed to be used without instructor intervention.

Resources.   The second element to consider in the instructional environment is the resources available to students. What materials will they have at hand? What materials will be available in libraries and laboratories? Will students have access to resources for easy communication with the instructor?

Another consideration is the quality of the instructional setting. Is the room comfortable? Can students get to the room easily? Will the room accommodate the nature and type of learning activities planned? Can students move the tables and chairs about in ways to make learning easy?

These are the types of concerns that an instructor needs to address when thinking about the learning environment. It is difficult to plan for a particular type of learning activity if the room cannot be adapted or changed in any way. For example, if the instructor plans a group activity in which students will need to move chairs and tables, can they do it without causing technical problems?

How Do You Determine the Quality of the Instruction?

Assessment will be discussed in Chapter 11, and evaluation will be discussed at greater length in Chapter 12. However, there is a need to look at questions an instructor might consider as part of the planning process. These questions revolve around considerations related to the strategies selected, the learners' interaction with the learning experience, and the learning environment.

In the instructional design process, formative evaluation becomes an important aspect. Two questions need to be considered. The first relates to reflection on the action or activity: "Is this approach going to work?" (Schon, 1987). To be an effective educator, it is important to consider what can happen within an instructional event. All experiences, both positive and negative, have some element of surprise. Perhaps expectations were not achieved; perhaps a serendipitous event led to an altogether different, but pleasant, outcome. Whatever the nature of the event, it is essential to reflect upon what has happened.

Reflection may take the form of critical assessment of the events, satisfying curiosity about the nature of those events (Macfarlane & Smaldino, 1997). Reflection may focus on the success of the learning situation. It helps the instructor understand the learning event. Once the instructor has reflected upon what took place, it is time to move on to the second question of the formative evaluation process.

The second question is, "How can I make this better?" The instructor needs to examine the instructional event in terms of what worked and what appears to have been a problem. The second phase of the formative evaluation is concerned with helping the instructor ensure a more successful educational experience for students. The instructor needs to consider not only the learning task, the instructional materials, and the teaching strategies, but also the role that the technology may have played in the instruction.

The instructor needs to consider the elements of technologies and their effect on the students. Did the hardware components of the system cause the problem? If so, what was the nature of the problem? Was there a temporary interference with the transmission? Was weather or some other noncontrollable phenomenon causing problems with the transmission? Can the hardware be improved? Can changes be made in the interactive instructional classroom to aid instruction in the future?

If the problem did not relate to the hardware, then what was the problem? Perhaps students needed to be better informed about how to use the equipment. It may be that students needed preparation for the lesson. Perhaps the instructor needed to prepare other types of handouts or manipulatives to ensure that the students could accomplish the tasks. Maybe the instructor needed to select an alternative teaching strategy to improve interactivity and student outcomes.

Because so many different factors affect the interactive learning environment, reflective teaching practices play a vital role in developing effective teaching practices. The process of determining what has transpired and how to change it creates a dynamic educational experience for both the instructor and the learners. Formative evaluation is essential for successful interactive distance learning experiences.

◆ OTHER ISSUES TO BE CONSIDERED

As with any planning, some of the aspects of the system that need to be considered are outside of the content, learners, and instructional setting. Three of these issues relate to student handouts, materials distribution, and the site facilitator.

Student Handouts

Even though the topic of student handouts is discussed at greater length in Chapter 8, it is also mentioned here because it is important for the instructor to think about handouts within the context of the planning process. The types of handouts will vary according to the age of the students and the content of the course. But whatever the type, it is important that the instructor realize that in a distance course, handouts are an essential communication link with students. Therefore, during the planning process, the instructor needs to invest time and energy in creating quality handouts for students.

Distribution of Materials

Even within a traditional class, the instructor is concerned with getting materials to the students. Often papers and books are distributed at the beginning of the class period. But when teaching at a distance, this task is rarely an easy one. Often the majority of the class is at a distance, and distribution of materials becomes a logistical nightmare.

An instructor needs to consider

◆ Getting the materials to the distant sites on time. A distribution network must be established for getting tests and other materials to those remote sites. The technology can be useful in transferring materials.
◆ Communicating with the students. Geographic separation between instructor and students does affect this communication.
◆ Dealing with time delays in material transfer. Students may have to wait a longer time than normally expected to receive written feedback. Instructors may elect to use other forms of telecommunications to facilitate this feedback.

Site Coordinators and Facilitators

The presence of a coordinator or facilitator at the distant sites is often an option. For many instructors and students, the presence of such a facilitator is important. Other instructors consider the extra person more work than necessary. The decision to have a coordinator or facilitator might be best made as it relates to the context of the course, the students, and the types of technology being used.

For example, if the students are on the young side or are unfamiliar with the distant learning environment, a facilitator might be valuable to get them started with the class. The facilitator can serve as an extension of the instructor. This person can help with distributing materials, with maintaining organization and keeping order, and with proctoring. This person can also help with the instruction.

Students need to understand the facilitator's role in the learning environment. They need to know what is expected of the facilitator. Further, the instructor needs to have input into the selection and evaluation of the on-site facilitator to ensure a quality experience for all.

◆ SUMMARY

It is essential that the instructor take the time to plan and organize the learning experience when engaged in teaching at a distance. The instructional design process provides the framework for planning. Instruction must be at a standard that is acceptable in all venues. The students should be engaged, and the instructor should be satisfied. Planning makes the difference in a successful learning environment.

Self-Test Questions

1. Define *instructional design*. Explain its importance to distance education.
2. Is it normally necessary for existing courses to be redesigned before offering them at a distance? Why?
3. Write an objective using the format presented in this chapter.
4. What purpose does evaluation play in instructional design for distance education?

Answers to Self-Test Questions

1. Instructional design is a systematic process for the development of learning materials.
2. Most often, existing courses do need to be redesigned before offering them at a distance.
3. Given: _____
   the learner will: _____
   according to: _____ .
4. Evaluation permits the instructional designer to continuously improve the course and course components. Design is not a one-time activity. Rather, it is cyclical, and evaluation information permits continuous improvement.

References

Dede, C. (1990, Spring). The evolution of distance learning: Technology-mediated interactive learning. *Journal of Research on Computing in Education,* 247–264.

Dick, W., & Carey, L. (1996). *The systematic design of instruction.* New York: HarperCollins Publishers.

Gardner, H. (1993). *Multiple intelligences.* New York: Basic Books.

Heinich, R., Molenda, M., Russell, J., & Smaldino, S. (1996). *Educational media and technologies for learning.* Columbus, OH: Merrill/Prentice Hall.

Herring, M., & Smaldino, S. (1997). *Planning for interactive distance education: A handbook.* Washington, DC: AECT Publications.

Macfarlane, C., & Smaldino, S. (1997). The electronic classroom at a distance. In R. Rittenhouse & D. Spillers (Eds.), *Modernizing the curriculum: The electronic classroom.* Springfield, MO: Charles Thomas Publishers.

McAlpine, L., & Weston, C. (1994). The attributes of instructional materials. *Performance Improvement Quarterly, 7*(1), 19–30.

Moore, M., & Kearsley, G. (1996). *Distance education: A systems view.* Belmont, CA: Wadsworth Company.

Schlosser, C., & Anderson, M. (1993). *Distance education: Review of the literature.* Ames, IA: Research Institute for Studies in Education.

Schon, D. (1987). *Educating the reflective practitioner.* San Francisco: Jossey-Bass.

Willis, B. (1994). *Distance education: Strategies and tools.* Englewood Cliffs, NJ: Educational Technology Publications.

chapter 7

The Distance Education Student

CHAPTER GOAL

The purpose of this chapter is to describe the characteristics and responsibilities of the distant learner.

CHAPTER OBJECTIVES

After reading and reviewing this chapter, you should be able to

1. Identify characteristics of the distance student.
2. Explain ways the student can be introduced at the beginning of class.
3. Describe the responsibilities of the student in a synchronous class.
4. Describe the responsibilities of the student in an asynchronous class.

◆ AN EMPHASIS ON THE STUDENT

Often in a distance learning situation, much emphasis is placed on the technology, ensuring the operations end of the process. The audience, or the distant learner, is often considered after the planning and organizing of the hardware, the content, and the instructional plan. But it is the learner who is the crucial member of the distance learning system. It is the learner who needs to be considered early in the planning and implementation of a distance learning experience. The more an instructor understands the members of the audience, the better the distance learning experience will be for all involved (Moore & Kearsley, 1996).

The distance learner can be of any age, have attained any educational level, and have a variety of educational needs. One common characteristic of the distance learner is an increased commitment to learning. For the most part, these learners are self-starters and appear to be highly motivated. Frequently, distance learners live in rural areas, although a distant site may involve students who live in or near metropolitan areas located sufficiently away from where a class is traditionally offered. The educational areas of need are usually specific and may represent low-incidence needs (i.e., learning a foreign language or a technical content area). Further impetus for distance learning can result from limited statewide resources (e.g., a specialized area teacher training program) that must be shared across diverse geographical regions.

One can conclude, after examining the various tools and approaches for distance learning, that they have one purpose: to provide a valuable learning experience to students who might not otherwise have access to learning. Dede (1990) suggests that distance education can provide assistance for schools in an array of ways. Students can be pooled into classes of sufficient size to create a critical mass, thus ensuring that a course will be able to continue based on economic measures. Students can aggregate for advanced courses in subjects not otherwise offered, creating an opportunity for extended learning. Distance education can be seen as an important method of responding to the growing pluralism of learners' backgrounds, characteristics, or unusual learning needs that may require or benefit from specialized instruction. Simply stated, there are a number of reasons to bring learners together at a distance. It is equally important to understand the intent of those learners when planning the process for delivery.

In any instructional situation it is important for the instructor to know as much as possible about the students in the class. Knowing the students in a class provides the instructor with an understanding of how to best approach instruction to ensure an optimum learning experience for all. In a distance learning setting, the instructor must learn about students at both the origination and distance sites. Knowledge of students can assist the distance educator in overcoming separation of teacher and student. It can ensure that the learning experience will be positive for all. And it will facilitate the design by the instructor to optimize the learning experience.

To begin with, the teacher must acquire some basic information about the class as a whole. In a synchronous-timed delivery course, knowing the number of sites and number of students at each site gives the teacher the "big picture." Equally important is information about subgroups such as urban or rural students as well as students from various cultural or social backgrounds represented within the class. Economics also plays a part in the nature of the class. Together, these factors provide the teacher with an overview of the class which can lead to learning about individuals in the class. Even in an asynchronous delivery mode, knowledge of the members of the class, even though they do not meet together, is crucial to design and delivery.

Each member of a class is an individual, although each individual may belong to one of the subgroups mentioned above. Each individual has a cultural identity as well as a socioeconomic "standing" in the community. However, each individual is unique and needs to be recognized for those unique characteristics. When the individual is considered, characteristics such as attitude or interest, prior experiences, cognitive abilities, and learning styles will all have an impact. Taking the time to learn about the individual will enhance the learning experience for that individual and for the class as a whole.

◆ ATTITUDE

The distance education literature from the past 20 years has suggested that one major difference between distance learners and traditional classroom learners is motivation (Office of Technology Assessment, 1989). In the majority of studies, distance learners were found to be highly motivated. Their reasons for participation in a distance learning setting varied from convenience for the nontraditional-aged student

Students of all ages can benefit from distance education.

to accessibility to coursework. Most commonly, distance education learners chose to be in the distance education classroom. They indicated that they actively seek these classroom settings to ensure the continuation of their education. Bozik (1996) found that graduate students enjoyed the opportunity to meet others from across the state during their programs of study. This was considered one of the most positive aspects of learning at a distance.

◆ EXPERIENCE

A second indicator of preference by students is prior experience (Bozik, 1996; Smith & Dunn, 1991). Students reported that once they took a distance course, they were willing to enroll in additional classes. Students felt satisfied with the quality of their learning experience, and the convenience factors reinforced their participation. These same students also indicated they would, if necessary, drive to a centralized campus to attend classes; however, this was not their preference. They wanted to continue as distance students. Students who experience a distance learning situation for the first time may indicate to the teacher a discomfort with the learning situation. An effective educator who utilizes technological tools in a nonintrusive manner can allay these fears and encourage students to take advantage of a unique and dynamic learning experience. But this takes time and patience on the part of the educator. It also assumes much in the way of responsibility on the part of the student to grow and adapt personal learning characteristics to distance learning situations.

◆ COGNITION

The third indicator of success is cognitive abilities (Smith & Dunn, 1991). Students of average or high ability at distance sites have demonstrated achievement at levels similar to or better than those of students in origination sites. In fact, this is true of students in distance education classes as a whole compared with students in traditional classrooms. This is not to suggest that students in distance classes are smarter; but capable students tend to succeed in distance learning situations. Students at a distance seem to assume more responsibility for their own learning earlier in the process than do those students who are enrolled in traditional classes.

◆ LEARNING STYLES

Finally, the fourth indicator of successful learning at a distance is learning styles. For some students the unique characteristics of distance learning tools facilitate better instruction than educational tools generally used in a traditional classroom. For example, in a distance classroom the teacher should place greater emphasis on providing visual cues, whether the technology is synchronous, such as audio only or two-way full-motion video (e.g., videotapes, overheads, concrete objects), or asynchronous, such as a complete Web-based course. When the instructor provides more visual cues, the visual learner may perform better in a distance education class. Auditory learners can focus on the instructor's words and generally listen better because there are fewer distractions, especially at sites with only one student. This situation does provide a challenge for the Web-based instructional situation. However, with the newer technologies, audio streaming is becoming less of a problem—as long as students have access to those new technologies. Students who display a reluctance to speak out or join discussions during class can find their "niche" by utilizing text-based communications through computer conferencing or completing written assignments. Even the needs of kinesthetic learners can be met with appropriate hands-on activities (Macfarlane & Stefanich, 1995).

All of this speaks to the need for the instructor to understand the characteristics of the members of the class. The more the distance education teacher knows about the individual student within the whole class, the more elegant the application of education tools to the learning situation. The instructor can learn about members of the class in a number of ways. Contacting instructors who have had students previously is one way of getting information. This works particularly well if a cohort group is moving through an extensive program of studies. As always, caution must be exercised when providing information about previous students in order not to pass on confidential information or to prejudice the teacher. Another way of getting information is simply to ask students directly about their own sense of what works for them.

A survey or similar type of information gathering device could be distributed to the students before the start of the class. This provides the instructor with information that might not be available through school records or other teachers. An additional way to get to know students is to create class-time opportunities for getting to know them. Not only does this provide additional information to the teacher, but also it gives the students a chance to get to know the other members of the class. For example, Macfarlane (Macfarlane & Smaldino, 1997) had four or five students bring a "me bag" to the television-based class. Following her example, students shared photos, examples of hobbies, and objects portraying various interests (e.g., a recently read book). Each student spent approximately 5 minutes doing this activity. In addition to learning more about each other, the students utilized classroom technology (e.g., overhead camera) to share the contents of their "bags." The outcome of this activity resulted in the class as a whole developing a strong sense of support for one another in the learning process. Finally, if possible, an instructor can visit or teach from each distance site. If not possible, private phone conversations and electronic mail are alternatives to spend individual time with students.

In essence, what is crucial is to become familiar with the students in the class and to address their needs as they have identified them. Further, by putting time into this type of discovery of information, the instructor will find that the class will function more as a unit than it otherwise would have. This makes it easier to engage learners in the activities and in the learning outcomes designed into the class structure.

◆ LEARNER RESPONSIBILITIES

Just as the instructor must take responsibility for learning about students, learners in the distance education classroom must assume ownership in their learning experiences (Macfarlane & Smaldino, 1997).

Microphones and Other Equipment.   Students will need to respond in class or to post responses in the correct forum, ask questions, or make presentations as the result of assignments; therefore, it is imperative that distant students learn to use the tools available in the distant classroom.

Usually an electronic classroom allows for two-way audio transmission regardless of video transmission. Thus, the first tool any student will need to learn to use is the microphone to relay verbal responses to the teacher and other students in the class as a whole. Usually this involves pressing a microphone button (i.e., press-to-talk), although it is possible that the microphones might be voice-activated. A few comments about microphone protocol are essential to managing this tool. In general, whoever pushes the microphone button "controls the airwaves." That is, no one else can make a comment that will be heard by the entire class until the first micro-

The roles of students change significantly when they learn from distant instructors, but the advantages of being able to have classes in advanced topics such as chemistry outweigh any problems.

phone button is released. Thus, students need to limit remarks so that others may also contribute to the discussion. Furthermore, the first one to press the mike is the first to talk. Occasionally, a microphone is pushed "on" accidentally by the pressure of a book or other classroom materials or a stray arm or elbow, or is activated by a cough or a conversation between individuals at a site. Background noise from an open mike usually alerts the instructor to this situation, but he or she may not be able to identify the source or resolve the problem because of the temporary inability to transmit auditorily. A written message (e.g., "please check your microphone") transmitted visually (e.g., as an overhead) can sometimes remedy the situation; or if not, a telephone call to each site may be necessary.

Even though voices are distinct, students must learn to identify themselves by name and site (e.g., "This is Bob at Cedar Falls") when they push the microphone to ask a question or make a comment. Eventually, most students will learn to recognize individual voices; however, the initial courtesy is necessary and should continue in order to avoid confusion and enhance recognition. One unique difficulty often occurs with learners in the origination-site classroom. These learners can see and hear the instructor without the need for audio or visual transmission. Thus, when they need to ask a question or make a comment, they often forget to press the mike button so classmates at distance sites can also hear. In fairness to other students, learners in the origination classroom must remember to press the mike button and to identify themselves if that is the given protocol of the class. Reminders from the teacher or reinforcement (e.g., a small piece of candy) when done without a prompt can help to alleviate this problem.

Other equipment such as overhead cameras, video players, and fax machines may be used by students with less frequency. Despite the sophistication of some technology found in a distance classroom, most students can be talked through operating instructions by the teacher or a trained technician. Early exposure to these tools (e.g., during their personal introductions) and modeling by the teacher can reduce anxiety and alleviate problems later on when students must use the equipment to present information as part of an assignment.

Attendance and Class Participation.

As in any instructional setting, class attendance is imperative. However, on occasion, learners may not be able to attend class due to conflicts, illness, or technical difficulties. In a video-based class one solution is to record the class and send the tape (video or audio) to the learner(s) who missed class. While no interaction is possible, at least learners do not lose out on content. It may be necessary to obtain the permission of all the class participants before making any recordings. It is best to obtain this permission in written form (Macfarlane & Smaldino, 1997).

Class participation, be it in a traditional class or a distance class, always enhances learning for students. The nature of the environment in distance sites has a significant impact on class participation. As mentioned earlier, some students do not like to respond either because of learning style or perhaps because of intimidation by the technology. Some students may ask fewer questions than in a traditional class.

Instructional strategies that encourage all students to provide answers can increase class participation. Teachers have also experimented with alternative answering strategies. For example, Harmin (1994) suggests for students in a television-based class that each student write the answer on a large card or "slate." Students can hold up their answers on cue. Voting on possible answers can also encourage active participation. An open hand or "thumbs up" can signal agreement or a vote for choice A; a closed fist or "thumbs down" can signal disagreement or a vote for choice B. During discussions some students need a brief period to prepare an adequate answer. Advance warning that a question is headed their way can ease discomfort and give the students time to think of an answer. Some learners feel intimidated by technology and are reluctant to respond to the teacher or initiate comments. The instructor needs to engage in strategies early in the course to alleviate this level of nonparticipation.

It is often the case that students at distance sites will talk with each other during class without sharing with the class. In a television-based environment, without a visual check the instructor may not know students are talking, a situation that would not happen in a traditional class or at the origination site. These "sidebar conversations" may occur as a result of a provocative piece of information presented during the class. That is, the content of the class can provoke an "in-house" discussion on the topic. Unfortunately, these comments are made to a few when the whole class could benefit. Students must be encouraged to share valid comments with the entire class. Occasionally, participants at distance sites engage in unrelated topics of conversation. Either way students not included or interested in the comments may be distracted by conversations at their site when two people talk with each other. Also, some may have difficulty hearing because of talking at their site. Out of respect for learners who are concentrating on the presentation or discussion, these conversations, whether task related or not, must not occur. We refer to this as "netiquette," that is, showing courtesy for the learning needs of others with respect to the technology.

In an asynchronous, text or graphical-based class, there are similar types of considerations related to the students' responsibilities. While they are not as specific, the directions will require some time. It is important that student's responsibilities be made clear.

Tone of Responses.   Since the student in an asynchronous class must respond to prompts and activities in a text format, it is essential that there be some ground rules about the nature of responses. Humor is one aspect of text that can be "lost" when others are reading the text. If humor is intended, it might be wise to have a protocol among the members of the class to identify the "humorous" section by special markers or by stating it as such (e.g., "A NOTE OF HUMOR: . . ."). Also within the context of the tone of responses, it is important that members of the class refrain from using inappropriate or unacceptable language. This is general courtesy among students, but is particularly important when these types of responses become archived, as might happen in a text-based setting.

Time for Class.   In an asynchronous class the class meeting time is a special issue. The fact that everyone does not have to be at the class at the same time is one of
the advantages of this type of class for very busy people who are unable to rearrange
their schedules. It is important that students understand the need to arrange a time
within their weekly schedule to "attend" class. Students must arrange their weekly
schedule to be able to "go to class" on a regular basis. This might be on a Saturday
night, or early on a weekday morning. The time selected is not important. What is
important is that the student arrange his or her schedule to be sure to complete the
class on a weekly basis.

There are a number of reasons to do this. First, if the course requires continual
input from the students as part of participation, then the student must be on-line on
a regular basis. If there are assignments, they must be completed in a timely fashion.
It is imperative that the instructor make it clear what students are expected to do to
complete a course, but it is the student's responsibility to adjust his or her schedule
accordingly.

Equipment Requirements.   A student who is planning to participate in an on-
line class must be certain that the equipment requirements match what is available to
use. If a student wishes to participate in a class that has very specific technical requirements, then those need to be clearly stated. But it is the student's responsibility to in-
quire if the requirements have not been identified.

Technical Know-How.   For some on-line classes, students need to know how to
use certain software packages, to use specific types of equipment (e.g., scanners), or to
follow technical procedures (e.g., FTPing a file to a Web site). The instructor may assume that students have this type of knowledge. Or the student may be required to attend special workshops or classes just to prepare for this type of class. It is ultimately the
student's responsibility to know how to do these things to ensure full participation in a
class.

Technical Difficulties.   In any situation where so much technology is involved,
there are bound to be problems. When tools do not work, the learner has the responsibility to notify the instructor so that adjustments can be made. Sometimes, a
technician can provide information to clear up the problem. At other times the system manager must be notified to provide assistance. It is the student's responsibility
to let the instructor know about problems. If the student does not assume this responsibility, the instructor might continue on under the assumption that the student is not participating because of other reasons. Students should not let a technical problem delay their participation in a course. Nor should they let it alter their
desire to participate.

Assignments.   It is the responsibility of the learner to complete assignments in a
timely manner and find an appropriate means to dispatch them to the instructor. Delay
in sending them in will result in delays in grading and in receiving feedback.

◆ SUMMARY

The learning experiences of students are the core of equivalency theory discussed previously. Learning experiences of students not only depend on the efforts and preparation of the instructor, but also are largely determined by the efforts and preparation of the distant learner. This chapter attempted to identify the characteristics, duties, and expectations that students may have when learning at a distance. Remember, learning experiences for learners should be equivalent, not necessarily equal. Also, a learning experience is provided by an instructor and used by a student. Teaching and learning are two sides of the same coin, often referred to as a learning experience.

Self-Test Questions

1. Identify some characteristics of the distant learner. Discuss why these characteristics are important and how they differ from the characteristics of the effective traditional learner.
2. How might an instructor obtain information about distant students? Why is this important?
3. What are some responsibilities of the distant student in a synchronous distance education class? Why are these responsibilities important?
4. What are some responsibilities of the distant student in an asynchronous distance education class? Are these different from those in a synchronous distance class?

Answers to Self-Test Questions

1. Characteristics might include ideas such as is a self-starter, is highly motivated, has above average ability, assumes responsibilities.
2. The instructor should consider the following: survey of students, require introductions, visits to distant sites.
3. The synchronous learner should learn to use the microphone, use proper microphone procedures, know how to gain attention while not interfering with others' questions, practice proper classroom etiquette.
4. The asynchronous learner should know how to use computers and computer communications software, be able to "understand" the intent of discussions that occur at different times, pay attention to deadlines and details, and be able to use resources provided to guide instruction.

References

Bozik, M. (1996). Student perceptions of a two-way interactive video class. *T.H.E. Journal, 24*(2), 99–100.

Dede, C. (1990). The evolution of distance learning: Technology-mediated interactive learning. *Journal of Research on Computing in Education, 22,* 247–264.

Harmin, M. (1994). *Inspiring active learning: A handbook for teachers.* Alexandria, VA: Association for Supervision and Curriculum Development.

Linking for Learning: A New Course for Education (1989, November). OTA Report Brief. Washington, DC: Office of Technology Assessment.

Macfarlane, C., & Smaldino, S. (1997). The electronic classroom at a distance. In R. Rittenhouse & D. Spillers (Eds.), *Modernizing the curriculum: The electronic classroom.* Springfield, MO: Charles Thomas Publisher.

Macfarlane, C., & Stefanich, G. (1995). Teaching science to persons with disabilities. In M. Herring, S. Smaldino, & A. Thompson (Eds.), *Interactive television preservice teacher education innovative applications: A monograph.* Teacher Education Alliance Iowa Star Schools Project (Grant No. 95-035). Iowa State University, Ames.

Moore, M., and Kearsley, G. (1996). *Distance education: A systems view.* Boston: Wadsworth Publishing Company.

Office of Technology Assessment (1989). *Linking for learning: A new course for education.* Washington, DC: U.S. Congress.

Smith, P., & Dunn, S. (1991). Human and quality considerations in high-tech education. *Telecommunications for Learning, 3,* 168–172.

chapter 8

Teaching at a Distance

CHAPTER GOAL

The purpose of this chapter is to provide guidance for the instructor when teaching at a distance.

CHAPTER OBJECTIVES

After reading and reviewing this chapter, you should be able to

1. Describe the responsibilities of the instructor in distance education.
2. Explain the importance of introductions at the beginning of class.
3. Describe the responsibilities of the student in a distance class.
4. Identify items to enhance delivery of instruction.
5. Discuss the preparation of visuals.

◆ ASPECTS OF DISTANCE EDUCATION

Distance education provides opportunities for instructors to extend and expand their classrooms beyond the confines of a building. It is also an opportunity to revisit techniques for teaching since distance education incorporates both place and time shifting (Herring & Smaldino, 1997). A *place shift* suggests that all the participants in the class are not in a single location, whereas a *time shift* implies that the instruction is not "live." Both these aspects of distance learning present instructional challenges to even the most experienced educators. Distance education is an opportunity to revisit the role of the instructor and the student in the learning environment.

◆ ROLE OF THE TEACHER

Lesson Organization

A primary role of the instructor in an educational setting is to provide guidance in the learning process (Herring & Smaldino, 1997). Student-centered learning is a direction that is taking a strong hold in education today. In particular, it is important in a distance education setting to center attention on the student and to focus the instruction away from the teacher and toward the learners.

After the initial planning and preparation for instruction is completed, it is time to concentrate on issues associated with the delivery of the instruction. One issue is the organization of content. Key elements of each lesson should be outlined. Cyrs and Smith (1990) recommend limiting the number of major concepts or points to be covered in a single lesson. They suggest incorporating no more than three or four major concepts or points in a 50-minute time period. While it may be possible to cover more points through lecture, doing so appears to be less successful in an interactive television session. Cyrs and Smith (1990) recommend that "teacher talk" be limited to 10 to 15 minutes and be varied by incorporating visuals and student interactions. Attention also should be given to the number and choice of visuals used in the lesson.

Another issue is time allotment. While the key elements of planning are essential regardless of the distance education format, the allotment of time for specific activities is crucial to ensure student success. Lessons should be planned to allow time for students to engage in the learning activities. In live interactive instruction, timing is critical because of an absolute time frame—transmission from the classroom is discontinued at the end of the scheduled period. Instructors cannot speak to the students as they head out the door!

In a time-shifted Internet-based learning environment, it is important to ensure the instructions are complete so that the learners are not struggling with how to use the technology or how to respond to tasks. It is important to focus on independent learning tasks, shifting the role of the instructor to that of manager of the prompts to encourage student learning.

Instructional Methods

Teaching methods should be chosen based on the characteristics of the instructor, students, content, and delivery system (Herring & Smaldino, 1997). Due to the increased responsibility for learning placed on the students at a distance, methods that focus on the learners and incorporate interactivity have been shown to be most successful (Souder, 1993).

Besides determining the appropriate instructional methods to be used in delivering the content, the instructor should also determine ways to involve the class at all instructional sites. There is no ideal way to accomplish this. With some adaptations, the same methods and techniques that are successful in a traditional classroom setting usually work as well in distance instruction, especially if they encourage student interaction.

The instructor is responsible for the learning environment created in the traditional and distance classroom settings. The technology incorporated in distance learning should be considered as a tool to enhance instruction and not as an end unto itself. Thus, instruction should include the fundamental elements of planning, including the effects of the technology in design. Using the technologies of distance education should not limit the choice of strategies used by teachers, but should open new possibilities for those who wish to enrich their teaching (Greenwood & McDevitt, 1987).

It has been suggested that if a strategy works in a regular classroom, it probably will work in distance instruction with some adjustment (Herring & Smaldino, 1997). It is important to consider a variety of techniques, but an instructor must remember to think of strategies that engage learners in active rather than passive learning experiences. It is useful to combine techniques. And instructors should not be afraid to experiment, to explore, to be creative in their teaching.

Teaching at a Distance

While few restrictions exist for the teacher in traditional 1990s classrooms, there are some commonsense expectations for those preparing to teach in a distance learning environment. This section reviews some basics to help the instructor teach at a distance.

Beginning the Class.   Developing rapport with students is important at the beginning of any class. Such rapport is essential to ensure a successful distance learning environment. This is especially true when the environment is computer-based. Students who participate in distance educational experiences have been found to form lasting friendships, developing a strong cohort focused on supporting each other to ensure a quality learning experience for all.

Although a class composed of students who might know one another might not require introductory activities, groups of strangers, such as people across a span of distance within the class setting, can certainly profit from getting to know one another. Instructors, all too typically, merely warm up their groups of students with simple introductions. For example: "Let's go around the room and state our names, hometown, major, and why we're here." While this type of introduction may have some value,

The teacher's role often changes to that of facilitator rather than presenter in many distance education systems.

often it becomes meaningless. Students become bored by the repetitiveness of the activity, especially if the introductions are offered by more than 15 people in a group (Herring & Smaldino, 1997). And this is very difficult to initiate in a computer-based environment. Instructors need to employ more directive and creative ways of helping the participants learn about one another.

More dynamic, experiential activities for introductions allow students to become acquainted with one another in more meaningful ways. There is a benefit to learning about attitudes, values, aspects of personality, expectations, etc., from the members of the class. And sometimes it is essential for the students to learn more than each others' names, hometown, etc. When it is necessary for students to form learning groups, knowing about the other members of the class is crucial.

Also, using elaborate techniques for introductions can reduce the lonely feeling that some students might be experiencing. It is important to finds ways to involve shy people. By investing time at the beginning of class for introductions, students will become more at ease with the setting and potentially will become more spontaneous in class participation (Herring & Smaldino, 1997). By engaging in meaningful, often fun activities at the beginning of the class, students' anxieties and tensions are reduced and students are more comfortable in participating in the class in the future. Strategies that engage learners at the beginning of the class focus the responsibility for learning on the learners.

Introduction strategies help the instructor demonstrate that the focus of the class is on the students, not on the instructor. Further, they give the instructor an opportunity to gather additional information about the members of the class. Are the members open to new experiences, fun-loving, nondefensive? Or are they cautious, sedate, inflexible? The level of energy that students exhibit in the initial phase of getting to know others helps the instructor decide on the instructional strategies to employ.

Several introduction strategies have been found to be highly effective (Herring & Smaldino, 1997). One is to have each participant meet someone new in the class, either within the same site or across sites, and then to provide an introduction of the person for the rest of the class. Another is to have each participant provide the information directly by way of "guided" or structured introductions. One very effective structured model is to identify specific topics that must be included in the introductions. For example, suggesting that each member of the class include "something personal," "something professional," and "something special" has been found to be beneficial to creating a learning community (Herring & Smaldino, 1997).

Structuring the Class.   In any instructional setting, students benefit when they have a clear view of such issues as class organization and student responsibilities. Class organization includes such items as class schedule, grouping for activities, and expectations for interaction. It is the responsibility of the instructor to ensure that students understand how the class is structured. Does the instructor begin with an activity that requires students to interact with each other? Or begin each class with a brief delivery of content? Or end each class with student reflections? These issues of format or structure are important to help students quickly and easily become involved in learning rather than focusing on trying to puzzle through the manner of delivery (Herring & Smaldino, 1997).

Instructors need to adhere to the predetermined schedules (Macfarlane & Smaldino, 1997). For synchronous settings, instructors need to maintain a class schedule that is congruous with the transmission schedule. For asynchronous distance learning settings, they need to post information and assignments in a timely fashion. They need to practice ways to use time wisely and to maintain the schedule of activities. Students need to know about the importance of presentation handouts if they are used and how to use them to benefit their learning.

Students need a clear understanding of their own responsibilities (Cyrs & Smith, 1990). They need to know what is expected of them in terms of preparation for class and participation in class activities. If students are expected to read assignments prior to class, then the instructor must plan to build on that material, not merely repeat it in class (Herring & Smaldino, 1997). Students will not read in advance if "the lecture is from the book." However, if the instructor has assigned a specific reading selection, then interactive activities related to that assignment will reinforce the need to read in advance.

Further, students need to know how their participation in class discussions is measured (personal communication, R. Muffoletto, spring, 1997). Students who are reluctant to engage in discussion or are unprepared should be prepared to accept the consequences of nonparticipation if a portion of assessment is dependent on a certain level of participation. Effort needs to be made to provide shy students with means for participating that is nonthreatening and that serves to ease them into feeling confident about their abilities to participate in discussions. Instructors must assume responsibility to meet the needs of students who might be reluctant learners.

Students need training in communication protocols. In an audio setting they need to be prepared to use microphones or other audio equipment. Further, they need to understand their responsibilities to be courteous and well-mannered, in both audio and text-based communication formats. Respect for others is an important part of working in groups, especially at a distance (Herring & Smaldino, 1997).

Also, students need to assume responsibility for initiating communication with the instructor. Because of the venue, the instructor and students may not meet in person, but rather must meet via the technology. If students are having difficulty with the course or need additional information or assistance, it is their responsibility to contact the instructor. But the instructor must provide them with contact information. It is crucial that students have convenient and reliable means of connecting with the instructor. An e-mail address or an 800 phone number is desirable as it will not inflict much expense on the students. But if neither of these is available easily, then an office or home phone number needs to be shared.

It is also desirable to provide some framework for contacting the instructor. If the instructor wishes to receive phone calls, then it is necessary to indicate when and where to call. An instructor who shares a personal or home phone number needs to be aware that students may well use that number. So if the instructor has preferred times to communicate with students, the students need to know that information.

Another related issue is what to do when there are technical difficulties. Provide students with alternatives. Students need to know what is expected of them. If, in a televised class, there are transmission problems, students need to know what to do about the session and assignments. If there are problems with an Internet-based class, students need a way to follow through with the learning tasks without penalty. When teaching with technology, always assume the worst and be pleasantly surprised when everything goes well.

Preparing for Remote Resources.

When preparing to work with students at a distance, it is necessary to consider the resources available to students. Resources that should be assessed include

1. Classroom equipment available for student use (e.g., computers, scanners, video equipment, cameras, projection devices)
2. Available computer software and resource people to assist students at a distance
3. Communication resources students can access (e.g., e-mail, 800 phone numbers, fax machines)
4. Library and classroom resources for homework and outside-of-class work
5. Availability of means for distribution and collection of coursework materials

This information will provide an instructor with the data necessary for creating equal educational opportunities for all students in the distance education classroom. It is important for students to feel they all have equal status in the class regardless of where they are located. If this means creating new, different ways of achieving the same tasks, then the instructor must engage in creative endeavors

(Macfarlane & Smaldino, 1997). For example, one instructor liked to begin each class period with a quick quiz to assess student knowledge of basic facts that had been assigned. However, in her distance class quick quizzes were not practical because of the time needed to send and receive quiz papers. The instructor decided on a timed recitation exercise in which students worked in pairs to check their knowledge of the facts (Macfarlane & Smaldino, 1997). The instructor found this to be such a successful means for checking students that she began to incorporate this technique in other classes, even those offered in traditional settings.

While many of the items previously identified deal with the mechanical side of the classroom resources, there is a human side to classroom resources. The presence of a facilitator is often considered optional, but this person can be important for the success of the distant instruction (Herring & Smaldino, 1997). A facilitator is generally an adult who has been hired by an educational institution to be a local contact for students. Facilitators' roles vary depending on their capabilities. They may be on-site during instruction, they may be available prior to and following transmissions, or they may be responsible for hardware and software performance.

Several issues should be considered when deciding if a facilitator is appropriate. What role will the facilitator have in conducting the class? Can facilitators assist with the teaching and learning process, or are they responsible for noninstructional aspects of the class? Can facilitators team-teach with the instructor, or is their duty to monitor the classroom, pass out papers, proctor exams, or manage on-line discussions?

No matter what the role of the facilitator, it is important to set up a time for discussion about expectations of each member of the team prior to starting the course, to avoid misunderstandings once the course begins. Further, it is important to share this information about the facilitator's role with students.

Another issue to consider is who selects the facilitators for the distant sites? If the facilitators are to be actively involved in the teaching and learning process, the instructor may wish to have input in the hiring. A good working relationship is essential for a successful distance learning experience.

Finally, the instructor must consider the issue of facilitator evaluation. Should the instructor have a say in the end-of-instruction evaluation of the facilitator? If the facilitator is an integral part of the teaching and learning process, there should be an opportunity for the instructor to identify the contributions of the facilitator.

Visuals for Learning.   At a distance, visuals are an important aspect of a quality learning experience. Research has demonstrated that the use of visuals clearly influences the learning experience of students (Cohen, Ebeling, & Kulik, 1981). Visuals play a role in providing a concrete reference for concepts and ideas. Providing a visual, even if it is just a list of concepts or ideas, helps the students to connect the spoken word with these ideas.

Also, visuals play a role in enhancing learning by simplifying information that is difficult to understand (Cohen, Ebeling, & Kulik, 1981). Students can focus on diagrams, graphics, and outlines while listening to the instructor or other students, to gain an understanding of complex topics. These types of visuals also help students by providing organization and structure to the topic.

Finally, visuals serve to provide redundancy in the learning process (Cohen, Ebeling, & Kulik, 1981). There is a benefit to including some redundant information for students. When spoken or written information is supplemented with visual information, learners have a greater chance of comprehending the material.

Interpreting Visuals.

Learners need to be guided in learning to decode or interpret visual information (Heinich, Molenda, Russell, & Smaldino, 1996). They need to develop skills in understanding the meaning attached to the use of certain types of icons or graphics. Age and developmental ability affect the way students interpret visual information. Younger students are more likely to single out specific elements rather than looking at the whole picture.

Several other issues are related to interpreting visuals. Cultural background can affect the way in which students interpret visuals. Different cultural groups may perceive visual information in different ways. It is essential for the instructor to be sensitive to the different cultural backgrounds of the students in any class.

Students often have a preference for the types of visuals they view. However, research indicates students do not always learn best from the types of visuals they prefer (Cohen, Ebeling, & Kulik, 1981). Most learners state they prefer color, but black and white visuals are equally effective. Many say they prefer photographs over line drawings, but these are often too complex to facilitate interpretation of the message. It might be better to use drawings to simplify the information. Instructors need to experiment with different types of visuals to identify which seem to help students in the learning process. If a disproportionate amount of time is spent in explaining the visual, it may indicate a need to simplify that particular visual.

The more often students engage in learning experiences using visual information, the more likely they will be successful in using visuals (Cohen, Ebeling, & Kulik, 1981). Providing students with frequent experiences with visuals, and guiding the students in their use, helps to increase the possibility of a successful application of visuals in the learning process.

Creating Visuals for Televised Instruction.

Instructors need to keep certain conventions in mind when creating visuals for televised instruction. Most educators are familiar with preparing transparencies for overhead projection in a traditional classroom. These follow standards in regard to font size and amount of information and are generally prepared in a vertical orientation. However, television uses a 3×4 ratio, horizontal orientation for its display. In addition to orientation, it is important to consider the design of the display (or visual). Good visual design tries to achieve at least four basic goals:

◆ Be legible.
◆ Be interpreted easily.
◆ Engage students.
◆ Focus attention.

In regard to legibility, it is important that all students can see the visual equally well. In the television arena, using the document camera or a prepared computer presentation can help ensure all can see the material.

Distance education classrooms often are equipped with special equipment, such as this electronic white board, so instructors can easily visualize concepts to distance learners.

When using prepared computer presentation programs, it is simple to prepare student handouts. Often these programs offer several options for student handouts, including an outline format or a set of reduced-size pictures of the actual screens. Providing the students, especially those at the distance sites, with a handout helps simplify note taking, and also ensures all can see the visuals clearly. Because some students have more difficulty taking notes in a distant class and focusing on the instruction, the pace of the class may be interrupted to accommodate these individuals. If everyone has copies of the visuals, it makes it easier for the teacher to keep the class moving along smoothly.

When designing visuals, three key design decisions must be considered:

1. Selecting the verbal and visual material
2. Choosing an underlying pattern for all displays
3. Arranging information within the pattern

The type of visual selected for the class depends on the learning task at hand. Visuals can be subdivided into three categories: realistic, analogic, and organizational (Heinich et al., 1996). Realistic visuals show the actual object under study. Analogic visuals convey a concept of topic by showing something else and implying a similarity. And organizational visuals include such things as flow diagrams, graphs, charts, and maps.

Designing Visuals.   The style of lettering should be consistent and should follow some simple conventions (Cohen, Ebeling, & Kulik, 1981). For informational purposes, a plain lettering style is recommended. A sans serif style (such as Helvetica) or a simple serif style (such as Palatino) should be used. Using more elaborate styles often can create visuals that are difficult to read. If you must use a fancy font, then make certain the students have a good-quality copy of the materials at all sites.

In addition to style, instructors need to be cautious when using all capital letters (Cohen, Ebeling, & Kulik, 1981). Whenever using all capitals, make certain it is only for short lines of text, such as a title. Do not use all capital letters for through text, as this style is hard to read and gives the impression of someone shouting.

Lettering size becomes somewhat less important when a distance education class has access to the document camera or when material can be forwarded using fax or computer-based technologies. However, it is important to note that when a line of text is too long, you cannot show it in its entirety without moving the text across the document camera (Herring & Smaldino, 1997). Use plenty of white space around any visual, thus ensuring that all can see clearly the particular element or part you want them to see. If you put too much information into too small a space, you may find it is difficult for the students to focus on important elements. It is better to use a larger font size (e.g., 24 or 36 point) and fewer words per line (e.g., a limit of six words per line). Further, it is suggested that a visual should have no more than six lines per page.

Color can add interest and ensure that students find the important information. Good color contrasts are important, such as dark lettering on a light background or light lettering on a dark background (Cohen, Ebeling, & Kulik, 1981). Make certain to use colors that are appropriate for television (e.g., blue is excellent on television; red is not).

Pattern is also critical when designing good visuals. Selecting a pattern for visuals that is easy to "read" will enhance the learning experience. Using shapes that are familiar to students, e.g., the shape of a circle to arrange the information, helps students to focus on the material. Make certain the visuals are balanced, that is, with equal weight (Cohen, Ebeling, & Kulik, 1981).

◆ SUMMARY

It is important to remember that distance education may be as new to the students as it is to the instructor. Preparing students for instruction is important in any teaching mode to maximize learning from class participation. But it is especially important to prepare students for settings where class participants are separated across distances. Students need to understand their responsibility to ensure a successful learning experience.

Teaching at a distance is a challenge. The instructor needs to be creative and imaginative in the design and structure of the course. One rule of thumb is that successful interactive learning experiences that work in a traditional classroom are adaptable to the distance learning environment. But they may require more than just some changes to the visuals or the handouts. They may require inventiveness and innovation.

Teaching at a distance can be a pleasurable experience for everyone involved, instructor and student alike. Keeping it interesting, and motivating the learners to remain active, can make it a valuable learning experience as well as fun.

Self-Test Questions

1. What are some of the organization factors that a teacher must consider when preparing to teach?
2. What strategies might be used to formalize introductions among students?
3. What elements of class structure need to be included when preparing to teach at a distance?
4. Why is it necessary to determine resources available at distant sites when preparing to teach at a distance?
5. What factors need to be considered when deciding to use a facilitator at a distant site?
6. What issues are examined when preparing visuals for distance education classes?

Finally, discuss these questions and answers in small groups and determine how the teacher's role changes and stays the same in a distance education environment.

Answers to Self-Test Questions

1. Organization of the content, time allotment, organization of the technology, and organization of the learning activities.
2. Responses might include student-to-student introductions among pairs of students, or whole group introductions using Powerpoint slides that include something personal and professional about oneself.
3. In structuring the class, it is important to ensure that students understand their responsibilities within the learning environment, understand the organization and structure of the learning activities, know the schedules and due dates, understand the process for responses in discussions, know the communication protocols, know how to contact the instructor and other students, and know what to do when there are technical difficulties.
4. It is necessary in order to know what hardware and software are available for students to use, what resources students will be able to access, what library and other related resources will be available outside of class time, and how coursework and related materials are distributed and collected.
5. The factors that need to be considered include what the role of the facilitator is, who selects the facilitator, and how the facilitator is evaluated.
6. Issues include the use of icons and graphics which may require instruction of their meaning; developmentally appropriate graphics for a particular age group; the cultural background of the students; legibility, contrast, and simplicity; the need for visuals to engage the students in learning; the use of visuals serve to focus attention.

References

Cohen, P., Ebeling, B., & Kulik, J. (1981, Spring). A meta-analysis of outcome studies of visual-based instruction. *Educational Communications and Technology Journal, 29*(1), 26–36.

Cyrs, T., & Smith, F. (1990). *Teleclass teaching.* Las Cruces, NM: Center for Education Development.

Greenwood, A. N., & McDevitt, M. A. (1987). *Multiple teaching strategies for use with an instructional telecommunications network.* Paper presented at the Society for Applied Learning, Orlando, FL.

Heinich, R., Molenda, M., Russell, J., & Smaldino, S. (1996). *Instructional media and the technologies for learning,* 5th ed. Columbus, OH: Merrill/Prentice Hall.

Herring, M., & Smaldino, S. (1997). *Planning for interactive distance education: A handbook.* Washington, DC: AECT Publications.

Macfarlane, C., & Smaldino, S. (1997). The electronic classroom at a distance. In R. Rittenhouse & D. Spillers (Eds.), *Modernizing the curriculum: The electronic classroom.* Springfield, MO: Charles Thomas Publishers.

Souder, W. E. (1993). The effectiveness of traditional vs. satellite delivery in three management of technology master's degree programs. *The American Journal of Distance Education, 4,* 37–53.

chapter 9

Handouts, Study Guides, and Visuals

CHAPTER GOAL

The purpose of this chapter is to present information about the effective use of printed materials in distance education

CHAPTER OBJECTIVES

After reading and reviewing this chapter, you should be able to

1. Develop a distance education course syllabus.
2. Use interactive study guides.
3. Apply graphic design principles.
4. Develop word pictures.
5. Use visual mnemonics.

◆ PRINTED MEDIA

Distance education has its roots in print-based correspondence study. The printed lesson was used to convey content information as well as to assess learning in correspondence study. Today many people give little credit to the effectiveness of printed materials. Educators sometimes use technological media to replace printed media, even though there is no real need to do so.

Printed materials can enhance teaching, learning, and managing in distance education. In particular, two kinds of instructor created print media can significantly improve the distance education environment—the course syllabus and the interactive study guide. Additionally, graphics design principles can be applied to develop study guides that use visual mnemonics and word pictures for the visualizations of key instructional ideas.

◆ DISTANCE EDUCATION SYLLABUS

The typical distance education course syllabus is similar to the syllabus used in any other course. The primary difference is in the specificity and completeness of the distance education syllabus as compared with a more traditional one. Normally, the distance education syllabus contains the following:

Course Logistics

◆ Course title
◆ Course meeting dates, times, and locations
◆ Instructor information, including name, office address, telephone number, e-mail address, biographical information, and emergency contact information
◆ Office hours
◆ Textbook and course materials

Course Policies

◆ Attendance policies
◆ Homework policies
◆ Participation information

Instructional Activities

◆ Class schedule with topic list (if the course is a synchronous one with regularly scheduled class sessions)
◆ Topic list and topic organizational concept map (if the course is an asynchronous one with topics that can be studied at the learner's discretion)
◆ Course goals and objectives
◆ Reading assignments with links to topics

◆ Discussion questions for readings (if special discussion sessions are scheduled on-line, then the time line for discussing certain topics can be included)
◆ Assignments
◆ Test and examination information
◆ Interactive study guides

Assessment Information

◆ Grading scheme
◆ Project evaluation criteria
◆ Grading contracts, if used
◆ Student precourse assessment
◆ Student postcourse assessment

Additional Information

◆ Student biographical information
◆ Project/assignment examples

The distance education syllabus should be available to students no later than the beginning of the first class, and probably should be distributed much earlier to prospective class members. Often, the syllabus is a recruiting tool for the distance education course. If the syllabus is available on-line, then the distant learners can access it from wherever they are located. The syllabus is a guide for the student, and can serve as an organizing document for the entire course. Many designers of asynchronous distance education courses use the syllabus to provide the overall structure for the content, delivery, and evaluation of the course.

◆ THE INTERACTIVE STUDY GUIDE

Tom Cyrs and Al Kent are often credited with proposing the interactive study guide (ISG) as an essential tool of the distance educator. Certainly they (especially Tom Cyrs, 1997) are staunch advocates of this technique. Basically, the interactive study guide is a structured note-taking system that leads the learner through a series of concepts and that requires some active and interactive involvement by the student (Figure 9–1).

There are several reasons why the handout, generally, and the interactive study guide handout, specifically, are important to the distance educator. First, the use of handouts improves student note taking and makes it more efficient. Second, the ISG is a management tool that directs course activities before, during, and after instruction. Finally, the ISG handout can be used in any classroom, including all categories of distance education systems.

The interactive study guide is a handout designed to be used by students. It is a highly organized set of student notes, graphics, pictures, graphs, charts, clip art, photographs, geometric shapes, activities, problems, and exercises. It is planned before a teleclass to assist students with note taking and to guide students through a variety of instructional events so they understand the structure of the content of the lesson. ISGs

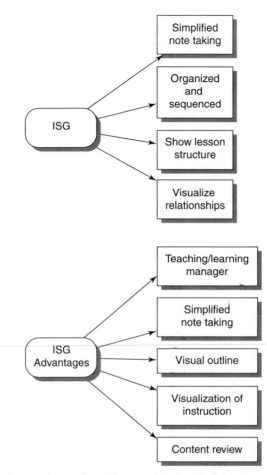

FIGURE 9–1   The interactive study guide is a critical tool of the distance educator.

are also meant to show the relationships among ideas and data presented during a class (Cyrs, 1997).

The ISG is different from other handouts because it is more organized and more systematically sequenced than other types. The ISG consists of two parts—the display (with the word picture) and the notes section (Figure 9–2). A series of displays are sequenced (numbered) in the order that they will be discussed in class. Each display corresponds to one idea or one visual element of the lesson. Sometimes a display is equated to a concept, but most often, displays are less general and more specific than a concept.

Well-designed displays are made up of word pictures that are graphic representations of concepts, principles, and information derived from various patterns to organize a lesson. The best word pictures are visual mnemonics that relate to the key ideas of

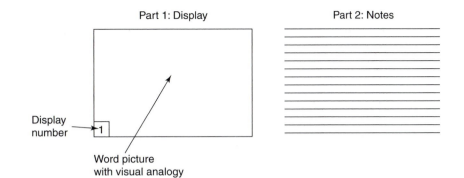

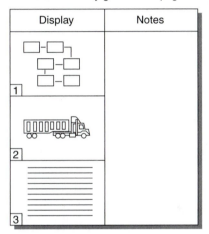

FIGURE 9–2   Interactive study guide—components.

the lesson. Mnemonics are ways to remember things, so visual mnemonics are visual ways to remember things.

The ISG is a series of displays presented from the top to the bottom on the left side of the handout page. Normally three to five displays are presented on each page of the ISG. A display is sometimes referred to as a "chunk" of information that is numbered and then referenced by the student (Cyrs, 1997). A display is similar to a paragraph of information in a written document, but the display attempts to present ideas visually rather than verbally, or at least with a combination of visual elements and words.

Displays can consist of

◆ Word pictures with fill-ins completed by the student
◆ Activities or exercises
◆ A set of directions
◆ A quote, poem, definition, or other short written item

- Problems—either verbal or numerical
- Summaries of data
- Tables or figures
- Photographs
- Drawings
- Self-test questions
- Lists

An ISG display can contain directions for students to accomplish a task outside of class that is external to the ISG itself. An effective display is clear, easy to understand, and useful to the learner.

Normally, a 50-minute class session would require approximately 10 displays in an ISG. In other words, displays should be complex enough to require about 5 minutes to explain, or conversely, simple enough to cover in 5 minutes. This is an estimate. Some displays may take much longer to deal with, and others much less time, but the 5-minute estimate is good for planning purposes.

The steps necessary to produce an interactive study guide are as follows:

- Identify the behavioral objectives for the lesson.
- Create a detailed outline of topics that relate to each objective.
- For narrative sections identify the key words.
- Use geometric shapes to show relationships or visuals to assist the learner in understanding each section.
- Create word pictures for the narrative sections by leaving blanks in the narrative where students will fill in the key words.
- Sequence the displays in the order that they will be presented or that they will be discussed.
- Develop subdisplays for topics that have more than one visual or word picture.
- Produce the ISG using proper graphic design principles.

The production of the ISG requires considerable planning. Once it is developed, the distance education course is considerably easier for the instructor to prepare for and to teach, and is more organized and easier for learners to follow, especially those in distance education courses where live, two-way interactive television is not available.

◆ GRAPHIC DESIGN PRINCIPLES

Interactive study guides are often used as the basis for interactive television graphics in distance education courses. For this reason it is important to design ISGs to conform to appropriate graphic design principles. The size, font, color and contrast, alignment, and use of uppercase and lowercase in written graphics are critical to successful design.

- **Size.** Letter size is very closely related to legibility. Large, bold lettering is easier to see and read than is smaller lettering. Certainly lettering should not be smaller

Univers Bold Caps

Univers Bold Caps and Lowercase

9 point   **LEGIBILITY**   **Legibility**

12 point   **LEGIBILITY**   **Legibility**

14 point   **LEGIBILITY**   **Legibility**

18 point   **LEGIBILITY**   **Legibility**

24 point   **LEGIBILITY**   **Legibility**

36 point   **LEGIBILITY**   **Legibility**

48 point   **LEGIBILITY**

           Legibility

72 point   **LEGIBILITY**

           Legibility

FIGURE 9–3   The type has to be large enough to be easy to read.

than 24 point (1/3 inch), and 32 to 36 point is preferable, especially if computer output is to be displayed on regular television monitors (Figure 9–3). Five words per line and five lines per page are a maximum for an ISG display or a screen of television information.

- ◆ **Font.** Sans serif fonts should be used instead of fonts with serifs, the thin extensions to letters often used in textbooks and printed documents. Serifs tend to be too fine for display on television. Bold fonts with thick stems display the best. Also, the same fonts should be used throughout a presentation, and no more than three different fonts should be used for any single display. Two font types work the best, when one is used for one category of information and the second is used for background or secondary information, for example. Fancy type faces and italics should be avoided unless there is an overriding reason for using them.
- ◆ **Color and Contrast.** Color is often misused in television. Colors should be bold and simple and should not be overdone. Some combinations, such as green and red, do not work well together. Avoid saturated colors like red. Use dark letters with a light background, or vice-versa. Many television instructors like to use bright colors on a black background for displaying computer screens of information. This approach produces very readable displays.
- ◆ **Alignment.** Centering text for television display is not as effective as aligning text to the left. Left-justified text seems to be most legible.
- ◆ **Capitalization.** The literature on readability is quite clear that uppercase and lowercase lettering, rather than all uppercase or all lowercase, reads the best.

Elements of Design

Literate, effective visuals for display as part of ISGs or for instructor-led presentations can be developed by applying the elements and principles of design. The elements of design (shown in Figure 9–4) are line, shape, space, texture, value, and color.

- ◆ *Line* is generally considered to be one-dimensional. Line has length but not width. Line portrays direction, presents objects, and defines the outer shape of something.
- ◆ *Shape* is used to symbolize objects or to show large or small spaces. Shapes have two dimensions, height and width.
- ◆ *Space* is either positive or negative. The outline of an object in a visual signifies its positive space. The most common negative shape of something is its background.
- ◆ *Texture* is the perceived or actual roughness or smoothness of a surface. Texture is used to help define shape or space.
- ◆ *Value* is the degree of lightness or darkness of a surface. Value is accomplished through shading. Value shows changes in space, and is often used to create the illusion of volume or solidity in a graphic object.
- ◆ *Color* is related to value and is used to visualize an object realistically or to differentiate an object from another object. Colors have hue, value, and intensity. *Hue* describes a specific color, such as red, green, or blue. *Value* is the lightness or darkness of a color. Yellow has the highest value. *Intensity* is the strength of a color, such as bright yellow or dull red. Intensity is determined by the purity of a color.

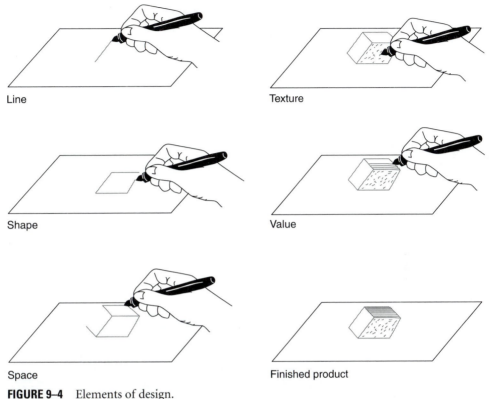

Line

Texture

Shape

Value

Space

Finished product

FIGURE 9–4   Elements of design.

Principles of Design

The elements of design are combined according to the guidelines provided by the principles of design. There are six principles: balance, center of interest, emphasis, unity, contrast, and rhythm.

◆ *Balance* is the sense of equilibrium in a visual. There are two kinds of balance—formal and informal (Figure 9–5). Generally, a visual should be balanced left to right and top to bottom. Formal balance means that objects of equal size and importance are placed at equivalent distances from the center of the visual (Figure 9–6). Informally balanced visuals are often more interesting to create and to view. Careful planning is important when informally balanced graphics are created. Several small images can be used to balance one large object, or words can be used to balance pictures (Figure 9–7). Small, brightly colored objects will balance larger, duller items.

◆ The *center of interest* is the visual focal point of the graphic and should relate to its purpose. Historically, well-designed visuals did not place the center of interest at

FIGURE 9–5   Formal and informal balance.

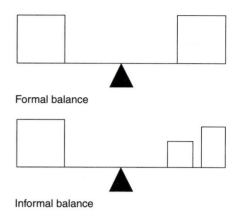

Formal balance

Informal balance

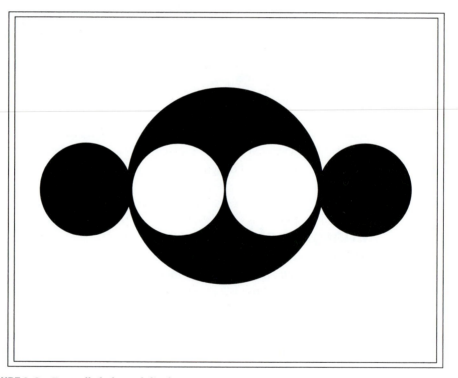

FIGURE 9–6   Formally balanced display.

the center of the picture. However, television places restrictions on the graphic designer. Since the area displayed on a television screen is relatively small and varies between television sets, it is probably safest to place the center of interest of a graphic at or near the center of the picture.

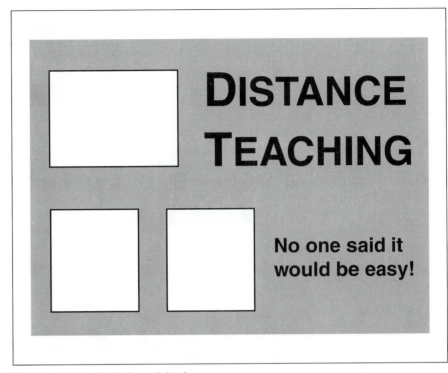

FIGURE 9–7   Informally balanced display.

◆ *Emphasis* is closely related to the center of interest. The key object should be emphasized so it is apparent to the viewer what is most important (Figure 9–8). There are several ways to emphasize the key element in a graphic:

1. Use pointers, such as arrows.
2. Use color to emphasize.
3. Use large objects at the center of interest.
4. Use different shapes for the center of interest.
5. Use more elements of design to create the center of interest for a graphic and fewer for less important elements.

◆ *Unity* means that a visual holds together to convey its purpose (Figure 9–9). If several graphics are used as part of a display, they should all convey or pertain to one meaning. Overlapping is a simple technique for promoting unity. Trees overlap buildings and each other. Houses overlap shrubs and people. A single background also promotes a feeling of unity. Another technique to promote the concept of unity is to place an outline or border around the elements of a display. Repetition of shapes, forms, and objects also can promote unity.

◆ *Contrast* refers to the characteristics of an object that cause it to stand out (Figure 9–10). Contrast is closely related to emphasis. Most often, contrast is achieved by

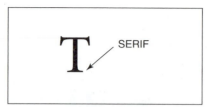

Arrow or pointers are effective.

A contrasting value can emphasize an area.

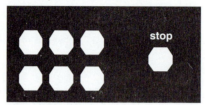

The placement of an item can cause it to be emphasized.

Size can be used.

FIGURE 9–8 Emphasis has to do with making the key item stand out.

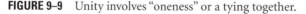

A "border" can be used to achieve unity.

Another technique is to use lines to unify.

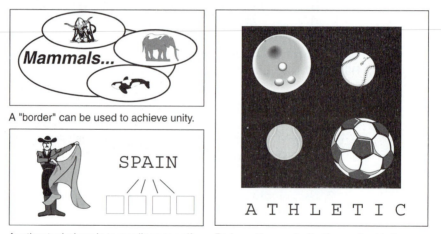

Perhaps the most effective method is to overlap a common shape.

FIGURE 9–9 Unity involves "oneness" or a tying together.

the use of light- or dark-valued objects. Shapes, forms, and textures can be used to create contrasts and make one object stand out while others seem to recede.

◆ *Rhythm* comes from repetition through variety, and is used to draw a viewer through the various objects in a visual (Figure 9–11). A row of houses in a display can present a sense of rhythm. The rhythm of a graphic helps tell the story of the picture by leading the viewer's eyes.

When light and dark values are used, contrast results.

Differences in size can create contrast.

FIGURE 9–10   The important parts of a display can be made to stand out (contrast) mainly through the use of color, size, value, and shape.

FIGURE 9–11   Rhythm results when an element is repeated in some systematic manner.

An effective graphic should provide visual information related to the topic being learned. The elements of design combined according to the principles of design can assist the distance educator in the development of effective interactive study guides and handouts that visually explain ideas and that facilitate understanding.

◆ WORD PICTURES

A word picture is a graphic representation of concepts, principles, and information. Each concept, principle, or item of information usually contains key words that can be shown in nodes. A node is a symbol that contains words or stands alone to represent some idea. A node is the central point around which subnodes originate (Cyrs, 1997). The best word picture is a visual mnemonic that helps the learner remember the concept, principle, or item.

Word pictures do not need to be self-explanatory. Rather, they often require additional verbal information. Key words are usually shown in the nodes. Key words are the most significant words in a statement that provide clues to the idea the statement is communicating. Word pictures are graphic organizers that put elements of ideas together in a visual way so the learner can understand the relationship between the elements.

Cyrs does an excellent job of explaining how word pictures are different from other ways of organizing information. Cyrs (1997) says about effective word pictures that

1. Emphasis should be placed on the types of symbols used.
2. They should cover chunks of information rather than entire documents.
3. Student attention can be maintained through the use of fill-ins.
4. They emphasize the logical sequence of the class presentation.
5. They provide a complete review of the class content.
6. They can also be used for display by overhead video cameras.
7. They are inexpensive to produce and duplicate.
8. They condense ideas into a few key words.
9. They should be designed to fit the format of television.
10. They apply principles of graphic design.
11. They emphasize communication via the visual sense.
12. They require the instructor to think visually rather than verbally.

Cyrs discusses a number of types of graphic organizers that can be incorporated into word pictures. They are semantic maps, mind maps, cognitive maps, structured overviews, outlines, patterned note taking, webbing, pyramiding, and information mapping.

◆ *Semantic maps* are two-dimensional diagrams that use arrangements of nodes and links to communicate ideas and to show the relationships among ideas. Semantic maps use primarily two structures—top down and bottom up (Johnson & Peterson, 1984).

◆ *Mind maps* use key words or phrases organized in a design that is nonlinear. Mind maps are based on the idea that individuals mentally organize information in a variety of structures, not just top down or bottom up. Rather, mind maps usually start at the center of a page and branch out as individual ideas are presented. Mind maps (Buzan, 1982) have the following characteristics:

The main ideas are clearly defined and placed in the center of the graphic.
The relative importance of a subidea is indicated by its proximity to the main idea.
Links between ideas are clearly indicated.
New information is easily added to a mind map because of its nonlinear structure.

◆ *Cognitive maps* (Diekhoff & Diekhoff, 1982) are organized around the relationship between ideas, and provide a graphic expression of the structure of a body of knowledge. Many confuse cognitive maps and mind maps. Cognitive maps are more structured and organized than mind maps and are usually developed by the instructor of a class.

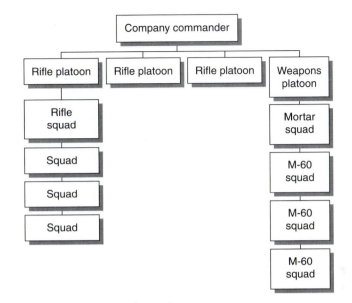

FIGURE 9–12   Word picture: Structural overview.

- *Structured overviews* use graphics and hierarchical structures showing the relationship of key ideas, concepts, and other information (Figure 9–12). Structured overviews are commonly used for readings or lectures. Austin and Dean-Guilford (1981) define the structured overview as a conceptualized visual-hierarchical type of diagram used to show concept interrelationships within written material.
- *Outlines* are visual displays that are useful in presenting concurrent ideas. Outlines are largely verbal, but use visual elements to present clusters of ideas in one display.
- *Patterned note taking* (Norton, 1981) is related to mind mapping. A key word or phrase is placed in the center of a space, and arrows and lines radiate out to subideas. Key words and phrases are used extensively. Lines are used to show relationships.
- *Webbing* is a graphic representation similar to other techniques discussed above. The main idea is at the center, and subordinate ideas radiate out like the spokes of a wheel. Webbing resembles semantic maps.
- *Pyramiding* shows the levels of ideas in a graphic way using a bottom-to-top model (Figure 9–13). Information is grouped according to a hierarchy, such as details at the bottom, concepts in the middle, and principles at the top.
- *Information mapping* is a method of bringing together current research into a comprehensive materials development and presentation approach. Maps are arranged hierarchically into blocks of information. Each block serves a separate purpose, but all relate to some central theme or idea.

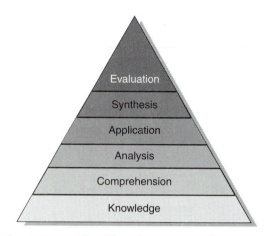

FIGURE 9–13   Word picture: Pyramiding Bloom's taxonomy of cognitive domain.

Cyrs (1997) provides an excellent list of organizational patterns for distance education classes. The strategies listed by Cyrs are wonderful starting points for those beginning to develop a personal approach to distance teaching. Several of the most useful approaches are

1. Problem solution. In this situation, students are presented with a real or contrived problem with elements provided about the situation that caused or have impact on the problem. Students are then asked, often in collaborative groups, to make observations about the situation and then propose alternative solutions including the consequences of each alternative. One effective technique for dramatizing the problem is to use "trigger films/videos," which are short (two to four minutes) scenarios dealing with the events that produced the problem. Students are then asked to respond to the problem. The film/video "triggers" a response. For example, a trigger film might dramatize a family in financial crisis with a stack of bills that are due at the end of the month. After watching the scenario unfold, financial counseling students would be required to work in small groups to develop a proposed solution to the situation depicted.

2. Time sequence. This presentation involves organizing information in a list or sequence of events that unfold chronologically. The sequence can be presented by the instructor, or the elements of the sequence can be presented visually and students can be asked to help order the elements and then explain the rationale for their decision. Examples of time sequences include developing film, completing a tax return, building a dog house, and baking a cake.

3. Definitions. When a presentation is based on definitions, there is usually a statement of the concept to be defined, a listing of its attributes, and examples of how the term, phrase, or item is used. For example, terms in a chemistry laboratory exercise might first be defined by the instructor before students work together to complete the sequence of activities involved in the laboratory experience. Definitions lend themselves particularly well to sequential interactive study guides.

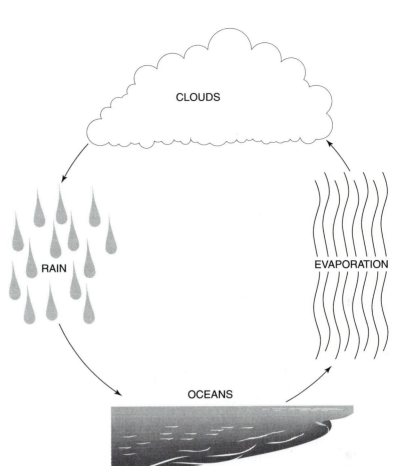

FIGURE 9–14   Word picture: Cause and effect—water cycle.

4. Cause and effect. In this approach an event and its causes or antecedents are presented (Figure 9–14). For example, the heavy rains in California would be discussed and would be followed by an exploration of why the rains occurred, such as the influence of El Niño water in the central Pacific Ocean. Actual or historic meteorological records could be used, as could weather reports in California newspapers.

◆ VISUAL ANALOGIES

An analogy is a way to describe something that is unfamiliar by comparing it with something familiar. The two things that are being compared seem to be different but have some similarities. Analogies help improve thinking and help learners understand new ideas by giving insights and by allowing new relationships to be explained.

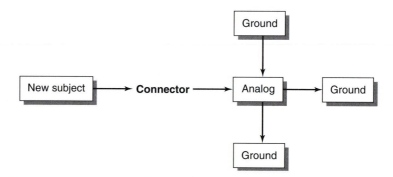

FIGURE 9–15   Components of an analogy.

According to Cyrs, analogies have four parts (Figure 9–15): the new subject, the analog, the connector between the analog and the new subject, and the ground.

◆ The *new subject* is the topic that is unfamiliar. The analogy is designed to help provide understanding of the new subject. Subjects normally are described by only a few words.

◆ The *analog* is familiar and is something that has been experienced by the learner. It is crucial that the learner knows the analog—the previously understood idea or concept.

◆ The *connector* shows the relationship between the two concepts: the new subject and the familiar idea, or analog. The connector is the critical element in the analogy and demonstrates the creativity of the author of the analogy. Connectors can be structural or functional.

   Structural relationships show the similarity in appearance and design of the two concepts.

   Examples of structural relationships include these: (a) Sharon is as creative as DaVinci. (b) Norman is as soft as a marshmallow. (c) Raindrops looked like balloons.

   Functional relationships describe what concepts do or how they work. Functional relationships show not only what the subject and the analog have in common but also what they do that is similar.

Connectors that often are used include the following:

. . . tastes like . . .
. . . resembles . . .
. . . is comparable to . . .
. . . feels like . . .
. . . looks like . . .
. . . is related to . . .
. . . is like . . .

Media are like delivery trucks. They permit the delivery of
ideas to learners.

FIGURE 9–16   Example: A visual analogy.

◆ The *ground* relates to the specific set of similarities and differences between the
unfamiliar and the familiar. The ground can be verbal or visual, but the more
concrete the ground, the more hints it provides and the more likely it will be that
the analogy will work. Pictures are often used to help make real the analogy (Figure
9–16). Some examples of a ground include these:

Football is like war—it requires strategy, tactics, planning, and trained individuals.
Distance teaching is like singing and playing the piano at the same time. It requires
   simultaneous verbal skills and physical dexterity.
Media are like delivery trucks, since media carry ideas.

There are five steps to follow when constructing visual analogies. First, identify
clearly what the new subject is, the idea that is not clearly known. Second, identify the
appropriate connector, such as "...is like ..." or "...is similar to. ..." Third, identify the
known analog—the familiar concept or thing that can be compared with the new idea.
Fourth, provide a ground for the comparison of the new and familiar ideas. Describe
the similarities and differences between the ideas. Finally, develop a visual way to
demonstrate the analogy and to provide learners with a visual mnemonic to help them
remember the relationship and to understand the new subject.

Analogies are difficult to develop. When a good analogy is identified, especially a
visual one, it can be the center of an elegant discussion of instructional content.
Naturally, the visual analogy should be incorporated as a word picture for an interactive study guide.

◆ **SUMMARY**

Printed handouts and teaching and learning materials are critically important to the effective practice of distance education. First, the course syllabus is the "glue" that holds
the course or the learning experience together. Sometimes the syllabus is expanded into
the course study guide, which is a document that provides the student with a level of
orientation to the distance education experience.

Second, the interactive study guide is a very important tool that provides the distant learner with a logical sequence for the distance education lesson. The interactive study guide is especially important when the student and instructor are in asynchronous communication or when fully interactive two-way television is not used.

Interactive study guides are made up of two ingredients—the display and the notes section. The display is made up of a series of word pictures, which are visuals and words that involve student interaction and which attempt to provide the learner with ways to remember the key ideas that are to be learned. In essence, the word pictures are visual mnemonics to help learners remember things.

Naturally, for visuals to be meaningful and instructional they need to be designed effectively. The guidelines for effective visual design should be followed.

Finally, printed materials are critical to the practice of distance education (Figure 9–17). Documents provide background information, amplify concepts, and give a sense of direction to instructional events. Printed materials are an important component of the distance education program.

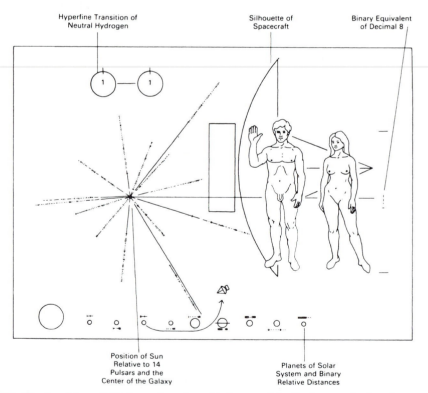

FIGURE 9–17   Speaking of distance education, this is a graphic display attached to the *Pioneer 10* spacecraft that is hurling into space. The designers of this display wanted to convey three ideas to whomever or whatever might find it thousands of years from now: (1) where the spacecraft came from, the earth, (2) who inhabited the earth, men and women, (3) that men and women are friendly.

Self-Test Questions

1. Define *visual analogy*. Why are analogies important?
2. Develop a visual mnemonic or word picture for these concepts:
   - Technology as productivity enhancer
   - Pythagorean theorem
   - Definition of distance education
3. Draw a line drawing using the five elements of design.
4. Write an analogy for these ideas:
   - Teaching
   - Golf
   - Learning
   - A pet dog
5. What is an interactive study guide, and what is it used for? Explain why study guides are important to the distance educator.

Answers to Self-Test Questions are on the following page.

Answers to Self-Test Questions

1. Visual analogies are ways to describe something unfamiliar by comparing it with something that is familiar using four elements—the new subject, the analog, the connector, and the ground.

2.

Technology as productivity enhancer

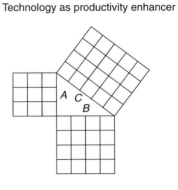

$A^2 + B^2 = C^2$
Pythagorean theorem

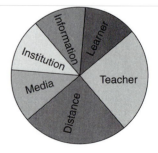

Distance education

3.

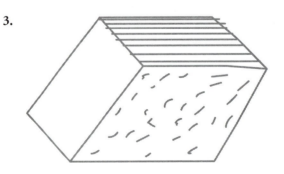

4. Sample answers:
    *   Teaching is like building a house. It involves materials and plans, and is successful if something useful results.
    *   Golf is like swimming—it is something you do individually, and in a special place.
    *   Learning is the same as living. We do it from birth to death, in a variety of locations and situations, and sometimes it is easy and sometimes it is difficult.
    *   A pet dog is like a friend. It is always glad to see us and we are glad to see it.
5. The interactive study guide is a handout designed to be used by students. It is a highly organized set of student notes, graphics, pictures, graphs, charts, clip art, photographs, geometric shapes, activities, problems, and exercises. It is planned before a teleclass to assist students with note taking and to guide students through a variety of instructional events so they understand the structure of the content of the lesson. The main advantage of the ISG is it keeps the students and the instructor moving together through the lesson.

References

Austin, R., & Dean-Guilford, M. (1981). Crashing content reading problems with reading strategies. Paper presented at the meeting of the Western College Reading Association, Dallas, TX. (ERIC Document Reproduction Service No. ED 204 703)

Buzan, T. (1982). *Use your head.* London: British Broadcasting Corporation.

Carrier, C. (1983). Notetaking research: Implications for the classroom. *Journal of Instructional Development, 6,* 19–26.

Diekhoff, G., & Diekhoff, K. (1982). Cognitive maps as a tool in communicating structural knowledge. *Educational Technology, 22,* 28–30.

Johnson, D., & Peterson, D. (1984). *Teaching reading vocabulary* (2nd ed.). New York: Holt.

Kiewra, K. (1987). Notetaking and review: The research and its implications. *Instructional Science, 16,* 233–249.

Norton, L. (1981). Patterned note-taking: An evaluation. *Visible Language, 15,* 67–85.

Smith, P., & Tompkins, G. (1988). Structured notetaking: A new strategy for content area teachers. *Journal of Reading, 32,* 46–53.

Additional Reading

Cyrs, T. (1997). *Teaching at a distance.* Las Cruces, NM: Center for Educational Development.

chapter 10

Distance Education, the World Wide Web, and the Internet

CHAPTER GOAL

The purpose of this chapter is to discuss the structure and functions of the Internet and describe the many ways it can be used in a distance education environment.

CHAPTER OBJECTIVES

After reading and reviewing this chapter, you should be able to

1. Describe current trends in the use of the Internet for distance education in K–12, higher education, and corporate training.
2. Discuss the evolution of the Internet and its functions that most directly relate to distance education, such as electronic mail, mailing lists, and the World Wide Web.
3. Describe how the structure of the Internet makes its functions available to nearly anyone with a telephone line and a sufficiently powerful computer.
4. Discuss why the Internet relates well to transformations taking place in the general paradigms for teaching and learning.
5. Define and differentiate between asynchronous learning networks and computer-mediated communication.
6. Discuss the advantages and limitations of Internet-based courses.
7. Recognize the major components of an on-line course and account for them in course development and delivery.
8. Select course activities that maximize active learning opportunities for students in an Internet-based distance education course.
9. Assist students in thinking critically in assessing the credibility and worth of information found on the World Wide Web.
10. Plan and develop a course Web site that enables students to achieve prescribed learning goals at a distance.

◆ THE IMPLICATIONS OF THE INTERNET FOR EDUCATION AND TRAINING

Of all the delivery technologies described in Chapter 4, none has more explosive growth potential for distance education than the Internet. Indeed, soon after the dawn of the 21st century, the Internet or one of its descendants will likely become the dominant distribution system for education and training at a distance across much of the industrialized world.

At the heart of this trend is improved access to the Internet. Through the mid-1990s, access was quite limited, but now more than 10,000 Internet service providers (ISPs) in over 120 countries make the Internet available to almost anyone in those nations with a sufficiently powerful computer and a telephone line, for modest monthly fees. In July 1998, the Irish consulting firm Nua estimated the worldwide total of Internet users at about 130 million, including 72 million in the United States and Canada, 32 million in Europe, 19 million in Asia and the Pacific island countries, and 7 million in South America (Nua Consultants and Developers, 1998). Nua noted that the Internet has become the fastest-growing communications medium of all time, reaching 50 million American users in just four years. By contrast, radio took 38 years and television 14 years to reach audiences of 50 million. As a result of the Internet's rapid growth, not only are more individuals given access to a remarkable array of education options, but students enrolled in those courses are only a few mouse clicks away from an information marketplace of unprecedented proportions. The implications for education and training are extraordinary.

The Internet and K–12 Education.   By early 1998, three-fourths of all primary and secondary schools in the United States were connected to the Internet, but this figure was misleading in that most schools had limited internal distribution to classrooms, computer laboratories, and library-media centers. The Universal Service Program (USP), established by the Telecommunications Act of 1996 to provide affordable access to the Internet for schools and libraries, promises to have a major impact on connecting the remaining buildings and enhancing student access within schools, especially in rural areas and inner cities. The USP requires service providers to offer their lowest rates to elementary and secondary schools and allows additional 20–90 percent discounts on top of those rates (known as the *E-rate*) for telecommunications services, Internet access, and internal networking. Service providers are then reimbursed from a multibillion dollar fund established as part of the program.

An increasing number of school districts are putting courses on the Web, either to supplement existing curricula, to promote course sharing among schools, or to reach students who cannot (for physical reasons) or do not (by choice) attend school in person. Some districts, among them the Eugene Public School District in Oregon and the Jefferson County Public School District in Colorado, planned to offer Web courses not only to their own students but to others nationwide. As with satellites and terrestrial video networks, the Internet thus has significant potential for delivering courses that smaller, underfunded districts may not have the resources to offer on their own.

Owston (1997) noted that alternative schools are beginning to make extensive use of Web technology to gain greater access to quality learning materials, and that Web-based courses also have high potential for adults attempting to complete their schooling through home study. In addition, some colleges and universities are now offering freshman-level courses on-line to allow students to get a head start on their postsecondary work while still enrolled in high school.

Home-schooled students in particular stand to benefit from courses and curricula offered on-line. The Web can help overcome two of the main limitations of home schooling—the lack of interaction with other students and, as with many alternative schools, limited access to high-quality learning materials (Owston, 1997). A new genre of educational institution, the "cyberschool," has arisen to provide 9–12 or K–12 curricula, with an emphasis on college preparation, completely via the Internet to home-schooled students nationwide. Private on-line schools such as Cyber High School in California and the Christa McAuliffe Academy in the state of Washington either are fully accredited or promise to seek appropriate accreditation as soon as they have graduated their first four-year classes. (As with any other product or service purchased through the Internet, a caveat emptor warning applies. Parents should fully investigate these schools before enrolling their children and paying tuition.)

Higher Education.   Although colleges and universities have been offering on-line instruction since the early 1980s, the World Wide Web has provided them with new means of reaching out not only to their traditional service areas but well beyond, as the Internet knows no state, province, or national borders. More than 800 U.S. colleges and universities now offer on-line courses for academic credit, and the majority of these programs are open to any student, anywhere, as long as entrance requirements are met and tuition is paid. Conventional brick-and-mortar institutions hardly hold the exclusive franchise on on-line degree and certificate programs. Proprietary (for-profit) institutions such as the University of Phoenix and Magellan University are enrolling large numbers of students via the Internet. Another important trend is the emergence of consortia of traditional colleges and universities to develop and deliver academic programs by a variety of nontraditional means. The Western Governors University, with affiliated public universities from Guam to Indiana, is the highest profile "campus without walls" institution yet established. Consortia such as the California Virtual University and the Southern Regional Electronic Campus have been set up to broker courses and degree programs developed by their member institutions.

Why does Internet-based distance education have such strong potential for academe? For one thing, the population of typical college-age students is expected to increase much faster over the next 20 years than campuses can find space to accommodate them, particularly in the Western states. Collectively, college students also are getting older. More than 40 percent of today's college students are "nontraditional," over 25 years of age, and these are the most likely to have Internet access either at home or at the workplace. Twenty-nine percent of the respondents to a 1997 national survey of Internet users conducted by the Emerging Technologies Research Group (ETRG) said they probably would engage in educational activities via the Internet, second only to banking (30 percent) among anticipated future on-line functions (Miller & Clemente, 1997).

The growing expense of traditional higher education is another important, related factor keeping some students home. Adjusted for inflation, the cost of attending a traditional residential college or university has doubled in the past 15 years. A recent survey by InterEd, a higher education research organization, found that over 1 million students in the United States were taking courses by distance education, many via the Internet, and that number was expected to triple by the turn of the century (Gubernick & Ebeling, 1997). With on-line courses, students can live at home and save on travel and the costs of maintaining two residences, and many can maintain their normal full-time jobs while completing their studies at their own pace and convenience.

Training and Development.   The need for learning does not cease when graduates enter the workforce. Oblinger and Rush (1997) predicted that by the year 2000, 95 percent of all workers will use some form of information technology in their jobs. They estimated that each employee will need to accumulate learning equivalent to 30 credit hours of instruction every seven years just to stay current. Executives of American Management Association member companies expected use of the Internet for training and development purposes to increase more than 270 percent between 1997 and 1999 (American Management Association, 1997). Bassi, Benson, and Cheney (1996) identified revolutionary advances in delivery technologies as one of the top 10 trends in corporate training. They noted the "almost unlimited" potential of the Internet for reaching multiple sites with training events, and that the Internet has "tremendous advantages over current CBT [computer-based training] technology in both cost and convenience."

Access in the workplace is generally not an issue. White-collar employees in most U.S. corporations either have direct access to the Internet or enjoy Internet-like functions through restricted-access company networks called *intranets,* and over half of all small businesses in the United States have Internet connections. An increasing number of partnerships are being established between corporate training units and higher education institutions, with universities providing customized training programs delivered via the Internet and videoconferencing.

◆ WHAT IS THE INTERNET?

A basic understanding of what the Internet is and how it works can be helpful to distance educators in their quest to use it effectively. The Internet is not a single, clearly defined entity, but a meganetwork of interconnected networks that share a common language, TCP-IP (transmission control protocol/Internet protocol). (A *protocol* is an electronic language that computers use to communicate with one another and exchange data. Protocols are roughly analogous to the languages humans use to communicate and exchange information.) In mid-1997, the BBN Corporation (1997), one of the Internet backbone network operators in the United States, estimated the worldwide total number of networks connected to the Internet to be 70,000. Moreover, these networks are in a perpetual state of evolution. Jack Rickard (1997), editor of *Boardwatch*

Magazine's Directory of Internet Service Providers, described the Internet as "a complicated matrix of connections in a constant state of upgrade with some 3,600 vendors making changes on a daily basis" (p. 1).

Internet Management

The Internet has no international headquarters or mailing address, no chief executive officer or board of directors, no stockholders to whom it must be accountable, and no toll-free number to call for information. This is not to say that the Internet is an anarchy, although some cynical observers may disagree. Much of the planning and coordination responsibility is assumed by the Internet Society, an international, nonprofit organization established for the purposes of "global cooperation and coordination for the Internet and its internetworking technologies and applications." Founded in 1991, the society facilitates the development and implementation of Internet standards and policies and holds oversight responsibilities over several important boards and task forces that address Internet issues.

Among these are the Internet Engineering Task Force (IETF), the protocol engineering and development arm of the Internet, and the Internet Architecture Board (IAB), responsible for the overall structure of the network. Addressing responsibilities are assumed by the Internet Assigned Numbers Authority (IANA) for Internet Protocol (IP) numbers (the four-element 123.456.78.90 addresses) and the Internet Network Information Center (InterNIC) for domain name system (DNS) addresses (somebody@somewhere.edu) and registration processes. Although some national governments restrict access and practice censorship, in general the existing oversight bodies are concerned with technical and network management matters rather than what information is placed on the Internet, who puts it there, and who has access to it. This is an important issue for students and teachers using the Internet for educational purposes, because no quality-control mechanism exists to ensure that information found on the Internet is accurate and unbiased, and that it may be freely viewed by the fainthearted.

Evolution of the Internet and Its Services

The Internet has its roots in the ARPANET, a network created in 1969 to link the computing systems of military and other government agencies to those of their research partners around the United States, including universities and corporate contractors. As the ARPANET grew, important technologies such as the TCP-IP, electronic mail, and Ethernet were developed to enhance its capabilities. In 1985, the National Science Foundation (NSF) established the NSFNET, a high-speed data transmission network that interconnected a series of NSF-funded supercomputers across the United States, and invited other networks running the TCP-IP to connect to it, including the ARPANET participants. This NSFNET national backbone and its affiliated networks became known as the Internet, and 1985 is generally regarded as the Internet's birth year. The ARPANET was absorbed into the Internet and ceased to exist in 1989.

A simultaneous but separate development was the evolution of the Because It's Time Network (BITNET), founded as a general-purpose academic network in 1981 by the City University of New York and Yale University. BITNET ultimately grew to include

about 600 educational institutions in the United States and was affiliated with networks in Canada, Europe, and other parts of the world. BITNET used a different protocol (RSCS/NJE) and therefore technically was not part of the Internet, but it interconnected with the Internet through "gateways" that functioned as translators between the two protocols. Mention of BITNET in this chapter is important for two reasons. First, BITNET was the first computer network available for widespread academic use. Hundreds of thousands of college faculty members and students became acquainted with international computing networks and their capabilities through BITNET. Second, BITNET mainframes hosted the LISTSERV mailing list management software that enabled both BITNET and Internet users to participate in on-line, asynchronous group discussions on thousands of topics. BITNET finally ceased operations in late 1996, as its functions also became absorbed into the Internet.

The Internet itself continued to expand through the 1980s, but for educators its primary functions remained electronic mail and on-line discussion groups, file transfers (using file transfer protocol, or ftp software), and remote access to computers ("remote login," commonly through telnet software). Use of the Internet at the K–12 level was minimal during this period, primarily because of access issues, although some schools were engaged in innovative e-mail exchange programs with other schools all over the globe.

In the early 1990s, two types of menu-driven server systems emerged that demonstrated the compelling nature of an on-line information database presented in a user-friendly environment—Wide-Area Information Server (WAIS) and Gopher. Thousands of Gopher sites were established worldwide, and for a time Gopher accounted for a substantial portion of all Internet traffic. WAIS and Gopher laid the groundwork for what was to become the "killer" application of the 90s, the World Wide Web (WWW).

The WWW was conceived by Tim Berners-Lee of the European Center for Particle Research (CERN) as a means of sharing data among scientists and was first used in 1989. The Web did not become a standard desktop icon until four years later, when the National Center for Supercomputing Applications (NCSA) at the University of Illinois unveiled Mosaic as an all-purpose WWW "browser." Within a year, more than 2 million persons around the world had downloaded Mosaic, and when Netscape appeared as the next-generation Web browser in late 1994, interest in the Web spread even more dramatically. As access grew, the number of Web sites on-line increased exponentially—from just 130 in June 1993 to 50,000 by November 1995 and over 3 million by mid-1998.

The World Wide Web brought the "point and click" technology of the desktop computer to the Internet. While such features as graphics, photographs, audio, and video were possible with Gopher, the Web was the first Internet application to integrate them into a single screen along with text. The use of multifont text also became possible. Perhaps the most dynamic feature of the Web was hypertext, the ability to link words, phrases, or graphics with other files, located on the same server or on someone else's server on the other side of the world. As a result, Web page developers could easily organize information from multiple sources and make any of it accessible to users with the single click of a mouse.

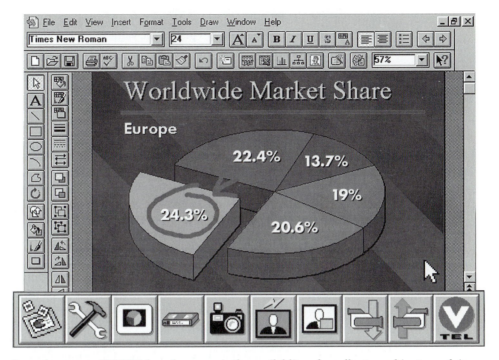

One advantage of WWW-based courses is the availablity of excellent graphics to explain key concepts.

The addressing system developed by Berners-Lee for the Web, ultimately called the uniform resource locator (URL), included three elements:

[protocol]://[host computer]/[file location]

The WWW protocol, hypertext transfer protocol (http), became the most popular by far, but the URL structure also permitted use of the Gopher, ftp, telnet, and WAIS protocols. The two elements following the double slash identified the name of the computer on the Internet upon which the desired information rested and the location of the information within the file structure of that computer. Browser vendors quickly added electronic mail capability and access to the popular Usenet newsgroups, making Web browsers all-purpose tools that revolutionized the way people used the Internet.

Before Mosaic and Netscape turned the Internet into a playground for the masses, interest had been limited primarily to the education and research communities. The rapid growth and powerful capabilities of the Internet quickly caught the attention of the commercial sector. A survey by the International Data Corporation (IDC) found that by the end of 1996, about 80 percent of all Fortune 500 companies had set up Web sites, up from 34 percent in 1995; and over half of all U.S. companies, regardless of size, had a Web presence (IDC, 1997). According to the IDC, commerce on the WWW expanded from a negligible amount in 1995 to $1.1 billion in 1996 and to an estimated $5.5 billion in 1997. Some estimates placed the value of Web commerce at over $300 billion by the year 2002.

Structure of the Internet

The potential for commercialization of the Internet led to a radical change in the network's architecture, as the National Science Foundation decided it should not continue to fund the backbone infrastructure in competition with private telecommunications carriers. A new structure was put in place by April 1995, and the NSFNET was retired. The transition to commercial backbone operators was seamless and unnoticed by most Internet users. Rickard (1997) described the current Internet structure in the United States as having five levels.

Level 1   Interconnect level network access points (NAPs). Four NAPs have been established—in San Francisco, Chicago, Washington, DC, and New York—where the national backbones interconnect and exchange data traffic. Four metropolitan area Ethernet (MAE) systems also serve as de facto NAPs, and the U.S. government operates three additional access points for its own traffic.

Level 2   National backbones. Rickard described a national Internet backbone provider as "a company that has physically located a high-speed TCP-IP router in a number of cities, and then leased high-speed data lines from long distance exchange carriers to link the routers—thus forming a national " 'backbone' connecting those cities" (p. 7). The winter 1998 *Boardwatch Directory of Internet Service Providers* listed 41 companies providing national backbone services in the United States alone, including CompuServe, IBM, MCI, and Sprint.

Level 3   Regional networks. Regional networks operate backbones on a smaller scale, typically within a state or among adjacent states, connecting to one or more national backbones. Rickard noted that many of the existing regional networks have been around since the NSFNET days.

Level 4   Internet service providers. This is perhaps the most important component for distance educators. The individual Internet service providers (ISPs) are connected to regional networks and provide dial-up or hard-wired access to the Internet at the local level. These are the companies that provide direct Internet access to schools, businesses, private homes, and other community entities such as libraries, churches, and government offices if not available through other networks. ISPs have been largely responsible for the worldwide Internet boom.

Level 5   Consumer and business market. Rickard included this level to illustrate that "each time a small office leases a line to an Internet Service Provider's point-of-presence, it has in fact extended the Internet by that number of linear feet" (p. 9). Dial-up ports maintained by companies and educational institutions so that employees and students can connect from home or on the road also extend the Internet.

Further Internet Discussion

Further discussion of the Internet is beyond the scope of this chapter. A list of Web sites that offer additional information about the Internet can be found at the end of this chapter. Unfortunately, as the World Wide Web continues to evolve, Web sites tend to come and go, or at least change their on-line locations. The URLs provided in the list were verified shortly before this book went to press, but readers are cautioned that long-term accuracy cannot be assured.

◆ OVERVIEW OF WWW/INTERNET-BASED DISTANCE EDUCATION

The emergence of the Internet as a delivery tool for distance learning comes at a time when education itself is undergoing a significant transformation. The teacher-centered "sage on the stage" model that has dominated education for centuries, or the "sage in a box" model (Bourne, McMaster, Rieger, & Campbell, 1997) as it often applies in video-based distance education, is slowly giving way to a learner-centered paradigm, with the teacher in the role of "guide on the side." Diana Oblinger (1994), Manager of Academic Programs and Strategy for IBM, observed the following transitions.

◆ From lecturing to coaching
◆ From taking attendance to logging on
◆ From distribution requirements to connected learning
◆ From credit hours to performance standards
◆ From competing to collaborating
◆ From library collections to network connections
◆ From passive learning to active learning
◆ From textbooks to customized materials

Barr and Tagg (1995) drew similar conclusions. They noted that the focus in the learner-centered paradigm shifts from the delivery of instruction and courses, passive learning, and competition to the creation of learning environments, active learning, and cooperation. Learning comes under the control of the student, the time at which learning takes place becomes variable, and a "live" teacher is no longer required. These are the very foundations upon which the concept of asynchronous learning networks (ALNs) is built. An emerging model for on-line distance education, ALNs attempt to move beyond the simple transfer of the conventional face-to-face classroom to the Internet. A well-conceived ALN-type course creates an on-line environment that includes all modes of learning appropriate for the specific educational goals being addressed. The idea that learning can take place at any time, anywhere, as in Coldeway's "different-time, different-place" context described in Chapter 1, is central to the ALN concept.

Not all use of the Internet has to be as sophisticated as a high-end ALN course. Courses offered through text-based applications have been around since the early days of BITNET and are still being offered. The Internet may also be used as a supplement to courses delivered primarily by video, audio, and even print. For example, courses offered through video networks often include on-line discussion groups as well as learning materials and assignments on the WWW.

Clarification of Terminology

Two terms frequently used to describe on-line learning systems are *asynchronous learning networks* and *computer-mediated communication.* The terms apply to similar concepts but have subtle differences.

Asynchronous Learning Networks.

An ALN is defined by the ALN Web site, maintained by the Center for Innovation in Engineering Education at Vanderbilt University, as "a people network for learning that is largely asynchronous. It combines self-study with substantial, rapid, asynchronous interactivity with others. In ALN learners use computer and communications technologies to work with remote learning resources, including coaches and other learners, but without the requirement to be on-line at the same time." The collaborative component is further emphasized by Odin (1997), who describes ALN as "any technology enabled collaborative learning environment using remote resources that can be accessed from anywhere at anytime and yet create a community of learners who are actively interacting, sharing ideas, learning, and helping each other learn."

ALNs represent the broader application of instructional technology described in this section. An ALN may include not only computer-based activities but also audio, video, print, and any other available tools for learning. Moreover, although asynchronous learning networks are frequently associated with distance education, an ALN may be employed as a component of a face-to-face course or as a nontraditional means of instruction with students or trainees within a single campus or company. This chapter is written primarily from the perspective of an ALN-type distance education delivery system.

Computer-Mediated Communication.

According to G. M. Santoro (1995), "Computer-Mediated Communication (CMC) is the name given to a large set of functions in which computers are used to support human communication. CMC can be defined narrowly or broadly, depending on how one defines human communication. At its narrowest, CMC refers to computer applications for direct human-to-human communication. . . . At its broadest, CMC can encompass virtually all computer uses" (p. 11). CMC thus is similar in many ways to asynchronous learning networks but is a slightly more narrowly defined term. ALNs use CMC as conversation, collaboration, and general learning tools but also employ noncomputer media such as fax machines and audio and video technologies (Sener, 1997). Like ALNs, CMC may also be used as a supplement to conventional face-to-face courses or video-based distance education.

Santoro (1995) described three broad categories of CMC functions. *Conferencing* provides direct communication among learners and with the instructor, using such tools as electronic mail, Internet mailing lists, newsgroups, and bulletin boards. *Informatics* is the term used by Santoro to refer to organized information resources maintained on-line to support learning, such as library catalogs, electronic reserves,

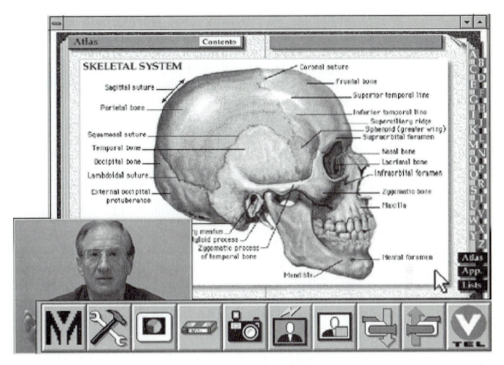

When WWW-based systems are used, learners can study any time and any place they choose.

on-line indexes and databases, and now the World Wide Web. *Computer-assisted instruction* (CAI) consists of the interactive learning and management tools that facilitate student achievement of course objectives. These may be accessed on-line or made available for use on the students' own computers.

Advantages of Internet-Based Courses

The advantages of Internet delivery of courses and training sessions, compared with conventional face-to-face teaching, are numerous.

◆ Unless access is deliberately restricted, courses could be available to any qualified individual in the world with a properly equipped computer and an Internet connection. Students can participate from school, home, office, or community locations.

◆ Asynchronous course components are available 24 hours a day, at the learner's convenience, and are time-zone independent.

◆ Students can work at their own pace.

◆ Course materials on the WWW and most group communications software are distributable across multiple computer platforms; it makes no difference if users are on PC/Windows or Macintosh computers.

◆ The technology is relatively easy for students to use.

◆ Learning resources are available across the entire Internet.

◆ On-line course materials, particularly those on course Web sites, are easy to update or modify, providing student access to current information.

◆ The Internet can provide a student-centered learning environment, if the materials and methods are designed to take advantage of the interactivity the Internet provides.

◆ The Internet promotes active learning and facilitates students' intellectual involvement with the course content.

◆ A well-conceived ALN course provides a variety of learning experiences and accommodates different learning styles.

◆ Students become skilled at using Internet resources, a factor that may improve employment options upon graduation.

◆ When personal identities remain concealed, all students, regardless of gender, ethnicity, appearance, or handicapping condition, are on equal ground.

◆ Corporate training programs conducted via the Internet can yield significant savings in employee time and travel costs, and training can be conducted on a "just in time" basis.

Limitations of Internet-Based Courses

The limitations of Internet course delivery may also be substantial.

◆ Access may still be a problem, especially in rural and lower socioeconomic areas, contributing to a technology "haves and have-nots" situation (Berge & Collins, 1995). Even if the Internet is available, many potential students do not have ready access to computers.

◆ Traffic congestion on the Internet can be a major problem, particularly at peak times during the day and among students dialing in via slow modems. The WWW is rapidly becoming known as the "World Wide Wait."

◆ Courses may focus on the technology rather than the content.

◆ Well-designed Internet-based courses may be labor-intensive to develop, requiring time and personnel resources not available to most instructors.

◆ The instructor may have to accept a new teaching paradigm, that of facilitator and manager of learning rather than as a dispenser of information.

◆ Although today's students as a whole are more technologically literate than ever before, many are technophobes who find the Internet confusing and intimidating.

◆ The active learning emphasis of Internet-based courses may be difficult for students conditioned by previous courses to be passive.

◆ Unless access restrictions are put in place, course materials and discussion groups on the Internet may attract undesired nonstudent participants. This is a problem in some Web courses that are not password-protected.

◆ Copyright violations on course Web pages sit in plain sight for viewing by the rights holders and their attorneys.

◆ Some topics may not adapt well to delivery by computer.

◆ Bandwidth limitations make it difficult to present advanced technologies, such as video, multimedia, and memory-intensive graphics, over the Internet.

◆ On-line courses require students to take more responsibility for their own learning. To be successful, students must be motivated, be self-directed, and have the self-discipline to participate (Hiltz, 1994). This is difficult for some students.

◆ While responses to questions may be instantaneous in the conventional classroom, feedback may be delayed by hours or even days in an asynchronous, on-line learning situation (Hiltz, 1994).

◆ The support infrastructure, providing training and technical assistance to both students and instructor, is often minimal or nonexistent. Instructional design support during the conceptualization and development of a course is also frequently unavailable.

Components of WWW/Internet-Based Courses

Delivery of instruction via the Internet, particularly complete courses for which academic credit is given, should be viewed within the broader context of an effective distance education system. Anthony Kaye (1981) identified four subsystems that compose such an endeavor. The *regulatory subsystem* consists of the management, decision-making, planning, funding, and evaluating processes, normally the responsibility of the administrators of the program and of the institution. The *course subsystem* includes course design and the production, distribution, and reception of the learning materials, along with management of the communications system maintained for course interaction. The *student subsystem* is responsible for admitting students and then managing and controlling their progress through the course. The *logistical subsystem* includes the purchasing and maintenance of equipment and software and the employment and training of personnel. As in any system, each of these subsystems must function effectively, both independently and in synchronization with the other subsystems, for the system as a whole to operate as it should.

This model provides insights into the factors that make an Internet course successful. Effective management is essential and depends heavily upon administrative support for funding, staffing, and resolution of issues that arise when an alternative instructional delivery system is introduced. For example, conventional colleges and universities are heavily bound by tradition. The credit hours awarded for a course are typically determined by the number of face-to-face contact hours. How are credit hours determined in an asynchronous, self-paced, on-line course with no face-to-face meetings? Can the campus curriculum committee be convinced that a proposed course designated for the Internet carries the same academic rigor as an on-campus course? If the admissions office requires that new students present evidence of measles shots, is this policy enforced for on-line students participating from Hong Kong and South Africa (suggesting perhaps that measles is contagious through cyberspace)? Conservative institutions can easily find any number of barriers to discourage innovative faculty from proposing courses in nontraditional structures.

Kaye's model identifies other issues that contribute to the success or failure of an on-line academic program, especially at the college level. If on-line courses are part of organized degree curricula, remote-site students who pay full tuition (and probably a distance education surcharge as well) should be entitled to the same level of support services as residential students, including advising and counseling. For example, a student who has been away from college for a few years may have rusty study skills. Assistance should be available on-line. Off-campus students should have access to financial aid, career exploration and placement services, and peer support groups. The logistical subsystem should provide technical support and training to students as well as faculty.

The course subsystem is particularly important. Any successful distance education program, whether delivered via the Internet, a video network, or any other technology, begins with well-conceived and well-organized courses. It is impossible to take weak teaching from the conventional classroom and improve it simply by moving it on-line. Placement of course materials on the Internet, such as the syllabus, lecture outlines, announcements, sample exams, assignment information, and study tips, does little more than change the distribution method for those resources. The Internet is at its best when its powerful capabilities are used to enhance learning, and these are the features that differentiate between mediocre teaching and highly effective teaching in an on-line environment. The course subsystem must account for the following.

Delivery of Course Content.

The traditional textbook may be equally appropriate in an on-line course. Course content may also be distributed via electronic mail or placed on a course Web page. Copyright-cleared videotapes or audiotapes, CD-ROMs, and computer disks may be part of the course materials purchased by students. During the course planning stage, the instructor needs to consider what behaviors are expected of the students at the end of the course (the learning objectives), what information is required for the students to meet those objectives, and what is the most effective, efficient means of getting that information to the students.

Active Learning Experiences.

Learning theorists today recognize that active learning is required before students can fully comprehend the course content and be able to apply it to life situations. As Chickering and Gamson (1987) explained, "Students do not learn much just by sitting in class listening to teachers, memorizing prepackaged assignments, and spitting out answers. They must talk about what they are learning, write about it, relate it to past experiences, apply it to their daily lives. They must make what they learn part of themselves" (p. 5). Students participate in active learning through interaction, either with the instructor and other students on a person-to-person basis via on-line discussions or with the subject matter of the course itself.

Numerous tools are available to facilitate on-line discussion and will be described below. Interactivity with the course content is best enabled on the World Wide Web through assignments that require students to make use of Web resources or custom-designed learning experiences requiring student intellectual activity. For example, animation tools that work with Web browsers can provide simulations to which students respond. Some wonderfully creative learning activities have been developed using "plug-ins," third-party software applications that extend the capabilities of a Web browser and allow instructors to include more complex learning materials in their course Web pages. Indeed, the Web offers extraordinary opportunities for simultaneous interaction with people and subject matter, such as student participation in ongoing dialog with astronauts or explorers during scientific expeditions, in conjunction with content-rich Web sites.

Access to Learning Resources.   Santoro (1995) listed *informatics,* organized on-line information resources, as one of the three primary components of a course offered by computer-mediated communication. An on-line course should provide remote students with a means of accessing all the resources necessary to complete course assignments. This is not as difficult a task as it might seem. Copyright-cleared materials can be placed directly on course Web pages. The Web itself provides a wealth of resources, including sites that provide search tools to help students identify books, periodical articles, and other print sources for potential use in course written assignments. More than 4,000 journals and newsletters are available on-line, most of which provide article abstracts if not full text. Those materials not on the Web can be obtained from local or regional public libraries, by interlibrary loan if necessary. If quick turnaround time is desired, on-line sources such as UnCover enable students to identify journal articles and order them through the Web for receipt via express package delivery services. The accessibility of these resources should be made known to students early in the course.

Submission of Course Assignments.   Means can be provided for the submission of course assignments. The postal service may be one option, depending upon the geographic distribution of the students. Many assignments can be submitted in electronic form, either as attachments to electronic mail messages or via input tools such as forms on course Web pages. Electronic submission results in the quickest feedback to students, particularly if the system provides for immediate evaluation.

Student Evaluation.   Every method of student assessment used by faculty in conventional face-to-face teaching should be available to a Web course instructor as well. The traditional objective test can be administered using the forms capability of a Web page, although this type of examination rarely reflects the actual application of course material in real-world situations, and exam security becomes a serious issue unless the course Web site permits the random selection of test items from a fairly large pool. (Nothing prevents the first students taking an on-line exam from sharing the questions with others.)

Other means of student evaluation, including essay and take-home exams, homework assignments, term papers and projects, class presentations (which may be delivered by e-mail or Web pages), and class participation, are equally appropriate for an on-line course. Self-evaluation may be an assessment component in the case of nontraditional students. A common criticism of on-line courses is that the instructor has no way of knowing if the student actually did the work, but the same question may be asked of many assignments in a conventional class as well.

On-Line Help.   As noted above, an effective support system for students is an essential component of an on-line course. Support begins with the instructor, who may conduct "virtual" office hours via electronic mail. Many faculty who teach Internet courses check their e-mail several times a day. On-line tutoring should be available from a course teaching assistant or central tutoring service on the campus. Advising, counseling, and other support services should also be provided, commensurate with those available to on-campus students.

Course Evaluation.   Course evaluation is particularly important in courses delivered by nontraditional means. Evaluation may be *formative* or *summative*. Formative evaluation is conducted for the purpose of identifying weaknesses and making improvements. If the course is to be offered again via the Internet, formative evaluation may be conducted at the end of the course. Under any circumstances, students should be surveyed during the course, preferably before midterm, to determine if changes can be made or additional assistance provided. Questions should be made specific to the course but should include the following general ideas.

◆ Are you having problems with the course delivery system? If yes, what are they?
◆ Are the course materials clear and helpful? If not, what suggestions can you make for improvement?
◆ Are the course communication tools working OK for you? If not, what problems have you encountered and how can they be fixed?
◆ Do you feel you are receiving feedback on a timely basis?
◆ Are you having problems communicating with the instructor?

Summative evaluation is normally conducted at the end of the course for the purpose of determining worth or merit. Administrators may use this information in decision making regarding subsequent iterations of the course and even institutional plans and policies related to future use of the Internet for distance education. Factors examined often include the level of student achievement, student satisfaction with the course, response to the course among potential students (did it reach the students expected to enroll?), performance of the Internet as a delivery system, and whether the course made or lost money.

◆ INTERNET COMMUNICATION TOOLS

Numerous tools are available to facilitate on-line learning, ranging from use of electronic mail and Internet mailing lists to fully integrated Web course software providing content presentation, communication systems, testing, and course management, all in the same package. To help illustrate the big picture of the types of tools available, this section is divided into Web and non-Web applications, with non-Web, computer conferencing tools further divided into synchronous and asynchronous systems, but these distinctions are not pure. A single course may use a variety of these tools, and applications such as World Wide Web browsers cross over these artificial boundaries.

Computer Conferencing (Non-Web)

Computer conferencing as a delivery system for distance education courses dates from 1981 and achieved fairly widespread use by the middle of that decade. It is still fairly common, although much activity now has shifted to the Web. Collins and Berge (1997) noted many advantages to computer conferencing as a tool for on-line learning, in-

Modern desk-top systems permit connecting multiple sites for conferences involving the instructor, content specialists, and students.

cluding convenience for both faculty and students, independence of time and distance, and the ability to create virtual communities of learners regardless of location. Among the disadvantages are the nature of computer conferencing as a text-based medium that tends to favor the well-educated and articulate, the potential for both students and teachers to go into information overload, and the need for technical support.

Synchronous Systems.

Synchronous activities are those in which the participants are on-line at the same time. Brainstorming and role playing are two functions particularly well suited for synchronous course tools, although the most common use is simple discussion of course content. Since synchronous activities must be scheduled in advance, they cancel the advantage of time independence. If students are separated by several time zones, finding convenient times for on-line meetings may be difficult.

Text-Based Systems.

The most common synchronous, text-based application is *chat,* available in a variety of forms. In a chat system, participants carry on a conversation in real time by keystroking their contributions. Some software posts the message after it has been typed, while others post it on a stroke-by-stroke basis, placing participants at the mercy of the slowest typist. Chat has been criticized because the messages often are not carefully considered and organized, and it is difficult to maintain the thread of a conversation.

A variation on chat is the MOO. MOO stands for MUD, object-oriented, with MUD an acronym for multiuser dimension or multiuser dungeon. MUDs originated with the Dungeons and Dragons game, in which the participants take roles in the game activities. Transferred to the Internet, MOOs are on-line, real-time, text-based, virtual reality environments in which each participant plays a role. MOOs have been devised for numerous scenarios and are accessed via telnet. Several variations on the MOO structure have evolved, including a WOO (Web, object-oriented).

Other Systems.

A wide variety of other systems have been developed for on-line conferencing via the Internet. Many of the more sophisticated were intended for use in the business community for meetings and corporate training. For example, Microsoft

NetMeeting is based on Internet videoconferencing technology, permits use of presentation graphics (Microsoft's own PowerPoint), and has a markerboard feature that allows participants to make on-screen pen strokes using the mouse. On-line videoconferencing is possible with a limited number of sites using products such as CU-SeeMe, developed by Cornell University and now marketed in an enhanced version by White Pine Software. CU-SeeMe requires that each participating site have a video camera mounted on or near the computer. Although functional cameras are available in the $300–400 range, this cost may be excessive for an individual student.

Another type of computer conferencing system is groupware, software that enables participants not only to converse but to share documents and collaborate on projects. Lotus Notes was the original groupware application, and numerous others are now on the market. Groupware is most commonly found in corporate settings rather than schools and colleges, although groupware features are incorporated into some of the integrated Web course tools to be discussed below.

Asynchronous Systems.

Asynchronous activities are those that do not take place in real time. Although most asynchronous, on-line courses maintain general schedules and set deadlines, within that framework students are able to participate at times convenient to them. This type of structure is particularly appropriate when students are spread across multiple time zones. Self-pacing and time for reflection before contributing to class discussions are important advantages of asynchronous course activities. The disadvantages include the lack of immediate feedback, the length of time required to carry on a discussion (often several days or longer), and the problem of information overload with an entire class posting messages on multiple discussion threads (Collins & Berge, 1997).

Electronic Mail and Mailing Lists.

By far, the most common asynchronous tool is electronic mail. E-mail on a one-to-one basis enables students to communicate directly with the instructor as well as with other students to discuss course questions and collaborate on projects. Group discussions can be maintained via Internet mailing lists (often inappropriately identified as "listservs"). A mailing list is exactly that—a computer file containing the e-mail addresses of subscribers interested in a specific topic, in this case the members of a class. Messages sent to the list mailing address are distributed by the listserver software to all subscribers on the list. Recipients can then reply back through the list to continue the discussion, with the response also distributed to all subscribers. Separate mailing lists may be established for individual work groups within the class.

The Web site Liszt (http://www.liszt.com/) maintains information about more than 80,000 publicly accessible Internet mailing lists. Lists are available on every conceivable topic from brine shrimp to tuba playing. Participation in one or more mailing lists on topics related to the course can provide excellent learning opportunities. Students can discuss current issues with professionals throughout the field and make important personal contacts.

Usenet Newsgroups.

Course discussions may also be maintained via Usenet newsgroups. Usenet (User's Network) is an independent network, not part of but accessible via the Internet, dedicated to on-line conversations on tens of thousands of topics.

A newsgroup can be established for a specific course. Students then access the newsgroup via a Web browser or newsgroup reader software.

Internet mailing lists and newsgroups have several important distinctions. Access to a mailing list can be controlled. Only subscribers receive the postings, which are distributed in the form of e-mail messages. Each list may be set so that subscriptions are closed (e.g., must be approved by the "list owner," which essentially keeps out non-class members) and so only subscribers can post (send messages) to the list. Mailing lists can be quite private. Newsgroups, on the other hand, are very public. Anyone who finds a newsgroup on Usenet can read the messages and contribute a posting, regardless of affiliation with or interest in the course. This may be a significant barrier if the course content includes sensitive or controversial material. Moreover, while mailing list messages come to the student via e-mail, students must remember to go to Usenet to read the course messages. The major advantage of Usenet over a mailing list is that a newsgroup normally requires less maintenance on the part of the teacher. Also, since newsgroups are open to public scrutiny, students may put more thought into their postings.

Computer Conferencing (Web)

Many of the computer conferencing systems that appeared during the past decade have been adapted for use with Web browsers. Software such as WebCaucus, CommonSpace, and Allaire Forums permits both large- and small-group communications to take place in on-line courses. These applications are especially beneficial when classes are broken into groups for discussions or collaborative projects. Woolley (1996) and LaLiberte and Woolley (1997) have written helpful summaries of Web conferencing tools and their functions. In addition, more than two dozen software products have come on the market since 1995 that provide fully integrated Web course development, delivery, and management systems. (These will be discussed below.) One-to-one electronic mail and group discussion tools, both synchronous (chat) and nonsynchronous, are common features of these products.

◆ TEACHING WITH THE WORLD WIDE WEB

With its broad capabilities and wealth of on-line resources, the Web has rapidly overtaken computer conferencing as the primary vehicle for on-line distance education. The Web may be a resource in an ALN-type course involving multiple technologies, or it could be a stand-alone delivery system.

The Web as a Learning Resource

During its most explosive growth period in 1996–1997, the Web was doubling in size about every 50 days, and a 1998 study by the NEC Research Institute counted more than 320 million Web pages (Kolata, 1998). While many of the new sites were student shrines to their favorite rock stars and others of dubious worth to young scholars, a wealth of

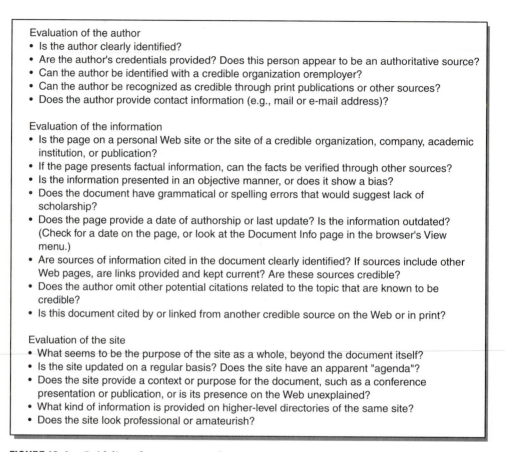

Evaluation of the author
- Is the author clearly identified?
- Are the author's credentials provided? Does this person appear to be an authoritative source?
- Can the author be identified with a credible organization oremployer?
- Can the author be recognized as credible through print publications or other sources?
- Does the author provide contact information (e.g., mail or e-mail address)?

Evaluation of the information
- Is the page on a personal Web site or the site of a credible organization, company, academic institution, or publication?
- If the page presents factual information, can the facts be verified through other sources?
- Is the information presented in an objective manner, or does it show a bias?
- Does the document have grammatical or spelling errors that would suggest lack of scholarship?
- Does the page provide a date of authorship or last update? Is the information outdated? (Check for a date on the page, or look at the Document Info page in the browser's View menu.)
- Are sources of information cited in the document clearly identified? If sources include other Web pages, are links provided and kept current? Are these sources credible?
- Does the author omit other potential citations related to the topic that are known to be credible?
- Is this document cited by or linked from another credible source on the Web or in print?

Evaluation of the site
- What seems to be the purpose of the site as a whole, beyond the document itself?
- Is the site updated on a regular basis? Does the site have an apparent "agenda"?
- Does the site provide a context or purpose for the document, such as a conference presentation or publication, or is its presence on the Web unexplained?
- What kind of information is provided on higher-level directories of the same site?
- Does the site look professional or amateurish?

FIGURE 10–1   Guidelines for screening information sources on WWW sites.

extraordinarily valuable resources has been placed on the Web in virtually every subject area. For example, the Internet was a prominent source of citations for this chapter. Internet technologies are changing so rapidly that most print publications on the topic (regretfully, including this one) have outdated material before they reach the bookstores. The most current source of information *about* the Internet *is* the Internet. The same is true with many other areas of study. But given the enormous quantity of unscreened and potentially erroneous or biased material on the Web, how can students sort out the wheat from the chaff? Assisting students in thinking critically when evaluating Web resources has become a major challenge for teachers. Figure 10–1 provides some guidelines to help with this process.

Dozens of search tools are available to assist students in locating desired information. Search tools may be classified into three general categories. A directory provides listings of sites organized in the form of a subject index, with many of the listed sites voluntarily submitted to the directory. A search vehicle is generally provided but only searches the directory's own database rather than the entire Web. Yahoo, LookSmart, and G.R.A.D.E.S. are examples of directory-type search tools. The second category, search engines, uses "robots" or "spiders" to search the Web for keywords specified by users. Even the most powerful of the search engines (HotBot) searches only about a third of the entire Web. Other search engines include AltaVista, Excite, InfoSeek, and Lycos. Meta search engines, the third category, search other search engines. Since search engines use different mechanisms for searching the Web and often provide different results, meta search engines can provide the most comprehensive list of hits. Examples of meta search engines include MetaCrawler, Highway61, Dogpile, Internet Sleuth, and All4One.

"Push" technology (also called channel-casting or web-casting) also has some promise for distance educators, although the initial high expectations for push technology have been largely unfulfilled. With the World Wide Web, users must seek out the information they desire, using search tools that typically turn up many more misses than hits. With push technology software such as PointCast and MyWay, service providers do the searching. They scan numerous news (such as Cable News Network, the *Wall Street Journal,* and the *New York Times*) and industry sources and "push" relevant articles to the user's client software via the Internet. The users specify the topics and industries to be scanned and set other parameters such as download times. Push technology allows class discussions and student projects to be based on the very latest information available, literally up-to-the-minute.

The Web as a Course Delivery Vehicle

In a distance education setting, a course that is completely on-line with no face-to-face meetings is often called a "virtual" course. Virtual courses without real-time chat components epitomize the concept of different time, different place, because students work largely independently, according to their own schedules. Communities of learners may be created via the communication tools, normally asynchronous, and group assignments involving students at various locations but communicating via small-group forums, e-mail, and even telephone, and sharing drafts through e-mail attachments, fax, or the postal service. Many faculty report that communities of learners are easier to form in virtual courses than in conventional face-to-face classes because of the necessity for students to become involved and communicate with one another.

Most virtual courses are now built around course Web sites. Every good Web course begins with a plan. In fact, the most critical steps in the development of a course for WWW delivery take place before the first page is authored. The teacher must think through not only how information (both administrative information and course content) is to be presented to students but, particularly, what learning activities will help students master the course material. In a sense, this is no different from a conventional course, but the delivery medium and the fact that students may be scattered over a broad geographic area change the teaching paradigm rather significantly. The importance of advance planning cannot be overemphasized.

Polyson, Saltzberg, and Godwin-Jones (1996) identified eight common components of quality course Web sites.

◆ An *on-line syllabus* enables the instructor to make changes as necessary and provides students with a complete and convenient means of obtaining current course information.

◆ *Personal home pages* can help to create communities of learners by enabling students to learn about each other, make contact, and share mutual interests.

◆ *Interactivity* can take the form of asynchronous chat sessions or asynchronous electronic mail, discussion groups, and/or bulletin boards.

◆ *Assignments* can be submitted via course Web sites and can be linked from content pages and the class schedule.

◆ An *announcements* section can provide course updates and other current information that students need to know.

◆ *Testing* modules can be provided in a variety of forms from simple self-help questions over content pages to complete unit mastery examinations.

◆ *Course management* features might include on-line grade books, test item analysis, course evaluation, and maintenance of student data such as user IDs and passwords, remote locations, and group assignments.

◆ *Course content* sections constitute the heart of the course and emphasize student intellectual involvement with the course material via active learning activities.

Content pages may contain not only text materials but also graphic illustrations, photographs, tables, audio, video, presentation graphics files (e.g., PowerPoint), animations, and virtual reality, as well as links to other Web sites relevant to the course topics.

Essential Site Design.   A course Web site must be designed so that students can easily navigate their way around it and move from any page or function to any other with no more than three or four mouse clicks. An easy-to-understand site organization is imperative, preferably with an index or table of contents accessible from every page. Navigation tools such as a list of internal links or Forward, Back, and Home buttons can be extremely helpful to students. Consistency in page design throughout the site also is important.

In addition to navigation tools and a clear title, each page could contain any of the following, depending upon the page function.

◆ Date of creation and revision
◆ Owner information (name and e-mail address)
◆ Page URL
◆ Copyright statement

The course "home page," the first page that students access, should contain links to the content presentation and communication components of the course, as well as to an index and/or table of contents. Assignment and quiz pages can be linked to from individual content pages or from the home page. The home page might also link to other pages of information that can be very helpful to students, such as the following.

◆ Course syllabus and schedule
◆ Technical requirements for the course, including computer specifications and a list of browser "plug-ins" or other software required for the course, and how to obtain these technical resources

- Instructions to students, including how to use the site and obtain assistance
- Biographical pages for each student enrolled in the course, to help students get acquainted with each other
- Course rules and policies
- Study guides
- Sample test bank
- Examples of assignments completed by past students in the course, to demonstrate expectations
- Course resources, such as archives of visual material found on content presentation pages
- Links to related Web sites

Authoring Course Web Pages.   All Web pages must be authored using hypertext markup language (HTML), the system of "tags" or codes that Web browsers read and interpret to display the appropriate information on our computer screens. While basic HTML is not difficult to master—correct use of 15 or 20 HTML tags is sufficient to create Web sites that are attractive and fully functional—most site creators now use Web page authoring tools such as PageMill, FrontPage, or HomePage. This software is relatively inexpensive and enables users to create fairly sophisticated Web sites with little training.

Integrated Web Course Systems.   Recognition of the World Wide Web's high potential for the delivery of instruction has led to an explosion of fully integrated Web course tools on the market. These products have in essence shifted many of the course design and page creation functions described above from the teacher to the software developer. These tools provide complete content presentation, communication, assignment submission, testing, and management functions in a secure environment, easily accessible to both instructor and students via a Web browser. They also provide standard page templates with convenient navigation tools that facilitate student movement around the site. Examples of these systems include LearningSpace, IntraKal, CourseInfo, TopClass, Web Course in a Box, and World Wide Web Course Tools (WebCT).

Using such a package, a typical student logs in, reads or downloads the current assignment, looks at the visuals, reads and responds to a thread of e-mail messages discussing the present topic, performs and submits the lab assignment for that material, takes a quiz or unit exam, sends a message to the instructor about the unfairness of question 8, and then logs off to surf elsewhere on the Web. The instructor logs in, modifies some upcoming course material to keep it updated, reads the student's complaint and runs an item analysis of the quiz to find out if that question has been a problem for other students, then clarifies the wording of the question and adjusts the grades accordingly, reads the e-mail messages posted to the course discussion group and sends a new message redirecting the train of thought, monitors how each student is doing in the course, and posts an announcement regarding the special guest participant next week. All this can be accomplished with a single piece of software.

Issues in Teaching Web Courses.   Teaching a course via the Web presents a number of issues that are nonexistent or of lesser concern in the conventional classroom.

Time commitment.   For example, the time commitment can be hefty in any Internet component of a course but can be extraordinary in Web-based teaching. Students must make a commitment to learn how to use the course delivery tools and adjust to a teaching and learning environment that is likely unfamiliar to them. They must take much more responsibility for their learning. In addition, they must develop the discipline to access the course communication tools on a regular basis (most likely daily) to read announcements and to keep from falling behind in discussions. For the faculty member, much more time is required for course planning and development. The teacher must also access the course site or communication tools daily to follow and orchestrate the discussions, receive assignments, solve problems, and serve other course management functions. Ongoing site maintenance and updating of links and student resources constitute another important teacher responsibility.

Security.   Course security is a significant issue. Faculty and administrators must decide whether, and how much of, a course should be open to the public and how much should be retained behind a password protection screen. Open access may be desirable for general information about the course and some content pages, as a means of attracting interest and possible fee-paying registrations. In some cases, all of the course content may be intended for the public—for example, university extension courses designed for outreach purposes but with participant assessment and fee-payment requirements for credentialing or receipt of continuing education credits. On the other hand, some components of Web-based courses should always be password-protected, including the grade book, quizzes and other student assessment measures, course communications (particularly chat room logs if controversial or sensitive information is discussed), and student biographies, photos, and other personal information.

Intellectual Property Rights.   As more and more schools and colleges engage in on-line course delivery, the intellectual property rights involved have become a major issue. At one level, as pointed out in Chapter 5, course developers must be sure that proper clearances are in hand for all copyrighted material posted on the Web site, including the work of former students. At a higher level is the basic matter of ownership of the intellectual property contained in the course. It has long been assumed at most locations that teachers/professors own the intellectual property expressed in conventional face-to-face courses. As these courses are developed for Web delivery and become in a sense "packaged," some institutions have taken the viewpoint that the courses are "works for hire," and therefore are the property of the school or college. This is not a popular stance among faculty unions. The ownership of on-line course materials and division of any royalties accrued should be negotiated between faculty and administration before any institution puts its courses on the Web.

Accessibility.   For many disabled students, "[t]he Web threatens to become the equivalent of a classroom building without an access ramp" (Young, 1998, p. A31). According to Young, many handicapped persons have found the Web so frustrating that they have stopped using it. While legal implications of the Americans with Disabilities Act (ADA) for educational institutions regarding course Web pages are unclear, course sites should be authored to maximize access opportunities for the disabled. For example, Web pages should be kept relatively simple. A page should contain no more text than necessary, especially preceding information of relative importance. The HTML coding for all images (including graphics and photographs) should contain "ALT" tags that provide brief text descriptions of the material. Audio and video files should be accompanied by optional links to pages containing transcripts for the hearing impaired. Burgstahler (1998) has provided additional suggestions for making Web pages universally accessible.

◆ THOUGHTS ON THE FUTURE OF ON-LINE LEARNING

As education itself is in a period of transition, so is distance learning. While distance education's roots are in the asynchronous form of correspondence study, the predominant electronic delivery systems of the 20th century have been synchronous—radio, telephone, broadcast television, audio networks, instructional television fixed service (ITFS), microwave networks, communications satellites, local cable systems, and compressed video and fiber-optic networks. The Internet can provide either form—asynchronous or synchronous—but for the most part it is used in an asynchronous mode; and as such, it has by far the greatest potential among all of today's delivery options for involving students intellectually with the course material in personal and productive ways.

The conclusion of Chapter 5 noted that the recent deregulation of the telecommunications industry will likely result in the blending of telephone, television cable, Internet access, and other electronic consumer services via a single connection to our homes, schools, and workplaces. On-line educational opportunities, whether for corporate executives, third graders, or nontraditional college students, will proliferate in this environment. We have only begun to explore the possibilities, but it is safe to say that the delivery of instruction by some form of networking, at all levels of education, will become more and more common as the 21st century progresses.

Self-Test Questions

1. Identify the major areas of potential growth for on-line distance education at the K–12 and higher education levels.
2. What international organization is responsible for planning and coordination of the Internet?
3. Why is BITNET significant in the history of on-line distance education?
4. What two software applications revolutionized the way people use the Internet?
5. In Rickard's description of the current Internet structure, which level promises to have the greatest impact on distance education, and why?
6. Differentiate between asynchronous learning networks and computer-mediated communication as delivery tools for distance education.

7. What are the four subsystems described by Anthony Kaye that must be accounted for in an Internet-based distance education course?
8. How can active learning experiences be built into an on-line course?
9. What are the primary advantages and disadvantages of synchronous activities in an on-line course with students spread over several time zones?
10. Under what circumstances would an instructor likely select a newsgroup over a mailing list as a tool for asynchronous course discussion?
11. What are two main advantages of the World Wide Web as a source of information for course assignments?
12. What three aspects of a Web document should be scrutinized in determining its credibility as a source of information?
13. What is the most imperative first step in developing a course Web site?
14. What is the advantage of using software such as WebCT or Web Course in a Box compared with developing a course Web site from scratch?
15. Name three important current issues in Web-based teaching.

Answers to Self-Test Questions

1. K–12: Promote course sharing among schools; provide curricula to home-schooled and alternative school children; enable adults to complete schooling through home study. Higher education: Provide courses and degree programs to students who are unable to attend college in residence; partner with industry in providing customized training programs via the Internet.
2. Internet Society.
3. BITNET introduced hundreds of thousands of college faculty members and students to international computing networks, hosted the LISTSERV mailing list management software, and enabled the first on-line courses in 1981.
4. Mosaic and Netscape.
5. Level 4, internet service providers, because they provide direct access to the Internet from homes, schools, local businesses, and other community locations.
6. ALNs incorporate CMC as conversation, collaboration, and general learning tools but may also employ noncomputer technologies; thus, asynchronous learning networks is a slightly broader term.
7. Regulatory, course, student, and logistical subsystems.
8. Active learning experiences may include technology-based interactive components integrated into course Web pages, assignments involving exploration and study of Web resources, synchronous and asynchronous on-line discussion groups, one-to-one on-line communication, conventional course assignments (e.g., research reports) incorporating Web sources, and a virtually infinite array of other activities.
9. Advantages: Provides live discussion opportunities similar to conventional classroom; creates virtual community of learners; effective for brainstorming and role playing. Disadvantages: Negates time independence and self-pacing features of on-line instruction; may be difficult to find on-line meeting time convenient

for all students; participants may be at the mercy of the slowest typist; text-based systems favor the well-educated and articulate.

10. Newsgroup might be a better choice if the instructor has minimal time for list management and the course content does not include sensitive or controversial material.
11. WWW contains a wealth of valuable information that may not be easily accessible elsewhere; Web may often be the most current source of information.
12. The author of the page, the information itself, and the overall site upon which the information rests.
13. Begin by planning the entire site, with special attention given to conceptualizing active learning activities.
14. Software provides content presentation, communication, assignment submission, testing, and course management functions in a secure environment, with standard page templates and navigation tools provided.
15. Any three of the following: time commitment required for students and instructor, course security, intellectual property rights, and accessibility of course materials to the disabled.

References

American Management Association (1997). *Business use of the Internet* [On-line]. New York: Author. Available: http://www.amanet.org/survey/netsurvey.htm.

Barr, R. B., & Tagg, J. (1995). From teaching to learning: A new paradigm for undergraduate education. *Change, 27*(6), 13–25.

Bassi, L. J., Benson, G., & Cheney, S. (1996). Position yourself for the future: The top ten trends. *Training & Development, 50*(11), 28–42.

BBN Corporation (1997). *Get smart: Customer tutorial* [On-line]. Available: http://www.bbn.com/getsmart/what.htm.

Berge, Z. L., & M. P. Collins. (1995). Overview and perspectives. In Z. L. Berge & M. P. Collins (Eds.), *Computer-mediated communication and the online classroom* (Vol. 1, pp. 1–10). Creskill, NJ: Hampton Press.

Bourne, J. F., McMaster, E., Rieger, J., & Campbell, J. O. (1997). Paradigms for online learning: A case study in the design and implementation of an asynchronous learning networks (ALN) course. *Journal of Asynchronous Learning Networks* [On-line] *1*(2). Available: http://www.aln.org/alnweb/journal/issue2/assee.htm.

Burgstahler, S. (1998). Making web pages universally accessible. *CMC Magazine* [On-line], January 1998. Available: http://www.december.com/cmc/mag/1998/jan/burg.html.

Chickering, A. W., and Gamson, Z. F. (1987). Seven principles for good practice in undergraduate education. *American Association for Higher Education Bulletin, 39*(7), 4–6.

Collins, M., & Berge, Z. (1997). *Facilitating discussion in online environments.* Workshop presented at the 13th Annual Conference on Distance Teaching and Learning, Madison, WI, August 1997.

Gubernick, L., & Ebeling, A. (1997, June 16). I got my degree through e-mail. *Forbes* [On-line], pp. 84–92. Available: http://www.forbes.com/forbes/97/0616/5912084a.htm.

Hiltz, S. R. (1994). *The virtual classroom: Learning without limits via computer networks.* Norwood, NJ: Ablex Publishing Corporation.

International Data Corporation (1997). *Information industry and technology update, 1997–98.* Framington, MA: Author.

Kaye, A. (1981). Origins and structures. In A. Kaye & G. Rumble (Eds.), *Distance teaching for higher and adult education* (pp. 15–31). London: Croom Helm.

Kolata, G. (1998). It's confirmed: Web's size bogs down searches. *The New York Times,* April 9, 1998, p. G3.

LaLiberte, D., & Woolley, D. (1997). Presentation features of text-based conferencing systems on the WWW. *CMC Magazine* [On-line], May 1997. Available: http://www.december.com/cmc/mag/1997/may/lalib.html.

Miller, T. E., & Clemente, P. C. (1997). *The 1997 American Internet users survey: Realities beyond the hype.* New York: Emerging Technologies Research Group.

Nua Consultants and Developers (1998). *How many online?* [On-line]. Dublin: Nua Consultants and Developers. Available: http://www.nua.ie/surveys/how_many_online/index.html.

Oblinger, D. G. (1994). *Transforming the academy to improve delivery of services: Redesign for reallocation* [On-line]. Available: http://www.hied.ibm.com/news/whitep/technote/hied/oblinger.txt.

Oblinger, D. G., & Rush, S. C. (1997). *The learning revolution: The challenge of information technology in the academy.* Bolton, MA: Anker Publishing Company.

Odin, J. K. (1997). *ALN: Pedagogical assumptions, instructional strategies, and software solutions* [On-line]. Available: http://www2.hawaii.edu/aln/aln_tex.htm.

Owston, R. D. (1997). The World Wide Web: A technology to enhance teaching and learning? *Educational Researcher, 26*(2), 27–33.

Polyson, S., Saltzberg, S., & Godwin-Jones, R. (1996). A practical guide to teaching with the World Wide Web. *Syllabus, 10*(2), 12–16.

Rickard, J. (1997, May). *Internet architecture* [On-line]. Available: http://boardwatch.internet.com/isp/internetarch.html.

Santoro, G. M. (1995). What is computer-mediated communication? In Z. L. Berge and M. P. Collins (Eds.), *Computer mediated communication and the online classroom* (Vol. 1, pp. 11–27). Creskill, NJ: Hampton Press.

Sener, J. (1997). Summary of the discussion on affordable ALNs: An online discussion. *ALN Magazine* [On-line], *1*(2). Available: http://www.aln.org/alnweb/magazine/issue2/sener_alntalk.htm.

Woolley, D. R. (1996, November). *Choosing web conferencing software* [On-line]. Available: http://thinkofit.com/webconf/wcchoice.htm.

Young, J. R. (1998, March 13). For students with disabilities, the web can be like a classroom without a ramp. *Chronicle of Higher Education,* p. A31.

Sources of Information About the Internet

An Atlas of Cyberspaces

http://www.geog.ucl.ac.uk/casa/martin/atlas/atlas.html
Atlas of maps and other graphic representations of the Internet, compiled by Martin
Dodge of University College London.

Internet Learner's Page

http://www.clark.net/pub/lschank/web/learn.html
Comprehensive source of Internet-related information, maintained by Larry
Schankman of Mansfield University.

Internet Mailing Lists Guides and Resources

http://www.nlc-bnc.ca/ifla/I/training/listserv/lists.htm ("I" is a capital i)
An extremely comprehensive source of information about Internet mailing lists,
maintained by the International Federation of Library Associations and
Institutions.

Internet Service Providers

http://boardwatch.internet.com/isp/
The on-line version of *Boardwatch Magazine's Directory of Internet Service Providers.*

Internet Society Home Page

http://www.isoc.org/
Information about the Internet itself and the society's mission and functions.

NetLearn: Internet Learning Resources

http://www.rgu.ac.uk/~sim/research/netlearn/callist.htm
Another comprehensive source of information about the Internet, from the School of
Information & Media, Robert Gordon University, Scotland.

Nua Internet Surveys: Latest Surveys

http://www.nua.ie/surveys/
Summaries of current Internet-related surveys conducted by research organizations
worldwide, compiled by the Irish consulting firm Nua Ltd.

Overview of the World Wide Web

http://www.cio.com/WebMaster/sem2_home.html
An "on-line seminar" describing what the WWW is and how it works, from
WebMaster Magazine.

What Exactly Is the Internet?

http://www.bbn.com/getsmart/what.htm
Another authoritative tutorial about the Internet, from the BBN Corporation, an
early ARPANET collaborator.

chapter 11

Assessment for Distance Education

CHAPTER GOAL

The purpose of this chapter is to present approaches for assessment of student learning.

CHAPTER OBJECTIVES

After reading and reviewing this chapter, you should be able to

1. Discuss the role of assessment in the instructional design process, especially for distance education.
2. Describe the characteristics of several types of traditional assessment activities and the appropriate uses of each.
3. Describe the characteristics of several types of alternative assessment activities and the appropriate uses of each.
4. Explain how the elements of assessment may be influenced by and integrated into a distance education environment.

◆ ASSESSING LEARNING GAINS

Mike is studying French via satellite and is preparing for his weekly conversation group during which he and other students talk with native speakers of the French language via audioconference. At 5:00 in the morning, Lakeisha logs on to a Web site set up for her U.S. government class to participate in a threaded discussion group that has been debating the purpose of the electoral college. Carlos opens his e-mail and finds his midterm essay test waiting, sent out this morning by his Renaissance literature professor, with instructions to complete the test and return it via e-mail within the next 24 hours. What do these students have in common? They're all involved in some form of learning assessment. Through their respective efforts, they are demonstrating their level of understanding of the subject matter. The above activities reflect the learning gains the individual students have made, and let their instructors know how well they're progressing.

While this chapter focuses on assessment in distance education, much of this discussion is not exclusive to distance education. Just as exemplary "distance" teaching resembles our best models of face-to-face teaching, assessing student achievement has a core of good practice that remains constant across a multitude of teaching/learning configurations.

◆ WHAT IS ASSESSMENT?

If assessment is a way to measure learning gains, what can we do with that measurement? Are there uses for the information? The answer is a definite yes. In fact, there are at least five ways that this knowledge can be used to facilitate learning, and there are many other uses that may indirectly influence the learning environment or help to formulate related policies. Some of the more "administrative" uses of assessment include program evaluation and improvement, justification for funding priorities, and reporting of long-term trends to state or federal entities. In a distance education environment, the results of assessment may sometimes be used to compare the academic performance of remote-site students with the performance of those at the origination site. Although this is not a particularly helpful comparison (we know that even if we could control the confounding variables, the results would very likely be "no significant difference"), it is often a necessary exercise to ease the worries of program administrators who must be able to "prove" that students at a distance are actually learning the material.

Probably the first use that comes to mind for student assessment is to enable the instructor to assign grades at the end of a course, unit, or lesson. While this is important (and, typically, is required of teachers) and often helpful in determining how to improve the instruction for future students, there are other, more direct, ways of enhancing teaching and learning.

Students gain a sense of control and can take on greater responsibility for their own learning if they know how well they're doing, compared with an established set of criteria. Frequent assessments, informal or otherwise, provide this scale. When the instructor has this information, he or she can provide remediation or correction where necessary, or determine if a student needs additional assistance. At the same time, this information helps the instructor to monitor the effectiveness of the instruction. If many students have difficulty with the same concept or skill, this could signal a lesson design problem. By using assessments carefully, the teacher can identify and address weaknesses or gaps in the instruction. When students encounter an assessment activity, they not only recall the needed concepts or skills, but reinforce them through application. This is especially important to remember if course content is highly sequential or hierarchical in nature. Frequent assessments help to emphasize the correct concepts and skills (necessary to advance through later material), and also pinpoint learner misconceptions that would eventually present obstacles to further progress.

Finally, assessments are often a motivational activity. Most learners want to do well, and knowing that they'll be held accountable for a body of knowledge or set of skills can be the nudge that keeps them on track. Many a teacher has adopted group discussions, pop quizzes, or in-class exercises to ensure that required readings or out-of-class assignments are completed on time.

Assessment and Evaluation

How does assessment differ from evaluation? These terms often are used synonymously, but in an instructional context they have different meanings and applications. Assessment, as explained above, denotes the measurement of progress toward a learning goal—for example, student performance compared with a desired level of proficiency at a task. In this chapter, the word *assessment* will be used specifically to refer to this process. Evaluation, on the other hand, suggests the attribution of significance or quality of the current status of a particular object or condition. As its root word, *value,* suggests, *evaluation* implies that a judgment will occur regarding the information that assessment activities provide. Summative evaluation of an instructional unit is a way of assigning value to a learning package; formative evaluation determines the level of quality of an unfinished product for purposes of revision and improvement. The techniques of assessment and evaluation may sometimes overlap, but their purposes make them distinct.

Assessment and Instructional Design

The role of assessment in the instructional design process is as a corollary to the development of learning objectives, and a precedent to the development and implementation of instructional strategies (Dick & Carey, 1995; Gagne, Briggs, & Wager, 1987). In this way, the assessment activities are matched to expectations, and instruction is then based on assessment plans. A less formal way of expressing this is: Figure out what learners should get out of the instruction, determine how you'll know whether or not they were successful, and then decide what they should do to reach that point. In this manner, "teaching to the test" becomes a desirable basis for instruction, because the test is a measure of what is considered important.

Unfortunately, this ideal is realized only occasionally, and assessments typically are created after the instruction is planned and often after it has been implemented. This doesn't preclude the use of objectives as a basis for determining progress, but care must be taken to ensure that the instruction has also been based on the same expectations and has not wandered from the original goals. If students prepare for an examination thinking, "What's going to be on this test?" or face an out-of-class assignment wondering what is expected of them, that may indicate that the objectives have been forgotten along the way. Those desired outcomes must act as a continuous thread that binds the instructional process together from beginning to end.

Characteristics of Good Assessments

As described in the previous section, assessment is one element of the teaching and learning process that grows from the determination of desired performance outcomes. It follows, therefore, that one of the characteristics of a good assessment tool is that it matches the objectives; learners know what to expect because they have already been made aware of what is important and how they will be expected to demonstrate their mastery of this knowledge or skill. The objectives, ideally, specify what the students will do to demonstrate their mastery of the content, how well they will be expected to perform this task, and under what special circumstances, if any, they should perform it.

Occasionally, instructors will find that a test item or exercise that they have created does not match the objectives, although they believe it to be an important skill or concept for learners to grasp. In this case, it makes sense to return to the list of objectives and consider the possibility that there are gaps or missing items. Herein is an excellent reason for creating assessment measures before implementing instruction. If there are gaps in the objectives list that become apparent only when developing an assessment activity, it is likely that the missing material will not have been included in the planned learning activities. Instructional design is conducted in an interactive manner that allows for enough flexibility to revise throughout the development process, but revisions during implementation are often more difficult and can confuse learners.

An assessment may, on the surface, match the objectives but still not reflect the student's progress. This characteristic, the degree to which an assessment provides an accurate estimate of learning gains, is known as *validity*. If a learner who has mastered the specified body of knowledge does poorly on the test, exercise, or project intended to measure this mastery, then that assessment is an invalid instrument or activity. Conversely, if learners who have not mastered the material perform well, then that assessment is not considered a valid predictor of learning, either. For example, test items intended to measure analogical reasoning may, instead, reflect the learner's reading ability if vocabulary level is not considered in test design. Or if a project is supposed to demonstrate the learner's understanding of due process in our judicial system, but an unrealistic time limit for completion is imposed, this assessment may indicate that some learners have not mastered the concepts when in fact they simply were not given adequate time to demonstrate their expertise.

A concept related to validity, and an important characteristic of good assessments, is *reliability*. Reliability refers to the stability of an instrument or activity; this could be thought of as how consistently the assessment measures learning gains. If students perform poorly, as a group, on one occasion and then do much better later, the predictability of this assessment is called into question. Or if learner mastery is measured by observation and scored by several different raters, the scores must be highly correlated to ensure consistency (also known as *interrater* reliability). Low reliability signals that the results are not dependable and could vary significantly from day to day.

A characteristic of good assessments that is especially important in distance education settings is *clarity* of expectations. This refers to how easy the assessment is for the learner to understand, whether the instructions are clearly written, and whether any special conditions are to be met. For many distant students, examinations will be proctored by someone other than the instructor ("I *think* this is supposed to be an 'open-book' test"), projects may be completed based only on the directions initially provided ("Well, she said we could pick any topic!"), and papers may be written according to instructions given in the course syllabus ("Was that 10 to 12 pages double-spaced or single-spaced?"). If the directions are not comprehensive, specific, and clearly worded, the assessment may ultimately prove useless.

Finally, while there are other criteria for judging the merits of a particular assessment, they all are designed to help answer the question "Does this assessment measure learning gains and allow an accurate generalization of results beyond the immediate situation?" In other words, a useful assessment reflects the learner's progress and understanding, as well as the transferability of skills and knowledge. The obvious purpose of an assessment is to document the direct results of instruction, but if the student performs a task in a learning environment but cannot do so elsewhere, the instruction has been futile.

Norm-Referenced and Criterion-Referenced Scoring

Once a student completes an assessment and it is scored or rated, there are two systems that are used to report this score. *Criterion-referenced scoring* is used when the rater compares the learner's performance with that of a predetermined set of standards, drawn from the learning objectives. The rater asks, "Did the learner master the content?" The score that is reported reflects this level of mastery. *Norm-referenced scoring*, however, reports these same ratings by comparing each student with the others who have completed the same assessment. The term *grading on a curve* reflects this type of scoring, and in this case the rater asks, "How well did the learner do compared with the others?"

There are appropriate uses for each type of scoring. If our concern, as teachers or instructional designers, is that each student master the course content, then their performance compared with one another is irrelevant; we need to ensure that they have performed well compared with our expectations by using criterion-referenced scoring. Norm-referenced scoring is used, appropriately, to report long-term trends and comparisons of extremely large groups of learners (e.g., nationwide or worldwide, in the case of some university preadmission examinations), but should never be used to determine grades or determine mastery of content. Grading on a curve just tells the teacher and learner how well students did relative to one another, but does not give a clue about whether anyone mastered any of the content.

◆ TRADITIONAL ASSESSMENT TOOLS

When considering how to determine if a student has achieved the desired level of content mastery, one of the first thoughts that might come to mind is to administer some kind of paper-and-pencil test. In this section, four of the more frequently used test styles—multiple choice, true/false, short answer or free response, and essay—will be described and their particular strengths and applications discussed.

Multiple-choice tests can be an efficient way to measure learning, especially if the objectives are written at a low level of cognitive effort, such as knowledge or comprehension, where students are expected merely to recall previously memorized information (e.g., state capitals, vocabulary words, or bones of the human skeleton). As objectives move up the cognitive processing scale toward analyzing and synthesizing (inferring relationships or creating models), multiple-choice test items get more difficult and time-consuming to create. Unfortunately, in many cases, instructors expect students to gain higher order thinking skills but then test them using items that only reflect comprehension, or maybe application, of the content area.

When writing multiple-choice items, the "stem" (usually written as a question or an incomplete statement) is presented along with one correct answer and several "distractors" (incorrect responses) in a list from which learners choose. Distractors should appear to be plausible answers and should include choices that are often confused with the correct answer, to ensure that students are discriminating among possible responses. When testing for higher order thinking, it may be necessary to direct students to select the "best answer" from those presented, rather than assume that there is only one correct answer to any given question. "All of the above" and "none of the above" responses should be avoided; these items and others that are unclear or obscure can be confusing and result in a score that does not reflect actual learning.

Multiple-choice questions can also be written with one stem and a list of responses from which students choose all that are correct. Or one set of responses can be used for several stems, with students selecting the correct response for each stem. In this case, there may be a mix of correct responses and distractors, and some of the responses might be appropriate answers for more than one stem.

One of the greatest advantages of multiple-choice testing is the ease of scoring and item analysis. These types of items (along with true/false) are considered "objective," because human judgment is unnecessary in scoring; i.e., an answer is either right or wrong and a subjective interpretation is not needed to determine the accuracy of each response. Where once nearly all multiple-choice tests were scored from optical scan forms ("bubble sheets") that were marked with the requisite No. 2 pencil, now inexpensive and easy-to-use testing packages that allow students to take the test electronically make even this obsolete. With appropriate password protection and student verification (to ensure that the person taking the test is, in fact, the one who is getting credit for it), these packages are a major leap forward for distant learners and their teachers. No more of the formerly inevitable turnaround wait time and massive stacks of papers to score and mark. However, as mentioned previously, multiple-choice tests are difficult and time-consuming to create unless the subject matter is at a very low level of cognitive difficulty. Other weaknesses include the possibility of students guessing correctly or responding to verbal associations that do not require an understanding of the content.

Another type of objective test item is the *true/false* (sometimes called *alternative response*) question. True/false items typically are used when objectives call for students to determine which of two possible responses is appropriate—whether a statement is true or false, fact or opinion, or some modification of this. One should use these items when there can be only two possible responses (yes or no, agree or disagree, valid or invalid, etc.), one of which is correct. If you find it difficult to create an unambiguous stem that clearly will have only two possible answers, consider using another type of test item. Like multiple-choice items, true/false questions can be clustered by providing a stem that asks students to identify specific responses from a list of several possible answers. For example, the stem might ask, "Which of the following are synonyms for the word *synchronous?* Responses to be marked as "yes" or "no" could include "concomitant, sequential, coincident, simultaneous, consecutive."

Some obvious advantages exist for true/false items: They provide for simple, easy-to-automate scoring; test administration can be handled more quickly (many items can be answered in a short amount of time); and results usually do not depend heavily on the reading ability of the student. Unfortunately, guessing offers the learner a 50% chance of success; and when the stem statement is false, it can be difficult to determine if learners actually know the right answer or if they just knew that the statement given was incorrect. (One way to mitigate this effect is to require test takers to rewrite a false stem so that it becomes a true statement. This, in turn, reduces the ease of scoring, however.) True/false items, to be effective, must be precisely written and free of irrelevant information or verbal clues to the correct response. And, finally, avoid designing the test so that students may miss items simply because they think they are being tricked in some way (the use of all "true" statements on a test, for example). While this might test the strength of the learners' convictions in their responses, it may not provide a realistic measurement of learning.

Short-answer test items (sometimes called *free-response items* or *supply items*) straddle the fence between objective and subjective assessments. These items are written either as direct questions requiring the learner the fill in a word or phrase or as statements in which a space has been left blank for the a brief written answer. Because students can fill in any answer, care must be taken to create items that are precise and not open to a wide variety of interpretations. In some distance education environments this is crucial; test proctors at remote sites cannot be expected to answer questions about particular test items and what the instructor meant to say. Like multiple-choice tests, free-response items are mostly useful when learners are expected to recall information from memory, rather than analyze or synthesize complex concepts.

An advantage of free-response items is that learners must actually know the correct answer, as opposed to recognizing it among choices in a list. Also, tests can be scored by teaching assistants or those who know little or nothing of the content area. Like multiple-choice tests, electronic versions of a free-response test are easily created and delivered via e-mail or Web site, but scoring is more difficult to accomplish electronically.

The scoring system must include the desired correct answer, answers that are synonyms for the correct answer, and the likely misspellings that could appear. In a large class, however, it might still be more efficient to use automatic scoring and deal with the resulting problems as they arise.

Essay questions, or *extended response items,* provide the instructor with the greatest degree of flexibility and can be used to assess higher order learning, such as analyzing concepts or designing plans. Students also have greater freedom in providing an answer that shows their level of understanding and ability to present an organized response. Questions must, however, be written with a clearly stated "assignment" for students to complete. Vaguely worded essay questions not only make scoring of responses difficult, but may not provide a valid assessment of whether the student has achieved the desired learning goals. Once the question has been written, a scoring rubric should be created to assist in grading answers so that, even though the rating is subjective in nature, it remains criterion-referenced, and answers are judged according to their accuracy and completeness, rather than whether they are better or worse than another student's answer. For many students, it may be helpful to suggest how much time should be spent on each item or approximately how long the answer should be, to help them organize their time and use it wisely. Students in a distance learning environment can easily take advantage of electronic delivery of questions (either directly through electronic mail or from a static Web site) and then submit their responses via e-mail.

The two main advantages of essay questions are flexibility and the option of testing for high levels of learning outcomes, but there are several disadvantages that should be considered. The most readily apparent of these is that scoring of essay responses is extremely difficult and time-consuming. Students who are "test savvy" may be skilled bluffers (for example, the student who writes extensively about what he or she knows and then attempts to fit it to the question, relevant or not), and good writers tend to score well on essays, regardless of actual content. Conversely, poor handwriting or bad spelling can also pull scores down unfairly, although having students write their essays using word processing software can eliminate (or at least reduce) this problem. Also, because of the time required to write the essay, only a limited amount of material can be covered. For this reason, many test design experts (Gronlund, 1998) suggest mixing objective items, such as multiple choice, with some free-response and essay items to increase the amount of material that can be covered on a single test.

Using Traditional Assessments

The traditional types of paper-and-pencil tests—multiple choice, true/false, short answer, and essay—can be used successfully in a distance education setting when they are designed and administered appropriately. Electronic versions of these instruments help with the problems of scoring and turnaround that have been the bane of many a program's existence; but until computing facilities are widely accessible, this form of delivery could limit student enrollments to those individuals who own a computer or have reliable access to one.

Although traditional assessment instruments typically are administered in a classroom with accompanying time limits, there are valid reasons to consider using take-home tests, especially if testing for higher order thinking. If an objective for the course or unit specifies that learners will apply concepts in tasks requiring analysis, for example, one option is to provide essay questions that meet this criterion. The pressure to memorize facts, names, or dates is relieved, and students will have a chance to revise their responses to more accurately reflect their knowledge of the content. Also, this more closely mimics our use of these cognitive skills in real life—rarely is there a brief, strict time limit for this type of task, and the use of available resources is encouraged, not forbidden. The wise instructor, however, will suggest a page limit or word limit for responses, thus avoiding the volumes of prose that some overeager learners would be happy to supply.

When selecting which types of assessments to use, consider the types of learning outcomes desired (as stated in the objectives), the time allowed for testing, and the time allowed for scoring. One rule of thumb states that the longer it takes to construct a test, the less time it will take to score. Valid and useful multiple-choice items are difficult to write but can be scored automatically, whereas essay questions take less time to write but are time-consuming to score.

◆ ALTERNATIVE ASSESSMENT

The types of assessment measures described above are considered traditional tests. *Alternative assessment,* as its name implies, is a method of gauging student progress in ways unlike those just described. In academic circles, this term has taken on an even more specific meaning, in which assessments are considered "alternative" not simply because they are dissimilar to traditional ideas, but because they represent a constructivist or cognitive processing learning philosophy. Three approaches—authentic assessment, performance-based assessment, and constructivist assessment—have come to the forefront of this movement, with areas overlapping in each category.

Authentic assessment refers to tasks that simulate real-world challenges. Ideally, the student is presented with the full array of expectations for a task and is expected to engage in activities that reflect a meaningful response. Wiggins (1990) described an effective authentic task as one that includes " 'ill-structured' challenges and roles that help students rehearse for the complex ambiguities of . . . adult and professional life." These types of assessments emphasize the transfer of skills to unfamiliar situations beyond the classroom.

Performance-based assessment is, in fact, what it sounds like it is: expecting the learner to perform a skill. In addition, it may include determining what the learner knows *about* the skill itself. Some also include the criterion that assessments focus on higher-order thinking and critical reasoning. Simply requiring that the student perform a science experiment, for example, does not guarantee that critical thinking will occur. Exploring how learners arrive at their answers or why they performed the task in the manner they did will provide evidence of the desired cognitive activity. Some performance assessments will reflect a process (giving a speech, for example) or have no tangible outcome (speaking a foreign language).

Assessment activities that reflect a *constructivist approach* encourage students to choose their own mode of expression, to work collaboratively with others, to think about their learning, and to rethink and revise their ideas as they build their cognitive structures (Herman, Aschbacher, & Winters, 1992). The emphasis is on the creation of personal meaning and divergent thinking, which poses some interesting challenges for the instructor who has experience only with more traditional forms of testing or projects. This need not mean that assessment activities lack scholarly rigor, however, and allowing for variance in learning style, memory, and developmental pace may, in fact, require that learners actually take on greater responsibility for their progress toward the instructional goal.

Assessments may incorporate characteristics of these approaches singly or in varying combinations, but, for the sake of clarity, the term *alternative assessment* will be understood to encompass these ideals. Some examples of alternative assessments include portfolios, projects, and problem-solving activities.

Portfolio assessment, a means of collecting and judging examples of student work, has received considerable attention in educational circles in the recent past. A portfolio can consist of a wide variety of materials (papers, videotapes, computer files, etc.) reflecting generalized learning across disciplines, or it can be a more specific gathering of content-based materials, such as tests, worksheets, or art projects. One of the key elements of portfolio creation is that the student decides (typically with an instructor's guidance) what materials to include in the portfolio. Self-reflection, leading to the development of standards and the determination of criteria to use in selecting these materials, are integral components of this process. Identifying what constitutes the student's "best" work represents a level of self-assessment that requires thoughtful consideration of learning goals and progress toward significant milestones.

The increasing attention given to portfolio development can be attributed to a shift away from learning as the accumulation of knowledge to a perspective that emphasizes the application of cognitive skills such as evaluating, problem solving, and analyzing. When education was seen, by learners and their prospective employers, as a discrete event encountered in school and then left behind after the conferring of a diploma or degree, the school transcript with its notations of courses taken and grades awarded was sufficient evidence of learning. Now, however, employers demand workers who not only can apply these important cognitive skills but will continue to learn on their own as the world's information base expands. The portfolio offers tangible evidence of what individuals can do as a result of learning and how well they apply this learning to a variety of challenges.

The assessment of the portfolio by a teacher or advisor can be a highly subjective process, but is often accomplished with the use of a standard rubric developed for that purpose. A rubric is simply a set of criteria against which products may be judged. It may include various performance levels ranging from a baseline of adequacy to higher levels that indicate excellence and work that demonstrates understanding beyond that required. For example, one criterion included in the scoring rubric may be that a wide variety of student projects be present or that the work be organized according to a thematic idea. In this way, systematic scoring of the portfolio helps to reduce the subjectivity of the final rating.

Projects constitute a large category of alternative assessment activities. These could include individual assignments as well as group activities, but they typically involve the creation of a product as the final result. Projects may be designed to simulate real-world challenges or be connected to the personal experiences of the learners, and can result in the development of plans, works of art, research proposals, multimedia presentations, or almost any other method of demonstrating mastery of a specific body of knowledge. Proponents of cognitive learning theory argue that when students are give the opportunity to design their own projects, individually or as a group, the potential benefits include improved performance, better management of one's own learning, increased motivation, and improved self-esteem (Herman, Aschbacher, & Winters, 1992).

One of the main advantages of group projects is that students learn to collaborate and work with others toward a common goal. Today's work world is dependent on teamwork; the social and interpersonal skills necessary for successful collaboration can be developed and honed through the use of activities that unite students with those of differing viewpoints, cultural backgrounds, and value systems. Projects also facilitate informal peer review of work. This can be a highly motivating force, and the benchmarking that it provides assists learners in self-evaluation and the definition of learning goals. Also, as the nature of classroom teaching and learning shifts from teacher-as-information-provider to teacher-as-facilitator, group work becomes a much more natural event. No one individual is seen as the center of attention, and the teacher can move to a more collaborative role, with students depending on each other to move the group toward its goals.

Another type of alternative assessment, *problem-based learning,* is actually an entire instructional strategy in which students are presented with a situation that they must then investigate to determine how to respond. For example, learners may be given a scenario or case study for analysis and then be required to recommend one or more strategies or solutions. (This approach has been used successfully in medical education for many years and is now being explored by other content areas.) Problem-based learning truly represents how challenges appear in real life; few of us are faced with dilemmas or untoward circumstances that we—coincidentally—have just spent several weeks researching. Instead, as in real life, students must learn about the problem itself, analyze its components, gather resources, and then synthesize this information to prepare a plan of action or recommended strategy. Individuals or groups may be assigned to a particular problem (or "case"), and the final result—the deliverable—may take the form of a presentation, written report, multimedia demonstration, or other tangible product.

Advantages and Disadvantages of Alternative Assessment

Alternative assessment, however it is applied, has advantages and disadvantages that may render it more or less appealing to the instructional designer or teacher. The advantages include the ability to simulate real-world settings, in which learners participate in activities that mimic those found in the workplace, home, or social environment. Transferability of skills to other environments may be strengthened by such challenges, and the relevance of course content may be heightened; and thus the classroom (in whatever configuration it takes) becomes just one link in the chain that connects learning and doing, theory and practice, goals and outcomes.

Workplace skills, such as teamwork, can be reinforced through instruction that emphasizes collaboration and assessment activities that reflect this perspective. Critical thinking, selection and evaluation of resources, effective interpersonal communication, and project planning are abilities characteristic of today's ideal citizen, worker, and learner. Instruction and assessment that require the acquisition, development, and use of such skills reflect a philosophy of education that includes lifelong learning as an essential goal.

Proponents of alternative assessment suggest that the content validity of "authentic" tasks is ensured because there is a direct link between the expected behavior and the ultimate goal of skill/learning transfer. Multiple-choice tests (or other "proxy" assessments) measure learning that we must infer can be applied to an unfamiliar or novel challenge. The claims of improved validity make sense for some categories of learning; consider the assessment of psychomotor tasks such as handwriting or objectives related to literary composition without observing the direct performance of their accomplishment. Determining the mastery of some learning outcomes may be dependent, also, on a specific set of circumstances or environmental constraints that simulate the transferability of skill; completing a federal income tax form within a predetermined time limit, or teaching someone else how to do so, can demonstrate abilities beyond basic skill levels that could not be judged without being observed under these circumstances.

One of the major disadvantages of alternative assessments is how difficult it can be to assign a score or rating to learner performance. Portfolios, for example, can be extremely time-consuming to evaluate. Each element in the collection of papers, videotapes, computer programs, or other pieces of "learning evidence" must be examined and scored to make a reliable judgment of completeness, quality, organization, or other desired criteria. Before this can be done, however, a comprehensive set of scoring guidelines must be developed. Herman, Aschbacher, and Winters (1992) suggested a nine-step process for the creation of a portfolio rubric that included such procedures as "Gather samples of students' and experts' work that portray a range of quality" after which you would "discuss characteristics of work that separate the excellent from the poor" and then "write descriptors for the important qualities." The amount of work represented by these steps includes only one-third of the total process, and the actual assessment itself has not yet begun. Unfortunately, without a finely detailed and clearly illustrated set of standards that would result from this sequence of steps, the subjectivity of the scoring process can result in unintentional bias or low interrater reliability. Finally, assuming that a reliable scoring procedure is created and implemented, how does a college or university compare a student's portfolio with the standardized tests traditionally required of applicants? And what institution has the personnel available to do so if it could?

Another disadvantage to the use of alternative assessments is their general unfamiliarity within traditional educational institutions. The little training that teachers get in the design of assessments cannot begin to prepare them adequately for the demands of such tasks. This "little training," however, is more than most college professors ever get, and their design of assessments is most likely to be guided by their experiences as students—under the tutelage of college professors who taught as those before them had. If the lack of awareness or understanding were the only reason for college faculty to turn away from alternative assessments, this could be remedied relatively easily; but accreditation concerns may also stand in the way of adopting such innovative practices. The standards by which postsecondary programs are judged are not casually or frequently revised, however, and traditional assessments that are understood and somewhat standardized across a profession or discipline may hinder any improvident "creativity" on the part of faculty.

One caveat regarding the use of alternative assessments must be offered. Educators should be cautious about abandoning tests that measure knowledge in favor of those that focus on thinking skills; this one-or-the-other approach creates a false dichotomy between content and its application that is counterproductive to creating a well-rounded learner. Pomperaug Regional School District 15 (1996) coined the term *process creep* to describe the insidious, and sometimes nearly unnoticed, orientation to process at the expense of connecting assessments with course content.

Finally, the terminology associated with alternative assessment has antagonized some educators and created an image problem for such practices. The use of the term *alternative* does not explain what these assessments are, but rather what they are not. Unfortunately, the use of this alienating jargon has given impetus to those who would relegate these procedures to a substandard or fringe element status. Terwilliger (1996) takes exception to the use of the term *authentic* to describe some assessment approaches as being "superior to others because they measure outcomes that are more 'genuine' or 'real.' " The assumption that a specific type of assessment is unequivocally more effective than another ignores the role of the instructional design process in developing measures to match the desired outcomes. This perspective is just as limiting as those that would shun alternative assessment out of hand and deserves no recognition.

◆ ASSESSMENT AND DISTANCE EDUCATION

Much of the information and content in this chapter could be applied to any instructional setting, regardless of where the participants are. As mentioned previously, explaining good assessment, like defining good teaching, requires an understanding and explication of a core of methodology that remains constant. There are, however, some elements of assessment that apply especially to the distance education environment. Although many K–12 schools have adopted distance education, adult learners make up the majority of students involved in such programs. These students may be returning to formal postsecondary education after being away from it for several years, they may be working full time, and they may have families to care for, as well as social or community obligations. They are, however, extremely motivated and eager to learn. For these learners, alternative assessments may be especially appropriate.

Assessment is possible at a distance, especially when live, two-way interactive systems are used. Students can complete their assignments and present them to classmates and the teacher.

Distance education students who are returning to formal education, in particular, derive great benefit from the use of *ongoing assessment.* Ongoing (sometimes called *embedded*) assessment activities are woven into the fabric of the instructional process so that determining student progress does not necessarily represent to students a threat, a disciplinary function, or a necessary evil, but simply occurs as another thread within the seamless pattern of day-to-day classroom events. One advantage of this approach is that any misconceptions held by learners that might interfere with later progress are identified and addressed before they become obstacles to further learning. A natural advantage for the instructor is that the dreaded "crunch" of grading that presents itself when assessments occur in large blocks is avoided; ongoing assessment provides information on student progress in smaller increments over the course of a unit, semester, or academic year (Hart, 1994; Wiley & Haertel, 1996).

Many distance delivery configurations do not provide the conditions for the creation of the informal learning group that develops almost automatically in traditional, face-to-face instruction. One characteristic of the learning group is that an unofficial benchmarking system, by which students compare their progress with that of the group, is created to provide feedback to individuals and enhance student motivation to keep pace with their peers. Ongoing assessment can provide this information and a motivational nudge through frequent feedback and reinforcement. For returning students who may be unsure of their competence in the classroom, these ongoing activities help them to achieve small successes early on without the stress of a major examination or assignment. Examples of ongoing assessments might include creating and implementing in-class exercises, holding students responsible for mediating discussions, or expecting students to participate in on-line, asynchronous discussion groups.

For many distance education teachers, large class sizes make formal assessment activities a daunting prospect. (Many distance education programs begin with a mission of making formal educational opportunities available to previously unserved markets, and find that these groups take advantage of the chance for learning in quantity!) Using *nongraded assessment measures* for part of the course, however, alleviates much of the strain of grading massive amounts of student work while still providing several of the benefits of traditional assessments. Spontaneous question-and-answer activities (either verbal or written, similar to pop quizzes) can be integrated easily into synchronous classroom instruction where they act to reinforce content, supply feedback on student progress to students and teacher, and provide motivational support. Students can check their own work and participate in the discussion of correct answers; the instructor may or may not choose to collect the anonymous "quizzes" to get a sense of the strengths and weaknesses of a particular lesson, but the pressure of grading and turnaround is relieved.

Self-paced assessment activities also offer benefits to distant learners. Without the pressure of time constraints, adult learners, who may have less-than-flexible schedules, have the opportunity to prepare papers, projects, or other tangible "deliverables" that demonstrate learning while not tying them to a rigid (and potentially unworkable) timetable. Unless learning goals require the student to create products within a specific time frame, it makes little sense to demand adherence to an inflexible program. Different learners require varying levels of external structure, but this may be considered a negotiable item based on performance and learning style. An example of this might be the assignment of a research paper with a series of milestone deadlines (topic and rough outline, first rough draft, second edited draft, etc.) jointly determined by the student and teacher.

Another issue of importance when assessing distant learners is the *fairness* of the assessment activity. Care must be taken to avoid penalizing remote-site students by requiring the use of resources not readily available to them or expecting them to adhere to a different set of time lines than students who are taking the course at the origination site. (In one regrettable instance, an instructor expected distant students to submit papers by mail earlier than on-site students turned theirs in at the origination site so that he would receive them all on the same day.) Distant students do not deserve special treatment on the basis of their location, nor should they be punished. Here again, adult students who have been absent from the classroom for some time may not have the same mental "set" that traditional students do, and terminology, procedures, and expectations should be defined as clearly as possible.

Also of concern is the issue of *diversity*. Many distance education programs, by mission and design, enroll a highly diverse group of learners. These differences (e.g., age, race, socioeconomic status) provide a richness to the learning group that might otherwise not occur and can offer many opportunities for cross-cultural interactions. Such differences may, however, pose a problem if the assessment of learning is biased in favor of "traditional" students—those who fit a preconceived notion of the type of person the instructor expects to have in the course. An example of this might be the instructor who uses examples or scenarios in course assignments that make sense only to young adults, a particular religious group, or native speakers of English. Unfortunately, the students affected might not speak up about the problem and will either perform unsatisfactorily (regardless of how well they know the content) or simply give up in frustration and drop the course.

As discussed earlier, one of the purposes of assessment is to provide *feedback* to learners. In some distance education environments, the turnaround time for tests, papers, or projects is long enough to interfere with the usefulness of the feedback, returning to the student's hands only after so much time has elapsed that the comments or corrections are nearly meaningless. Also, because the opportunities for personal communication between the teacher and learner may be limited, feedback must be clear, detailed, and constructive. Unlike the student who can linger after class to ask "What did you mean by this squiggly line?" the distant learner is left to ponder the underlines, circles, arrows, and sometimes cryptic notes provided as guidance for further assignments or revisions.

◆ SUMMARY

Assessment is the means of measuring learning gains and can be used to improve the teaching-learning process. Determining content mastery and transferability of skills helps teachers and students identify gaps in learning; it gives feedback to the teacher about the instruction and feedback to the student on strengths and weaknesses in performance. It also can reinforce content and identify misconceptions, as well as act as a motivating force that prods learners toward content mastery.

Traditional assessments, those that are most often identified as "paper-and-pencil tests," can be used to gauge a student's learning of a large body of content and can focus on the comprehension and application of information when declarative knowledge is the objective. Or a narrower slice of content can be explored in greater depth with assessment instruments that require higher order thinking skills, such as analysis, synthesis, or evaluation. Each type of activity has its appropriate uses and should be selected according to desired outcomes, amount of time available for assessment, and level of the students' intellectual and developmental maturity.

Alternative assessments are those activities that are not identified as traditional and that are guided by the philosophies of constructivism, performance assessment, and authentic assessment. These include, but are not limited to, portfolio development, individual or group projects, and problem-based learning. Alternative assessment is not yet well-accepted in many educational institutions and will only catch on as the movement grows and becomes more stable.

Although most of what this chapter has included could apply to any instructional environment, there are elements of assessment that are of special concern for instructional designers, teachers, and learners (many of whom are adults returning to formal education) involved in distance education. These considerations include the use of ongoing, nongraded, or self-paced assessments; the fairness of the assessment activity;

awareness of the diversity of the student group; and the provision of detailed, timely, and abundant feedback to learners.

Some final conclusions and recommendations remain. First, assessment must be an integrated and transparent component of the instructional process. If extensive effort and resources go into designing activities that measure higher order thinking but the instruction does not guide learners in achieving this level of cognition, the assessment and the learners will fail (Baker & O'Neil, 1996). Everyone involved must be aware of what the expectations are and how learners will achieve them. If our testing is to reflect what is important and "make concrete what is valued by the educational system" (Bank Street College of Education, 1990), testing cannot be a secret.

Distance education can serve as a catalyst for change and growth in the education arena. By rethinking our ideas about what a classroom is, what teaching and learning are, where learning can occur, and how to measure it most effectively, we can use the best of what we know that works and discover new ways to facilitate this change. Distance education can be more than doing the same old things in many places instead of just one, and we need not feel bound to emulate worn-out models. Assessment, as a component of the instructional design process, can explore new ideas and refine the old as we reflect on our best practices for teaching and learning in whatever environmental configurations may confront us in the future.

Self-Test Questions

1. Although instructional design models prescribe the development of assessment instruments or activities prior to instruction, in reality, many (if not most) teachers wait until after instruction. What are some reasons for this, and how might this affect the assessment results?

2. Traditional assessments are often based on the student's ability to recall or comprehend information. How might these be designed, instead, to reflect higher order skills such as synthesizing? What are some examples of knowledge or comprehension-level tasks that could be converted to a higher level of assessment to better reflect student learning and transfer of skills to a real-world situation?

3. Proponents of alternative assessments suggest that, to obtain an accurate picture of student progress, sampling student performance over time is necessary. What implications does this present for one-time, standardized testing programs (e.g., the SAT examination) used for university admission? What potential policy implications might this present at the university level if the decision is made to accept portfolios as a substitute for high school transcripts when making admission decisions?

4. Norm-referenced testing is a widely accepted method of assigning grades and determining certification or licensing qualifications. What might be the arguments for and against this type of scoring? (*Food for thought:* Would you want to take an airplane ride with a pilot whose skill level was assessed based on how well she performed compared with her classmates or compared with a set standard of excellence?)

Answers to Self-Test Questions

1. Classic instructional design approaches require a clear statement of what is to be learned and a minimum level of competence that is expected. In many situations this approach is very effective. However, during instruction and learning it is often the case that new ideas are developed and new competencies are identified. Additionally, sometimes content areas are not adequately covered or are determined to be of minimal importance. For these reasons and others, many educators feel that assessment items and criteria should be developed after instruction has occurred.

2. Traditional assessments often concentrate on lower levels of cognitive learning because it is easier to measure knowledge and comprehension. Increasingly, educators are realizing that application, syntheses, and evaluation competencies are important. Assessment strategies that require a demonstration of the ability to apply what has been learned, such as by participating in teams that develop solution strategies to real world problems, are ways to assess high levels learning. Instead of asking students to define terms, it might be better to ask students to use new terms in a verbal presentation that discusses how the terms apply to a certain job situation.

3. Alternative assessments determine students' progress by providing a way for them to actually show that they can use the new knowledge they have learned. Actually, many feel that one-time testing determines very little about what a person knows, and others look at a person's entire collection of school grades, activities, and test scores as a kind of traditional portfolio. Concerns for fairness and completeness of assessment are balanced against efficiency and timeliness.

4. Norm-referenced testing basically pits learners against one another instead of against some standard. Advocates of norm-referenced assessment state that this is how the real world assesses people, so that is how schools should assess them also. Others state that a level of competence should be met in order to be considered competent (certainly the airline pilot would need to be able to demonstrate competence to some level, not just as compared with other would-be pilots). From a practical standpoint, both norm- and criterion-referenced assessments will probably be used most often in most courses.

References

Baker, E., & O'Neil, H. (1996). Performance assessment and equity. In M. Kane & R. Mitchell (Eds.), *Implementing performance assessment: Promises, problems, and challenges.* Mahwah, NJ: Lawrence Erlbaum.

Bank Street College of Education (1990). *Applications in educational assessment: Future technologies.* Washington, DC: Office of Technology Assessment. (ERIC Document Reproduction Service No. ED 340 773)

Dick, W., & Carey, L. (1995). *The systematic design of instruction.* Glenview, IL: Scott Foresman.

Gagne, R., Briggs, L., & Wager, W. (1987). *Principles of instructional design.* New York: Holt, Rinehart & Winston.

Gronlund, N. (1998). *Assessment of student achievement* (6th ed.). Boston: Allyn & Bacon.

Hart, D. (1994). *Authentic assessment: A handbook for educators.* Menlo Park, CA: Addison-Wesley.

Herman, J., Aschbacher, P., & Winters, L. (1992). *A practical guide to alternative assessment.* Alexandria, VA: Association for Supervision and Curriculum Development.

Pomperaug Regional School District 15 (1996). *A teacher's guide to performance-based learning and assessment.* Alexandria, VA: Association for Supervision and Curriculum Development.

Terwilliger, J. (1996). *Semantics, psychometrics, and assessment reform: A close look at "authentic" tests.* Paper presented at the Annual Meeting of the National Council on Measurement in Education, New York. (ERIC Document Reproduction Service No. ED 397 123)

Wiggins, G. (1990). *The case for authentic assessment.* Washington, DC: ERIC Clearinghouse on Tests, Measurement, and Evaluation. (ERIC Document Reproduction Service No. ED 328 611)

Wiley, D., & Haertel, E. (1996). Extended assessment tasks: Purposes, definitions, scoring, and accuracy. In M. Kane & R. Mitchell (Eds.), *Implementing performance assessment: Promises, problems, and challenges.* Mahwah, NJ: Lawrence Erlbaum.

chapter 12

Evaluating Teaching and Learning at a Distance

CHAPTER GOAL:

The purpose of this chapter is to present two approaches for evaluation of distance education programs and systems.

CHAPTER OBJECTIVES:

After reading and reviewing this chapter, you should be able to

1. Differentiate between research and evaluation.
2. Define evaluation.
3. Explain the six categories of evaluation information including measures of activity, efficiency, outcomes, program aims, policy, and organizations.
4. Describe the AEIOU approach to evaluation and its five levels—accountability, effectiveness, impact, organizational context, and unanticipated consequences.

◆ RESEARCH AND EVALUATION

> The best way to find things out is not to ask questions at all. If you fire off a
> question, it is like firing off a gun—bang it goes, and everything takes flight
> and runs for shelter. But if you sit quite still and pretend not to be looking,
> all the little facts will come and peck around your feet, situations will venture
> forth from thickets, and intentions will creep out and sun themselves on a
> stone; and if you are very patient, you will see and understand a great deal
> more than a person with a gun does. (Huxley, 1982, p. 20)

This marvelous quote from Huxley's *The Flame Trees of Thika* illustrates a metaphorical rationale for a major refocusing of procedures for evaluation of distance education systems. Traditional evaluation models have concentrated on the empirical and quantitative procedures that have been practiced for decades (Stufflebeam & Shinkfield, 1985; Worthen & Sanders, 1987). More recently, evaluators of distance education programs have begun to propose more qualitative models that include the collection of many nonnumerical types of information.

Because it is easy to think of them as being the same thing, it is important to differentiate between theory-based research and evaluation. Hanson and Maushak (1996) have provided an excellent review of distance education literature including research on and about distance education. Hanson summarized distance education research as follows:

- ◆ Distance education is just as effective as traditional education in regards to learner outcomes.
- ◆ Distance education learners generally have more favorable attitudes toward distance education than traditional learners, and distance learners feel they learn as well as nondistant students.

The research clearly shows that distance education is an effective method for teaching and learning (Hanson & Maushak, 1996).

Evaluation, as contrasted to research, is the systematic investigation of the worth or merit of an object. Program evaluation is the systematic investigation of the worth of an ongoing or continuing distance education activity (Joint Committee on Standards for Educational Evaluation, 1994). This chapter focuses on approaches to evaluation for the purpose of improving distance education and determining the worth of distance education activities. Additional information related to evaluation and distance education is available in Cyrs and Smith (1990), Willis (1994), Fitz-Gibbon and Morris (1987), Worthen and Sanders (1987), and Rossi and Freeman (1993).

◆ EVALUATION AND THE OPEN UNIVERSITY

Program evaluation at the Open University of Great Britain is the systematic investigation of the merit of a particular distance education program, curriculum, or teaching method, and how it might be improved compared with alternatives. As part of evaluation procedures for distance education by the Open University (Woodley &

Kirkwood, 1986), two alternative strategies have been merged. The first is the traditional, positivist-empiricist approach to evaluation. This represents an attempt to apply the rules and procedures of the physical sciences to evaluation. The second is a more eclectic view of evaluation that incorporates qualitative and naturalistic techniques for the evaluation of distance education.

The traditional strategy normally includes an experiment that determines the effectiveness of a distance education strategy. The distance education project is structured from its beginning with the requirements of the evaluator in mind. Carefully matched samples are picked, controls are established, and variables are selected for which comparison data will be collected. Next, objective tests of variables are selected or constructed. Data are collected before, during, and always after the instructional event or procedures. Then the evaluator takes the data and prepares the evaluation report, which is submitted weeks or months later.

The primary outcome of this type of evaluation is the comparison of the data collected from the two or more categories of learners. For example, the distant learners are compared with those taught locally, and conclusions about the effectiveness of the distance education activity are made.

This approach represents the traditional process for the evaluation of distance education. Recently at the Open University and elsewhere, a countermovement has emerged (House, 1986). Advocates of this counterapproach are united in one primary way. They are opposed to the traditional, quantitative procedures for evaluation.

Increasingly, evaluation activities are incorporating more naturalistic methodologies with holistic perspectives. This second perspective for evaluation uses focus groups, interviews, observations, and journals to collect evaluation information in order to obtain a rich and colorful understanding of events related to the distance education activity.

From a practical standpoint, most evaluators now use a combination of quantitative and qualitative measures. Certainly, there is a need to quantify and count. Just as certainly, there is a need to understand opinions and hear perspectives.

According to Woodley and Kirkwood (1986), six categories of evaluation information can be collected about distance education activities.

1. **Measures of activity.**   These measures are counts of the numbers of events, people, and objects. Administrative records often provide data for activity questions. Activity questions are ones such as
   - How many courses were produced?
   - How many students were served?
   - How many potential students were turned away?
2. **Measures of efficiency.**   Measures of efficiency are closely related to measures of activity, and often administrative records can be the source of efficiency information. Efficiency questions often asked are ones such as
   - How many students successfully completed the course?
   - What was the average student's workload?
   - How many students enrolled in additional courses?
   - How much did the course cost?
   - How much tuition was generated?

3. **Measures of outcomes.**   Measures of adequate learning are usually considered the most important measures of outcomes of distance education activities. Often interviews with learners are used to supplement course grades in order to find students' perceptions about a distance education activity. Mail surveys are also efficient ways to collect outcome information from distant learners. Other outcome measures include documenting the borrowing and use of courses and course materials by other institutions as an indicator of effectiveness, and the enrollment by students in additional, similar courses as indicators of a preliminary course's success.

4. **Measures of program aims.**   Some distance teaching programs specify their aims in terms of what and whom they intend to teach, and evaluation information is collected to establish the extent to which these aims were met. One common aim of distance education programs is to reach learners who otherwise would not be students. Surveys of learners can be used to collect this type of information.

5. **Measures of policy.**   Evaluation in the policy area often takes the form of market research. Surveys of prospective students and employers can be used to determine the demand for distance education activities.

    Policy evaluation can also include monitoring. Students can be surveyed to determine if tuition is too high, if appropriate courses are being offered, and if there are impediments to course success, such as the lack of access to computers or the library.

    Sometimes policy evaluation can be used to determine the success of experimental programs, such as those for low achievers or for students who normally are not qualified for a program. The purpose of policy evaluation is to identify procedures that are needed or that need to be changed, and to develop new policies.

6. **Measures of organizations.**   Sometimes it is important to evaluate a distance education institution in terms of its internal organization and procedures. Evaluators sometimes are asked to monitor the process of course development or program delivery to help an organization be more efficient. This category of evaluation requires on-site visits, interviews, and sometimes the use of journals by key organization leaders.

These six categories of evaluation are not used for every distance education activity. Certainly, some modest evaluation activity is almost always necessary. It is important that the activities of evaluators be matched to programmatic needs. Woodley and Kirkwood (1986) have summarized evaluation in distance education as being a fairly eclectic process that utilizes procedures that should match program needs to evaluation activities.

◆ **THE AEIOU APPROACH**

Recently, Fortune and Keith (1992) and Sweeney and Sorensen (1994) have proposed the AEIOU approach for program evaluation, especially the evaluation of distance education projects. The effectiveness of this approach has been demonstrated in evaluating the activities of the Iowa Distance Education Alliance Star Schools Project (Simonson, 1995; Sorensen & Sweeney, 1994; Sorensen, 1995, 1997; Sweeney, 1995), a multiyear, statewide distance education activity. Additionally, the model has been used to evaluate a number of other innovative projects such as the Iowa Chemistry Education Alliance (1995), the Iowa General Chemistry Network (1994), and the DaVinci Project: Interactive Multimedia for Art and Chemistry (Simonson & Schlosser, 1995).

The AEIOU approach is similar to Woodley and Kirkwood's in that it is an eclectic one that uses quantitative and qualitative methodologies. It has two primary purposes as an evaluation strategy. First, the model provides formative information to the staff about the implementation of their project. Second, it provides summative information about the value of the project and its activities.

The AEIOU evaluation process provides a framework for identifying key questions necessary for effective evaluation. Some evaluation plans use only parts of the framework, while other, more comprehensive plans use all components. Some examples of evaluation questions asked in comprehensive distance education projects include the following:

COMPONENT 1   *ACCOUNTABILITY*

Did the project planners do what they said they were going to do?

This is the first step in determining the effectiveness of the project or course and is targeted at determining if the project's objectives and activities were completed. Evaluation questions typically center on the completion of a specific activity and often are answered "yes" or "no." Additionally, counts of numbers of people, things, and activities are often collected.

Questions such as the following are often asked to determine project accountability.

◆ Were the appropriate number of class sessions held?
◆ How many students were enrolled?
◆ How many copies of program materials were produced, and how many were distributed?

Methods Used: Accountability information is often collected from project administrative records. Project leaders are often asked to provide documentation of the level of completion of each of the projects goals, objectives, and activities. Sometimes evaluators interview project staff to collect accountability data.

COMPONENT 2   *EFFECTIVENESS*

How well done was the project?

This component of the evaluation process attempts to place some value on the project's activities. Effectiveness questions often focus on participant attitudes and knowledge. Obviously, grades, achievement tests, and attitude inventories are measures of effectiveness. Less obvious are other ways to determine quality. Often, raters are asked to review course materials and course presentations to determine their effectiveness, and student course evaluations can be used to collect reactions from distance education participants.

Examples of questions to determine effectiveness include

◆ Were the in-service participants satisfied with their distance education instruction?
◆ Did the students learn what they were supposed to learn?
◆ Did the teachers feel adequately prepared to teach distant learners?

Methods Used: Standardized measures of achievement and attitude are traditionally used to determine program effectiveness. Surveys of students and faculty can be used to ask questions related to perceptions about the appropriateness of a project or program. Focus groups (Morgan, 1988) also provide valuable information. Participants are systematically asked to respond to questions about the program. Finally, journals are sometimes kept by project participants and then analyzed to determine the day-to-day effectiveness of an ongoing program.

COMPONENT 3   *IMPACT*

Did the project, course, or program make a difference?

During this phase of the evaluation, questions focus on identifying the changes that resulted from the project's activities, and are tied to the stated outcomes of the project or course. In other words, if the project had not happened, what of importance would not have occurred? A key element of measurement of impact is the collection of longitudinal data. The impact of distance education courses is often determined by following learners' progress in subsequent courses or in the workplace to determine if what was learned in the distance education course was useful.

Impact is extremely difficult to determine because determinants of impact are difficult to identify. Often evaluators use follow-up studies to determine the impressions made on project participants, and sometimes in distance education programs learners are followed and questioned by evaluators in subsequent courses and activities.

Questions might include

◆ Did students register for additional distance education courses?
◆ Has the use of the distance education system increased?
◆ Have policies and procedures related to the use of the distance education system been developed or changed?

Methods Used: Qualitative measures provide the most information to the evaluator interested in program impact. Standardized tests, record data, and surveys are sometimes used. Also, interviews, focus groups, and direct observations are used to identify a program's impact.

COMPONENT 4   *ORGANIZATIONAL CONTEXT*

What structures, policies, or events in the organization or environment helped or hindered the project in accomplishing its goals?

This component of evaluation has traditionally not been important even though evaluators have often hinted in their reports about organizational policies that either hindered or helped a program. Recently, however, distance educators have become very interested in organizational policy analysis in order to determine barriers to the successful implementation of distance education systems, especially when those systems are new activities of traditional educational organizations, such as large public universities.

The focus of this component of the evaluation is on identifying those contextual or environmental factors that contributed to, or detracted from, the project's or course's ability to conduct activities. Usually these factors are beyond the control of the project's participants. Effective evaluation of organizational context requires the evaluator to be intimately involved with the project or course in order to have a good understanding of the environment in which the project or course operates.

Questions typically addressed in evaluating organizational context include

◆ What factors made it difficult to implement the project or to successfully complete the course?
◆ What contributed most to the success or failure of the project or the students in the course?
◆ What should be done differently to improve things and make the course more effective?

Methods Used: Organizational context evaluation uses interviews of key personnel such as faculty or students, focus groups made up of those impacted by a program, and document analysis that identifies policies and procedures that influence a program or course. Direct participation in program activities by the evaluator is also important. Sometimes evaluators enroll in distance education courses. More often, a student is asked to complete a journal while enrolled in a course. By participating, the evaluator is confronted directly with the organizational context in which a program exists, and can comment on this context firsthand.

COMPONENT 5   *UNANTICIPATED CONSEQUENCES*

What changes or consequences of importance happened as a result of the project that were not expected?

This component of the AEIOU approach is to identify unexpected changes of either a positive or negative nature that occurred as a direct or indirect result of the project or course. Effective evaluators have long been interested in reporting anecdotal information about the project or program that they were evaluating. It is only recently that this category of information has become recognized as important, largely because of the positive influence on evaluation of qualitative procedures. Often evaluators, especially internal evaluators who are actively involved in the project's or course's implementation, have many opportunities to observe successes and failures during the trial-and-error process of beginning a new program. Unanticipated consequences of developing new or modified programs, especially in the dynamic field of distance education, are a rich source of information about why some projects are successful and others are not. Central to the measurement of unanticipated outcomes is the collection of ex post facto data.

Examples of questions asked include

- Have relationships between collaborators or students changed in ways not expected?
- Have related, complementary projects been developed?
- Were unexpected linkages developed between groups or participants?
- Was the distance education system used in unanticipated ways?
- Did the distance education system have impact on student learning other than that expected?

Methods Used: Interviews, focus groups, journals, and surveys that ask for narrative information can be used to identify interesting and potentially important consequences of implementing a new program. Often, evaluators must interact with project participants or course students on a regular basis to learn about the little successes and failures that less sensitive procedures overlook. Active and continuous involvement by evaluators permits them to learn about the project as it occurs.

Sweeney (1995) advocates an eclectic approach to evaluation, an approach also supported by Worthen and Sanders (1987). The AEIOU model is a dynamic one that permits the evaluator to tailor the process of program evaluation to the specific situation being studied.

◆ PROGRAM EVALUATION: AN EXAMPLE

In 1993, it was decided that a three-phase plan should be implemented to establish distance education classrooms throughout the state of Iowa. For the first phase, 15 area community colleges, 3 public universities, and Iowa Public Television had classrooms built and connected with fiber-optic cables capable of carrying 48 full-motion video signals in addition to virtually unlimited voice and data information. The second phase of the plan connected a classroom site in any of Iowa's 99 counties that was not already served by a community college site. These classrooms were connected with 12 fiber-optic cables. A total of 103 sites were built and connected as part of phases one and two. During phase three, additional sites were connected throughout the state. Recently, over 600 sites were connected to this distance education infrastructure, which was named the Iowa Communications Network (ICN).

As part of the implementation plan for the ICN, a comprehensive evaluation program was put into action. This program utilized the AEIOU approach and collected data from thousands of sources and individuals. The evaluation approach went through several stages during the five years it was used. First, evaluators concentrated on evaluating the construction, connection, and implementation of the ICN's physical infrastructure. Records related to classroom design, construction schedules, and dollars spent were collected and reviewed, and summary results were reported. This related to the accountability component of the AEIOU approach.

Next, those involved in the decision-making process for establishing the network were interviewed and completed surveys. Evaluators used the results to develop reports on the effectiveness of the processes used to construct the ICN. To determine impact, evaluators conducted follow-up investigations of classroom utilization and examined records of how the system was used.

The program evaluators examined many interesting organizational issues, such as who made decisions about where classrooms were located, how funds were obtained and spent, and who controlled access to the system. Finally, program evaluators identified unanticipated outcomes. One of the most significant was the infusion of several millions of dollars from federal, state, and local sources to support the development of the network. How these funds were obtained and used added to the importance of the evaluation report.

Once the network was built and a plan for its continued growth was put into place, evaluators shifted their primary focus to the human side of the growth of distance education in the state. Staff development, technical training, curriculum revisions, and school restructuring became the focus of network planners and funding agencies, so program evaluators used the AEIOU model to obtain information about these activities. The approach was used to provide formative information about the development of programs and their impact on teachers and learners, and also to provide information on outcomes, or summative information, to document the successes and failures of various program activities.

A true understanding of activities of evaluators of this statewide, multiyear project can only be gained by reviewing the yearly reports they submitted. However, it is important to note that the evaluation plan provided the following information:

Accountability.   Evaluators checked records, interviewed staff, and visited classrooms to determine the status of the development of the ICN, both as a physical system and as a tool used by teachers to deliver courses to distant learners. The accountability focus shifted during the project as its activities shifted from construction to implementation and finally to maintenance.

Effectiveness.   Evaluators conducted interviews and focus groups to determine what impact the availability of the ICN had on classroom education. Surveys were sent and reports were generated that helped education leaders to better understand what role distance education was playing.

Impact.   As the network became widely available and the number of courses and activities increased, it became possible to determine the impact of the ICN and distance education events on education in the state. Students were tested and grades reported. Most of the achievement data showed that learning occurred and good grades were obtained. More important, the availability of new learning experiences grew considerably.

Organizational context.   From the beginning of the ICN project, the role of the state as compared with local educational organizations was a focus of evaluation activities. One outcome was to identify where cooperation between agencies was necessary, such as in scheduling, and where local control, such as in course selection, should be maintained. Project evaluators identified and reported on what the data seemed to indicate were the barriers and the contributors to the effective growth and utilization of the ICN.

Unanticipated outcomes.   During the project, scores of unanticipated outcomes were identified and reported. Among the most interesting were

- The movement of the ICN into the role of Internet service provider
- The role of the ICN in attracting external grants
- The role of distance education and the ICN in the movement to restructure schools
- The impact of the ICN on positive attitudes toward technology in education
- The emerging role of the public television station in Iowa education

There were also many other unanticipated outcomes. The AEIOU approach was useful in helping the state's educators in evaluating the role of distance education as an approach and the ICN as an infrastructure. Evaluation played a significant part in the positive implementation and use of this new technology in the state of Iowa.

◆ SUMMARY

As distance education in the United States increases in importance, evaluation will continue to be a critical component of the process of improvement. Certainly, the literature is clear. Eclectic models of evaluation such as the ones advocated by Woodley and Kirkwood (1986) and Sweeney (1995) are most applicable to distance education program evaluation. Quantitative and qualitative procedures should be used by evaluators. Distance education programs and even single courses should be accountable to their goals, should be at least as effective as alternative approaches, and should have a positive impact. Evaluators should attempt when possible to identify what organizational contexts support effective distance education systems, and unanticipated events both should be shared with interested readers and should be used to improve courses.

If you are very patient, you will see and understand . . .

Self-Test Questions

1. What term means "the systematic investigation of the worth or merit of an object"?
2. The systematic investigation of the merit of a particular distance education program, curriculum, or teaching method is a purpose of which of the following:

    a. Research about distance education
    b. Program evaluation, especially at the open university
    c. Curriculum building in the AEIOU approach
    d. Activity planning and evaluation
    e. Organizational context research

3. What are measures of activity?
4. When costs are identified and compared with tuition, the evaluator is determining which type of measure?
5. Give the five levels of the AEIOU approach.
6. True/False. Eclectic models of evaluation are increasingly the preferable ones.

Answers to Self-Test Questions

1. Evaluation.
2. b.
3. Counts of numbers of events, people, and objects.
4. Measures of efficiency.
5. The five levels are accountability, effectiveness, impact, organizational context, and unanticipated outcomes.
6. True.

References

Cyrs, T., & Smith, F. (1990). *Teleclass teaching: A resource guide* (2nd ed.). Las Cruces, NM: Center for Educational Development.

Fitz-Gibbon, C., & Morris, L. (1987). *How to design a program evaluation.* Newbury Park, CA: Sage.

Fortune, J., & Keith, P. (1992). *Program evaluation for Buchanan County Even Start.* Blacksburg, VA: College of Education, Virginia Polytechnic Institute and State University.

Hanson, D., & Maushak, N. (1996). *Distance education: Review of the literature* (2nd ed.). Ames, IA: Research Institute for Studies in Education.

House, E. (Ed.) (1986). *New directions in educational evaluation.* Lewes, England: Falmer Press.

Huxley, E. (1982). *The flame trees of Thika: Memories of an African childhood.* London: Chatto and Windus.

Iowa Chemistry Education Alliance (1995). Ames, IA: Research Institute for Studies in Education.

Iowa General Chemistry Network (1994). Ames, IA: Iowa State University.

Joint Committee on Standards for Educational Evaluation (1994). *The program evaluation standards* (2nd ed.). Thousand Oaks, CA: Sage.

Morgan, D. (1988). *Focus groups as qualitative research.* Newbury Park, CA: Sage.

Rossi, P., & Freeman, H. (1993). *Evaluation: A systematic approach.* Newbury Park, CA: Sage.

Simonson, M., & Schlosser, C. (1995). More than fiber: Distance education in Iowa. *Tech Trends, 40*(3), 13–15.

Sorensen, C. (1996). *Final evaluation report: Iowa distance education alliance.* Ames, IA: Research Institute for Studies in Education.

Sorensen, C. K. (1997). Localizing national standards for evaluation of distance education: An example from a multistate project. In C. L. Dillon and R. Cintron (Eds.), *Building a working policy for distance education.* New Directions for Community Colleges, #9, pp. 53–82.

Stufflebeam, D., & Shinkfield, A. (1985). *Systematic evaluation.* Boston: Kluwer-Nijhoff.

Sweeney, J. (1995). *Vision 2020: Evaluation report.* Ames, IA: Research Institute for Studies in Education.

Willis, B. (Ed.) (1994). *Distance education: Strategies and tools.* Englewood Cliffs, NJ: Educational Technology Publications.

Woodley, A., & Kirkwood, A. (1986). *Evaluation in distance learning.* Paper 10. Resources in Education. (ERIC Document Reproduction Service No. ED 304 122)

Worthen, B., & Sanders, J. (1987). *Educational evaluation.* London; Longman.

Suggested Readings

Cronbach, L. (1982). Designing evaluations of educational and social programs. San Francisco: Jossey-Bass.

Simonson, M., & Schlosser, C. (1995). *The DaVinci Project.* Iowa Computer Using Educators Conference, Des Moines.

index